BIBLICAL HAPAX LEGOMENA IN THE LIGHT OF AKKADIAN AND UGARITIC

SOCIETY
OF BIBLICAL
LITERATURE

DISSERTATION SERIES

edited by
Howard C. Kee
and
Douglas A. Knight

Number 37
BIBLICAL HAPAX LEGOMENA IN THE LIGHT OF AKKADIAN AND UGARITIC
by
Harold R. (Chaim) Cohen

Harold R. (Chaim) Cohen

BIBLICAL HAPAX LEGOMENA IN THE LIGHT OF AKKADIAN AND UGARITIC

Scholars Press

Distributed by
Scholars Press
PO Box 5207
Missoula, Montana 59806

BIBLICAL HAPAX LEGOMENA IN THE LIGHT OF AKKADIAN AND UGARITIC

Harold R. (Chaim) Cohen
Department of Bible
Tel-Aviv University
Ramat-Aviv, Israel

Ph. D., 1975
Columbia University, New York

Sponsor:
Moshe Held

Library of Congress Cataloging in Publication Data

Cohen, Harold R
Biblical hapax legomena in the light of Akkadian and Ugaritic.

(Dissertation series—Society of Biblical literature ; no. 37)
Originally presented as the author's thesis, Columbia, 1975.
Bibliography: p.
Includes index.
1. Hebrew language—Etymology. 2. Bible. O.T.—Language, style. 3. Assyro-Babylonian literature—Relation to the Old Testament. 4. Ugaritic literature—Relation to the Old Testament. I. Title. II. Series: Society of Biblical literature. Dissertation series ; no. 37.
PJ4801.C6 1977 492.4'2 77-13422
ISBN 0-89130-195-X

Printed in the United States of America
1 2 3 4 5
Edwards Brothers, Inc.
Ann Arbor, Michigan 48104

To my Parents

and

To Sandy, Yoav and Aliza

אשרי הגבר אשר מלא את אשפתו מהם (Ps 127:5)

TABLE OF CONTENTS

TABLE OF ABBREVIATIONS*

AD	G. R. Driver, *Aramaic Documents of the Fifth Century B.C.* (Oxford, 1957)
AF	H. Zimmern, *Akkadische Fremdwörter als Beweis für babylonischen Kultureinfluss* (Leipzig, 1917)
AfO	*Archiv für Orientforschung*
AHW	W. von Soden, *Akkadisches Handwörterbuch* (Wiesbaden, 1959-.)
AIA	S. A. Kaufman, *The Akkadian Influences on Aramaic* (Chicago, 1974)
AJSL	*American Journal of Semitic Languages and Literatures*
AKF	M. Burchardt, *Die altkanaanäischen Fremdworte und Eigennamen im Aegyptischen* II (Leipzig, 1910)
ANEP	J. P. Pritchard (ed.), *The Ancient Near East in Pictures Relating to the Old Testament* (2nd ed.; Princeton, 1969)
ANET	J. B. Pritchard (ed.), *Ancient Near Eastern Texts Relating to the Old Testament* (3rd ed.; Princeton, 1969)
AnSt	*Anatolian Studies*
AP	A. Cowley, *Aramaic Papyri of the Fifth Century B.C.* (Oxford, 1923)
ArOr	*Archiv orientální*
AS	Fr. Delitzsch, *Assyrische Studien* I (Leipzig, 1874)
AW I	W. von Soden, "Aramäische Wörter in neu-assyrischen und neu- und spätbabylonischen Texten. Ein Vorbericht. I," *Orientalia* 35 (1966), 1-20
AW II	W. von Soden, "Aramaische Wörter in neu-assyrischen und neu- und spätbabylonischen Texten. Ein Vorbericht. II," *Orientalia* 37 (1968), 261-71
BA	*Biblical Archeologist*
BASOR	*Bulletin of the American Schools of Oriental Research*

---

*All Akkadian texts are cited according to the abbreviations listed in *CAD*, L, vi-xviii.

BASS	Beiträge zur Assyriologie und semitischen Sprachwissenschaft
BDB	F. Brown, S. R. Driver, and C. A. Briggs, *A Hebrew and English Lexicon of the Old Testament* (Oxford, 1929)
BHS	*Biblia Hebraica Stuttgartensia*
BJPES	*Bulletin of the Jewish Palestine Exploration Society*
BZ	*Biblische Zeitschrift*
CAD	*The Assyrian Dictionary of the Oriental Institute of the University of Chicago* (Glückstadt, 1956-.)
CBQ	*Catholic Biblical Quarterly*
CIOT	E. Schrader, *The Cuneiform Inscriptions and the Old Testament* I-II (London, 1885)
CMHE	F. M. Cross, *Canaanite Myth and Hebrew Epic* (Cambridge, 1973)
CML	G. R. Driver, *Canaanite Myths and Legends* (Edinburgh, 1956)
CPOT	J. Barr, *Comparative Philology and the Text of the Old Testament* (Oxford, 1968)
CTA	A. Herdner, *Corpus des tablettes en cunéiformes alphabétiques découvertes à Ras Shamra-Ugarit de 1929 à 1939* (Paris, 1963)
DISO	C.-F. Jean and J. Hoftijzer, *Dictionnaire des inscriptions sémitiques de l'ouest* (Leiden, 1965)
EI	*Eretz Israel*
EM	אנציקלופדיה מקראית I-VI (Jerusalem, 1949-.)
EncJud	*Encyclopaedia Judaica* I-XVI (Jerusalem, 1971)
ESO	W. F. Albright, *The Vocalization of the Egyptian Syllabic Orthography* (New Haven, 1934)
FFM	J. M. Sasson, "Flora, Fauna and Minerals," *Ras Shamra Parallels* I (Rome, 1972), 385-452
FWOT	M. Ellenbogen, *Foreign Words in the Old Testament* (London, 1962)
GAG	W. von Soden, *Grundriss der akkadischen Grammatik* (Rome, 1952)
GKC	E. Kautzsch (ed.), and A. E. Cowley (tr.), *Gesenius' Hebrew Grammar* (reprint; London, 1966)
HALAT	W. Baumgartner et al., *Hebräisches und aramäisches Lexikon zum Alten Testament* (Leiden, 1967-.)
HTR	*Harvard Theological Review*

HUCA	*Hebrew Union College Annual*
IFCM	A. F. Rainey, "Institutions: Family, Civil, and Military," *Ras Shamra Parallels* II (Rome, 1975), 71-107
JANESCU	*Journal of the Ancient Near Eastern Society of Columbia University*
JAOS	*Journal of the American Oriental Society*
Jastrow	M. Jastrow, *A Dictionary of the Targumim, the Talmud Babli and Yerushalmi, and the Midrashic Literature* I-II (New York, 1950)
JBL	*Journal of Biblical Literature*
JCS	*Journal of Cuneiform Studies*
JEA	*Journal of Egyptian Archaeology*
JESHO	*Journal of Economic and Social History of the Orient*
JNES	*Journal of Near Eastern Studies*
JPOS	*Journal of the Palestine Oriental Society*
JPS Torah	*The Torah* (Philadelphia, 1962)
JPS Torah Notes	H. M. Orlinsky, *Notes on the New Translation of the Torah* (Philadelphia, 1969)
JQR	*Jewish Quarterly Review*
JSS	*Journal of Semitic Studies*
JTS	*Journal of Theological Studies*
KAI	H. Donner and W. Röllig, *Kanaanäische und aramäische Inschriften* I-III (Wiesbaden, 1966-69)
KB I	L. Koehler and W. Baumgartner, *Lexicon in Veteris Testamenti libros* (Leiden, 1958)
KB II	L. Koehler and W. Baumgartner, *Supplementum ad Lexicon in Veteris Testamenti libros* (Leiden, 1958)
Lane	E. W. Lane, *An Arabic-English Lexicon* I-VIII (reprint; Beirut, 1968)
LKK	H. L. Ginsberg, *The Legend of King Keret* (New Haven, 1946)
LP	A. Schoors, "Literary Phrases," *Ras Shamra Parallels* I (Rome, 1972), 3-70
MA	W. Muss-Arnoldt, *Assyrisch-englisch-deutsches Handwörterbuch* I-II (Berlin, 1905)
MH	Middle Hebrew
MLC	T. H. Gaster, *Myth, Legend, and Custom in the Old Testament* (New York, 1969)
MT	Masoretic Text
MVAG	Mitteilungen der Vorderasiatisch-ägyptischen Gesellschaft

NEB	*New English Bible* (Oxford, 1970)
NSGJ	A. C. M. Blommerde, *Northwest Semitic Grammar and Job* (Rome, 1969)
OLT	H. J. Kasovsky, אוצר לשון התלמוד I-XXVIII (Jerusalem, 1954-.)
OLZ	*Orientalistische Literaturzeitung*
OTS	*Oudtestamentische Studiën*
PEPI	S. Gevirtz, *Patterns in the Early Poetry of Israel* (Chicago, 1963)
PEQ	*Palestine Exploration Quarterly*
PRU II	Ch. Virolleaud, *Le Palais royal d'Ugarit* II (Paris, 1957)
PRU V	Ch. Virolleaud, *Le Palais royal d'Ugarit* V (Paris, 1965)
RA	*Revue d'assyriologie et d'archéologie orientale*
RB	*Revue biblique*
RHA	*Revue hittite et asianique*
RLA	E. Ebeling et al., *Reallexikon der Assyriologie* (Leipzig, 1932-.)
RSV	*Revised Standard Version* (reprint; New York, 1962)
SAYP	F. M. Cross, Jr., and D. N. Freedman, *Studies in Ancient Yahwistic Poetry* (Montana, 1975)
SHL	L. G. Zelson, "A Study of *Hapax Legomena* in the Hebrew Pentateuch" (Unpublished Ph.D. dissertation; University of Wisconsin, 1924)
SP	J. C. de Moor, *The Seasonal Pattern in the Ugaritic Myth of Ba'lu* (Neukirchen-Vluyn, 1971)
SUL	M. Held, "Studies in Ugaritic Lexicography and Poetic Style" (Unpublished Ph.D. dissertation; Johns Hopkins University, 1957)
TZ	*Theologische Zeitschrift*
UF	*Ugarit-Forschungen*
Ugaritica V	Ch. Virolleaud, *Ugaritica* V (Paris, 1968)
UHP	M. Dahood, *Ugaritic-Hebrew Philology* (Rome, 1965)
UHPP I	M. Dahood, "Ugaritic-Hebrew Parallel Pairs," *Ras Shamra Parallels* I (Rome, 1972), 73-382
UHPP II	M. Dahood, "Ugaritic-Hebrew Parallel Pairs," *Ras Shamra Parallels* II (Rome, 1975), 3-39
UT	C. H. Gordon, *Ugaritic Textbook* I-III (Rome, 1965)

VT	*Vetus Testamentum*
VTSup	*Vetus Testamentum*, Supplements
WAS	A. Erman and H. Grapow, *Wörterbuch der aegyptischen Sprache* I-VII (reprint; Berlin, 1971)
WO	*Die Welt des Orients*
WUS	J. Aistleitner, *Wörterbuch der ugaritischen Sprache* (Berlin, 1963)
WZKM	*Wiener Zeitschrift für die Kunde des Morgenlandes*
YGC	W. F. Albright, *Yahweh and the Gods of Canaan* (New York, 1969)
ZA	*Zeitschrift für Assyriologie*
ZAW	*Zeitschrift für die alttestamentliche Wissenschaft*
ZDMG	*Zeitschrift der Deutschen Morgenländischen Gesellschaft*
ZK	*Zeitschrift für Keilschriftforschung und verwandte Gebiete*
ZKM	*Zeitschrift für die Kunde des Morgenlandes*
מחברת מנחם	Z. Pilipowski, מחברת מנחם (reprint; Jerusalem, n.d.)
מלון הלשון העברית	E. ben Yehuda, מלון הלשון העברית I-VIII (New York/London, 1960)
ענת	M. D. Cassuto, האלה ענת (Jerusalem, 1951)
פשוטו של מקרא	N. H. Tur-Sinai, פשוטו של מקרא I-IV/2 (Jerusalem, 1962-67)
תשובות דונש	Z. Pilipowski, ספר תשובות דונש (reprint; Jerusalem, n.d.)

PREFACE

The present study, in its original form, was presented as a dissertation to the Faculty of Philosophy of Columbia University in 1975. Then, as now in its somewhat revised form, its purpose was to place the study of biblical *hapax legomena* on a sound scholarly basis. In the present volume (which will hopefully be followed by at least one other), two complete lists of biblical *hapax legomena* are presented (totaling some 480 words), and all biblical *hapax legomena* which have reasonably certain cognates in Akkadian and/or Ugaritic are discussed (about 90 words). In the two introductory chapters, a functional definition for biblical *hapax legomena* is sought and found, and a methodological discussion then leads to the proposal and defense of a new method for dealing with these difficult words. A history of biblical *hapax legomena* research from the period of the Masoretes to the present day is included in the discussion. In Appendix II where the biblical *hapax legomena* are listed, the notes have for purposes of clarity and ready reference been included at the appropriate place in the text, rather than gathered as end-notes as is done elsewhere.

I was introduced to the study of biblical *hapax legomena*, as I was to the study of the Bible and the Ancient Near East, by my mentor Professor Moshe Held. It was my great privilege to study first as an undergraduate and then as a graduate student with him at both Columbia University and at the Jewish Theological Seminary. At the latter institution, it was also my great privilege to study with one of the deans of modern biblical scholarship, Professor H. L. Ginsberg, who took a special interest in this work and who, through his refusal to compromise with what he felt were imperfections, is responsible in no small way for whatever achievements and progress have been made in this study. To the other members of my doctoral committee, Professor David Marcus, Professor Theodor H. Gaster and Professor John Schmidt, I am greatly indebted not only for their many efforts in improving the present work, but even more so for all I have learned from them through the years. I would here like to thank also the Faculty of the Humanities of Tel-Aviv University for providing me with a grant which covered the cost of my trip to the United States in January 1975 for the purpose of defending the original form of the present work and receiving the Ph.D.

After having been in Israel and teaching at Tel-Aviv University for some three years, it was my good fortune to have this work in its present revised form accepted for publication in the SBL Dissertation Series. I would here like to thank Professors Leander E. Keck, James L. Crenshaw and Douglas A. Knight, all of whom corresponded with me concerning this matter, for all their help and encouragement. Professor Knight, as editor of this series, was especially helpful in many diverse ways. I am also very grateful to Joann Burnich, the Scholars Press typist, for a difficult job well done!

Many of my colleagues both at Tel-Aviv University and at other Israeli universities have read this work in its original form and have made suggestions for its improvement. Here I would like to thank especially Professors M. Greenberg, J. Licht, S. M. Paul and H. Tadmor for their efforts on my behalf. I owe a great deal moreover to Professor Moshe Weinfeld who went over the original manuscript with great thoroughness and contributed many valuable suggestions which have improved this work considerably.

Finally, to my parents, my wife and my children, I dedicate this work as a token of love and gratitude.

Ramat-Aviv, Israel
Pesach, April 7, 1977

Harold R. (Chaim) Cohen

Postscript, August 15, 1978

This study now becomes a final tribute to the memory of my beloved father, Bernard Cohen ז"ל, who was my first Hebrew teacher and who constantly encouraged me in my academic work in every possible way. He was buried in Israel on the eve of Rosh-Hashanah, 5738.

זכר צדיק לברכה

CHAPTER I

INTRODUCTION

A. The Origin of the Term *Hapax Legomenon*

The term *hapax legomenon* is of Greek origin and means literally "once said."[1] It was first used by early Homeric scholars at Alexandria in their marginal notes to the Homeric epics, in order to classify words used only once.[2] The first attempt at such a classification was made by Zenodotus of Ephesus (ca. 325-234 B.C.E.),[3] who was the first librarian at Alexandria. It was not, however, until Aristarchus of Samothrace (ca. 220-145 B.C.E.)[4] that the term was used consistently and scientifically.[5] Somewhat later, Apollonius the Sophist (ca. end of first century C.E.),[6] drawing to a large extent upon the marginal notes of Aristarchus,[7] utilized the term in his *Lexicon Homericum*.[8]

It should not be assumed that the term *hapax legomenon* was the only term or even the most common term utilized to classify words appearing only once in the Homeric poems. In fact, several other terms were similarly employed,[9] the most common being *hapax eirēmenon* which also means literally "once said."[10] According to Martinazzoli,[11] of Apollonius' fifty-five notations in his *Lexicon Homericum* of words which appear only once in the Homeric poems, fifty are noted as *hapax eirēmenon*.

Thus, *hapax legomenon*, though not the most common term used in antiquity for a word appearing once in an ancient text, finds its historical roots in the scholia and lexicons of Homeric scholars at Alexandria and elsewhere. Its usage was in no way different from that of other lexicographical terms introduced in this period such as the similar term *dis legomenon* "twice said,"[12] referring to words which appeared once in the Iliad and once in the Odyssey.

B. Previous Definitions of the Term *Hapax Legomenon* in Biblical Research

The term *hapax legomenon* has been defined by biblical scholars through the ages in many diverse ways. Some of these definitions are explicitly stated by their authors as referring to *hapax legomena*, while others (especially those of the earlier periods) are implicit, and can only be reconstructed on the basis of the principle of selection apparently utilized to isolate the relevant words. In order to facilitate discussion, these definitions have been divided below into three periods of composition, namely: 1. The Masoretic Period; 2. The Period of the Early Hebrew Grammarians; and 3. The Modern Period.

1. The Masoretic Period[13]

Of all the terms utilized by the Masoretes in the Masorah Parva[14] the ל׳ (or ל̇)[15] was clearly the most common.[16] This abbreviation stood for the Aramaic particle of non-existence לית or ליתא meaning "there is none (other)."[17] It served to indicate unique forms and expressions, and its ultimate purpose like that of most other Masoretic notations was to guard the extant text from scribal error.[18] For example, among the forms and expressions labeled with the ל׳ by the Masoretes in Genesis 1 are the following:[19]

> את השמים (1:1); מרחפת (1:2); למים (1:6); יקוו (1:9); ותראה (1:9); ולמקוה (1:10); תדשא (1:11); את המאור (1:16); ואת המאור (1:16); ישרצו (1:20); וכבשה (1:28).

As is apparent from these examples, this term did not distinguish between common verbs (ותראה, וכבשה) and rare verbs (תדשא, יקוו, מרחפת), or common nouns (את השמים, למים) and rare nouns (ולמקוה). Rather, the principle of selection utilized by the Masoretes seems to have been that of uniqueness of form or expression. As illustrated by the above examples, this uniqueness could be either syntactical (e.g., both את המאור and ואת המאור)[20] or morphological (e.g., ישרצו).[21] Several scholars consider this notation to be the first attempt at isolating biblical *hapax legomena*.[22]

2. The Period of the Early Hebrew Grammarians[23]

The interpretation of rare biblical words was part of the major theological controversy between the Rabbanites and the Karaites in the Middle Ages.[24] The central issue of that controversy was whether or not the Oral Torah was indispensable for understanding and interpreting the Written Torah. The Rabbanites, accepting the premise that the Oral Torah was a natural continuation of the Written Torah, tried to show that these rare biblical words could only be interpreted in terms of their meaning in MH.[25] The Karaites, on the other hand, rejecting the Oral Torah in toto, attempted to demonstrate that these rare words could be sufficiently explained by their original biblical contexts.[26] Although not immediately recognized as such by modern scholars,[27] the composition כתאב אלסבעין לפט׳ה by Saadiah Gaon[28] was the first to treat these rare biblical words in this fashion.[29] Four other works or parts of works soon followed, three emulating Saadiah's approach (Rabbanite) and one diametrically opposed to it (Karaite).[30] Thus, a total of five works or parts of works from the Middle Ages are presently known to have been devoted to this subject. Since these five works share many commonly selected rare words,[31] and since none of them sufficiently defines their principle of selection,[32] we must again deduce that common principle from the types of words chosen. What follows is a list of these five works[33] and an attempt to deduce their common principle of selection:

a) Saadiah Gaon (Rabbanite) - כתאב אלסבעין לפט׳ה[34]
b) Judah ibn Quraysh (Rabbanite) - רסאלה, part two[35]
c) [Yitzḥa]q ben M[ ][36] (Rabbanite) - שאלות עתיקות, chap. הה[37]
d) Menaḥem ibn Saruq (Karaite) - מחברת מנחם, entry גלב[38]
e) Judah ben Ḥayyūj (Rabbanite) - כתאב אלנתף, Judg 14:9[39]

At the beginning of the address to Saadiah's composition, it is explicitly stated that the words involved are isolated in the Bible.[40] Likewise, Menaḥem ibn Saruq tells us in his introductory statement that he is dealing with מלים אשר אין להם דמיון "Words which are not attested elsewhere (in the Bible)."[41] Thus it is clear that these authors themselves considered the words with which they were about to deal as *hapax legomena*. The polemical nature of their work, however, forced them to select words which were attested in MH (Rabbanite), or words which were thought to be easily understood from their context (Karaite). Often these words, while rare in the Bible, were attested there more than once.[42] It is probable that the definition of *hapax legomenon* was thus broadened by these authors to include certain key biblical words, occurring more than once, which were felt to be polemically indispensable. Only in this way can we understand how the authors of these five works, intending to deal with *hapax legomena*, could include both words which occur once in the Bible and rare biblical words which occur more than once. Among the words selected which occur only once are the following:[43] צרכך,[44] נחתך,[45] מפנק,[46] אטון,[47] גלבים,[48] חרצנים,[49] אשך,[50] גבעל,[51] זג,[52] לטאה,[53] אקר,[54] בהט.[55] Among the words selected which occur more than once are the following: טפלו,[56] מצרים,[57] לויתן,[58] חלמיש,[59] מלק,[60] סמדר,[61] טרחכם,[62] כבר,[63] פקעים,[64] כימה,[65] נעצוץ,[66] כומז,[67] אריתי.[68] The stretching of the definition of *hapax legomenon* by these authors is another indication that these works were of a much more polemical than linguistic nature.[69]

3. The Modern Period

While definitions of the term *hapax legomenon* were not explicitly stated in the relevant works of the two periods so far discussed, this is fortunately not the case in the modern period, in which we find studies on *hapax legomena* together with explicit definitions from the beginning of this century up to the present day.

The first modern study specifically devoted to biblical *hapax legomena* was written by A. S. Yahuda in 1903.[70] Yahuda, before proceeding with his interpretation of individual words, defined the term *hapax legomenon* to include all words fulfilling any of the following criteria:[71]

a) single occurrence of root;
b) single occurrence of form;
c) only two occurrences of root in same form with same meaning;
d) only two occurrences of root in different forms but with same meaning;
e) root and form occur frequently but meaning is unique.

Perhaps the most popular and surely the most often cited definition[72] was that of I. M. Casanowicz in the Jewish Encyclopedia,[73] who divided biblical *hapax legomena* into two groups:

a) *absolute or strict hapax legomena*, i.e., words which "are either absolutely new coinages of roots, or which cannot be derived in their formation or in their specific meaning from other occurring stems."[74]

b) *unique forms*, i.e., words which, "while appearing once only as a form, can easily be connected with other existing words."[75]

He then gave a list of all the "absolute" *hapax legomena* in the Bible with an English translation for each one, and a chart indicating the number of "absolute" *hapax legomena* as well as the total number of *hapax legomena* (including "unique forms") for each biblical book.[76]

The next important attempt at a new definition was in the thesis of L. G. Zelson.[77] Zelson considered only Casanowicz' "absolute or strict *hapax legomena*" as relevant to a proper definition, and added "words that are repeated in parallel passages, generally in identical phrases...and words used more than once but that are limited to single passages."[78] After providing this new definition, he then proceeded to analyze all the *hapax legomena* in the Pentateuch in order to arrive at a satisfactory interpretation for each one.[79]

Between 1928 and 1949, four encyclopedia articles were written on *hapax legomena* in the Bible.[80] Clearly the most original and far-reaching of these articles was that of N. H. Tur-Sinai (Torczyner).[81] While not arriving at a new definition, Tur-Sinai dealt mainly with methodology and the origins of biblical *hapax legomena*. He gave many examples demonstrating that a number of these words were not originally *hapax legomena*, and that their present unique status in the Bible is due to scribal error.[82] Such words are now appropriately called "ghost words."[83]

In the last two decades, several articles have been written on biblical *hapax legomena*,[84] but no new definitions have been suggested. Most scholars still follow Casanowicz at least by implication.[85] Perhaps the most important of these articles is that of H. Rabin.[86] Rabin suggested that the real uniqueness of these words lay in their occurrence in but one context. Scholars could not use the regular method of comparison of different contexts in order to determine the meaning of these words.[87] He went on to suggest that although it is not customary to include as *hapax legomena* words that appear two or more times in parallel passages or in the same single context, the clarification of such words is subject to the same limitations because they too occur in only one context.[88] Nevertheless, he did not go so far as to posit a new definition and consistently used the definition of Casanowicz throughout the article.[89] This correlation of the uniqueness of the *hapax legomenon* with the one context in which it occurs was mentioned again by J. Blau, but again was not considered very significant.[90] As we will attempt to show in the third part of this chapter, it is precisely this correlation which must be used as the fundamental basis upon which to build a satisfactory functional definition for biblical *hapax legomena*.

C. The Present Definition

In order to postulate a functional definition for the term *hapax legomenon* in biblical research, it is necessary to isolate a group of rare biblical words which all share a certain functional uniqueness, and which truly could be described as occurring but once. This "functional uniqueness" should in some way be related to difficulties in the philological interpretation of these words, since the term *hapax legomenon* is historically rooted in lexicographical research, the ultimate purpose of which was to facilitate philological interpretation.[91]

Neither the principle of selection of the Masoretic ליתא[92] nor that of the rare words chosen by the Rabbanite and Karaite scholars of the Middle Ages[93] fulfill the conditions set forth above. The former has nothing to do with philological interpretation,[94] while the latter were selected for polemical reasons and, as a result, do not all share a "certain functional uniqueness."[95] Most of the definitions of the modern period[96] also do not qualify. All definitions which include Casanowicz' "unique forms"[97] are unacceptable because many of these "unique forms" present no philological difficulty whatsoever.[98]

The key to a proper definition of the term *hapax legomenon* in biblical research is the identification of the "functional uniqueness" of these words with the single context in which the root of each word occurs. The definition of the term *hapax legomenon* in biblical research would then be as follows: *Any biblical word whose root occurs in but one context.* This definition would exclude the following:

a) Casanowicz' "unique forms"[99] since the roots of such words each occur in more than one context.

b) Proper names of all kinds since these are philologically independent of their context.

Included would be the following:

a) Casanowicz' "absolute or strict hapax legomena."[100]

b) Words which occur more than once in parallel verses.[101]

c) Words which occur more than once in the same single context.[102]

d) Bonafide homonyms whose homonymic root occurs in but one context.[103]

The definition presented here was first proposed by L. G. Zelson some fifty years ago,[104] but was subsequently ignored by modern biblical scholarship.[105] Despite the realization by both H. Rabin[106] and J. Blau[107] that the uniqueness of the biblical *hapax legomenon* lay in its occurrence in but one context, neither of them thought this quality of sufficient importance to serve as the key to a proper definition.[108] This definition is, however, the only one of all those dealt with in part two of this chapter which satisfies the conditions set forth above.[109] As such, it is the definition accepted in this study. Henceforth, all references to the term *hapax legomenon* cited below will refer to this definition exclusively.

NOTES

CHAPTER I

[1]*Hapax* is an adverb meaning "once" (H. G. Liddell and R. Scott, *A Greek-English Lexicon* [Oxford, 1940], 178) and *legomenon* is a passive present participle, neuter singular form of the verb λέγω "say, speak" (ibid., 1034).

[2]These marginal notes have survived in the Homeric scholia assembled by later Homeric scholars. See the summary given by J. E. Sandys, *A History of Classical Scholarship* I (reprint; New York, 1958), 141-42. For the specific scholia involved, see F. Martinazzoli, *Hapax Legomenon* I/2 (Rome, 1957), 11 and the bibliography cited in n. 2.

[3]For the work of Zenodotus in general, see Sandys, *Classical Scholarship* I, 119-21. For his usage of the term *hapax legomenon*, see Martinazzoli, *Hapax Legomenon* I/2, 12-13 and the bibliography cited on p. 13, n. 4.

[4]For the work of Aristarchus in general, see Sandys, *Classical Scholarship* I, 131-36. For his exegetical work on the Homeric poems, see especially A. Roemer, *Die Homerexegese Aristarchs in ihren Grundzügen*, ed. E. Belzner (Paderborn, 1924).

[5]The first scholars to realize that the scientific isolation of *hapax legomena* was a characteristic of Aristarchean Homerology were K. Lehrs, *De Aristarchi Studiis Homericia* (Königsberg, 1833), and A. Ludwich, *Aristarchs Homerische Textkritik* (Leipzig, 1884-85). See Martinazzoli, *Hapax Legomenon* I/2, 11-13, n. 3.

[6]For the work of Apollonius the Sophist in general, see Sandys, *Classical Scholarship* I, 296.

[7]See H. Gattiker, *Das Verhältnis des Homerlexikons des Apollonius Sophistes zu den Homerscholien* (Zürich, 1945), and Martinazzoli, *Hapax Legomenon* I/2, 19 with the bibliography listed in n. 22.

[8]The standard edition of this lexicon is L. Leyde, *De Apollonii Sophistae Lexico Homerico* (Leipzig, 1884). The utilization of the term *hapax legomenon* and similar terms in the *Lexicon Homericum* is the subject of Martinazzoli's work, *Hapax Legomenon* I/2, which is subtitled "Il Lexicon Homericum di Apollonio Sofista."

[9]For the other terms utilized, see Martinazzoli, *Hapax Legomenon* I/2, 23-25.

[10]See ibid., 24, n. 3, where it is stated that modern scholars prefer *hapax legomenon* to *hapax eirēmenon* because the meaning of the former is more transparent than that of the

latter which is a passive form of the less common verb εἴρω "say, speak, tell" (Liddell and Scott, *Lexicon*, 491).

[11]Martinazzoli, *Hapax Legomenon* I/2, 33.

[12]This term was also used by Apollonius the Sophist in his *Lexicon Homericum*. See Martinazzoli, *Hapax Legomenon* I/2, 64-65.

[13]For the work of the Masoretes in general, see now the excellent article by A. Dotan, "Masorah," *EncJud* XVI, 1401-82, with detailed bibliography on pp. 1479-82.

[14]For a discussion of the Masoretic notations in the Masorah Parva, see E. Levita, *Massoreth Ha-Massoreth*, ed. C. D. Ginsburg (reprint; New York, 1968); G. E. Weil in *BHS* VII, XI-XV; E. Würthwein, *Der Text des Alten Testaments* (4th ed.; Stuttgart, 1973), 31-32; Dotan, "Masorah," 1421-22; M. H. Segal, מבוא המקרא IV (Jerusalem, 1965), 906-908; Y. Ring, מבוא לספרות התנ"ך (Tel-Aviv, 1967), 161-63.

[15]For the usage of the ל׳ specifically, see Levita, *Massoreth Ha-Massoreth*, 245; *BHS* VII, XIII; Würthwein, *Der Text*, 32; Dotan, "Masorah," 1422; Segal, מבוא המקרא IV, 907; Ring, מבוא לספרות התנ"ך, 161.

[16]See Levita, *Massoreth Ha-Massoreth*, 245: "Now I shall begin by explaining the word לית 'not extant,' since the Massorites use it more than any other expression."

[17]For references, see Jastrow II, 710 and *OLT* XXII, 1042-65. Note especially the Targum to Job 9:33 which renders לא יש with לא אית. As this example illustrates, לית or ליתא is a contraction of לא + אית which was perhaps inspired by Akkadian *laššu* (= *lā* + *išû*) "is not, are not." The latter, previously thought to be almost completely restricted to Assyrian (*GAG*, §111a; W. von Soden, *Ergänzungen zu GAG* [Rome, 1969], 25 [to §111a]; *AHW*, 539), has now been shown to occur also in Old Babylonian, Middle Babylonian, Standard Babylonian and Boghazkeui Akkadian (see *CAD*, L, 108-10). Note for example in Old Babylonian, W. G. Lambert and A. R. Millard, *Atra-Ḫasīs* (Oxford, 1969), 94:18: [*šapāt e*]*ṭūtu Šamaš laššu* "The darkness was dense, there was no sun." Compare Gilg. IX:v:36 (and parallels): *šapāt ekl*[*etumma ul ib*]*ašši nūru* "The darkness is dense and there is no light." As this example clearly shows, *ul ibašši* often replaces *laššu* in Old Babylonian as does *yānu* in all other periods and peripheral Akkadian. See *CAD*, I/J, 323-24. Only in the form *laššu* and in the Akkadian of the Amarna letters does *išû* have the meaning "to be" (= Akkadian *bašû*). In all other cases, *išû* means "to have." Note finally the usage of suffixes with Aramaic לית (e.g., Targum on Esth 3:8: ליתהון "they are not" rendering אינם) which is paralleled by the stative forms *laššuwāku* "I am not" and *laššuāti* "you (fem.) were not" in Old Assyrian (see *CAD*, L, 110; *AHW*, 539; von Soden, *Ergänzungen zu GAG*, 25 [to §111a]).

[18]See, e.g., Würthwein, *Der Text*, 32; Segal, מבוא המקרא IV, 907; Ring, מבוא לספרות התנ"ך, 161.

[19]The edition of the Masorah Parva utilized here is that of G. E. Weil in *BHS* (see the foreword by K. Elliger, W. Rudolph, and G. E. Weil in *BHS* VII, IX-XV).

[20]The substantive מאור "luminary" is well attested (e.g., Gen 1:14, 15, 16; Ezek 32:8; Ps 74:16), but both the forms את המאור and ואת המאור are syntactically unique.

[21]The verb שרץ is likewise well attested (e.g., Gen 1:20, 21; 8:17; 9:7; Exod 1:7; 7:28; Ezek 47:9; Ps 105:30), but the form ישרצו is morphologically unique.

[22]G. E. Weil in *BHS* VII, XIII ("hapax"); Würthwein, *Der Text*, 32 ("hapax legomenon").

[23]On this period in general, see H. Hirschfeld, *Literary History of Hebrew Grammarians and Lexicographers* (London, 1926), and now the excellent article by D. Tene, "Linguistic Literature, Hebrew," *EncJud* XVI, 1352-90 with comprehensive bibliography on pp. 1400-1401. Here it should be noted that such medieval commentators as Rashi, Rashbam, Abraham ibn Ezra and Radaq all paid special attention to the phenomenon of biblical *hapax legomena* and often designated words belonging to this group (together with other rare words and forms) by such key phrases as the following:
1. אין לו דמיון/דומה "It (the word) has no equivalent" (Rashi, Abraham ibn Ezra)
2. אין לו/לה חבר "It (the word) has no counterpart" (Rashbam, Abraham ibn Ezra, Radaq)
3. אין רע לו/אין לו רע "It (the word) has no counterpart" (Abraham ibn Ezra)
4. אין לו אח/אחות "It (the word) has no counterpart" (Abraham ibn Ezra)
5. מלה זרה "A unique word" (Abraham ibn Ezra).

As may be surmised from the above list, Abraham ibn Ezra noted biblical *hapax legomena* much more often than his fellow commentators in medieval times. In fact, E. Z. Melammed has located about 180 instances in Abraham ibn Ezra's commentaries in which biblical words are designated biblical *hapax legomena* according to one of the above (or less frequently other similar) expressions. For this point and for many examples of each of the phrases translated above, see E. Z. Melammed, מפרשי המקרא-דרכיהם ושיטותיהם (Jerusalem, 1975), 419, 479, 623-26, 648-52, 847-49.

[24]For this controversy in general, see especially S. Baron, *A Social and Religious History of the Jews* V (New York, 1957), 209-85.

[25]For the Rabbanite approach to these rare biblical words, see A. Geiger, *Wissenschaftliche Zeitschrift* V (1844), 323, n. 3; B. Klar, מחקרים ועיונים (Tel-Aviv, 1954), 260-66; N. Allony, ספר דים "מיכה בשבעים מלים בודדות לרס"ג" (Jerusalem, 1958), 365-66; idem, "המלים הבודדות בשאלות עתיקות", *HUCA* 30 (1959), ב-ד;

idem, ספר טור-סיני, "ישעיהו בשבעים מלים בודדות לרס"ג" (Jerusalem, 1960), 282-84; idem, "ירמיהו בשבעים מלים בודדות לרס"ג", *Bet Miqra* 7/2 (1962), 46-49; idem, ספר זיידל, "הקדמת רס"ג לספרו שבעים המלים הבודדות" (Jerusalem, 1962), 234-39; A. Scheiber, "Fernere Fragmente aus שאלות עתיקות", *HUCA* 36 (1965), 230; N. Allony, ספר ייבין, "שבעים מלים בודדות ברסאלה ליהודה אבן קריש" (Jerusalem, 1970), 412-14, 419-21; idem, "קטע חדש מספר הקרחה לר׳ יהודה חיוג׳" appended to P. Kokovzov, מספרי הבלשנות העברית בימי הבינים (reprint; Jerusalem, 1970), ה-ו.

[26]See N. Allony, "השקפות קראיות במחברת מנחם והמלים הבודדות בערך גלב", אוצר יהודי ספרד V (1962), 21-49.

[27]The Rabbanite-Karaite controversy was not immediately recognized as being the raison d'être of this composition. Many modern scholars thought the work to be simply comparative philology for its own sake. See, e.g., L. Dukes, "Erklärung seltener biblischer Wörter von Saadias Gaon," *ZKM* 5 (1844), 115-17; H. Ewald and L. Dukes, *Beiträge zur Geschichte der ältesten Auslegung und Spracherklärung des Alten Testamentes* (Stuttgart, 1844), 39; M. Steinschneider, *Die arabische Literatur der Judea* (reprint; Hildesheim, 1964), 60; H. Malter, *Saadia Gaon, His Life and Works* (Philadelphia, 1921), 138-41, 306-308. A. Geiger was the first to suggest that the Rabbanite-Karaite controversy was the impetus behind this work (Geiger, *Wissenschaftliche Zeitschrift* V [1844], 323, n. 3), and B. Klar later fully developed this point (Klar, מחקרים ועיונים, 260-66).

[28]For bibliography, see n. 34.

[29]The main purpose of this work has now been made abundantly clear from the recently found introduction to this composition by Saadiah himself. Saadiah states (Allony, "הקדמת רס"ג", 241, lines 8-15 and Hebrew translation on p. 244) that he has noticed some Jews (i.e., Karaites) who distinguish between the written and the oral law, and between the language of the Bible and the language of the people which is not in the Bible, denying the sanctity of the latter in each case. However, he claims, he has found many biblical words which cannot be satisfactorily understood except through comparison with the language spoken by the people and the Oral Law (i.e., MH).

[30]See the statement made by Menaḥem in מחברת מנחם under the entry גלב (מחברת מנחם, 56):

> אין למלה זו דמיון בתורה אבל ענינה
> יורה עליה...ויש בתורה מלין אשר אין
> להם דמיון אבל ענינם יורה עליהם.
>
> This word appears in the Bible only here, but its context sheds light upon it...and there are (other) words in the Bible which appear only once, but their contexts shed light on them (as well).

[31]See the list in Appendix I which includes all the *hapax legomena* (according to the definition to be presented below) dealt with in these five works, and the chart by Allony,

"רסאלה", 415, which tabulates the number of words each of the first four works have in common with each other. For the fifth work, that of Judah ben Ḥayyūj, which is very fragmentary and so far includes only ten words, see the discussion by Allony, "ספר הקרחה", ו, who tabulates that four of these ten words are utilized by Saadiah, five are utilized by Judah ibn Quraysh, one is utilized in שאלות עתיקות, and there is none utilized in מחברת מנחם.

[32]Only in the case of Saadiah are we given any indication, even in a general way, as to the principle of selection utilized (see Saadiah's introduction to his work cited above in n. 29, and especially the section paraphrased in the same note).

[33]See Allony, "ספר הקרחה", ה.

[34]This work was first brought to the attention of the scholarly world in 1844 and was published four different times in that year: Dukes, "Erklärung," 115-36; Ewald and Dukes, *Beiträge*, 39-40, 110-15; Geiger, *Wissenschaftliche Zeitschrift* V (1844), 317-24; A. Jellink in Y. Benjacob, דברים עתיקים (Leipzig, 1844), 3-11. Since then, several other editions with further explanatory notes have been published: S. Buber, בית אוצר הספרות I (1887), 33-52; D. Fink, לשון למודים III (Berlin, 1926), 34-36; S. A. Wertheimer, באור תשעים מלות בודדות בתנ"ך (Jerusalem, 1931). New fragments were then published by B. Klar and N. Allony: Klar, מחקרים ועיונים, 259-75; N. Allony, "שני קטעים נוספים מהנוסח המקורי של שבעים מלים בודדות", *Sinai* 37 (1955), 245-60. To N. Allony again, we owe the publication of many additional fragments together with the critical edition of this work: N. Allony, "כתאב אלסבעין לפט׳ה לרב סעדיה גאון", *Ignace Goldziher Memorial Volume* II (Jerusalem, 1958), 1-48 (Hebrew section). Allony has also published a Hebrew translation of Saadiah's introduction with copious notes, as well as several articles on Saadiah's interpretation of these words in the light of modern biblical scholarship: "הקדמת רס"ג", 233-52; "מיכה", 362-66; "ישעיהו", 279-88; "ירמיהו", 43-49.

[35]The standard edition of this work is J. J. L. Bargès and D. B. Goldberg, *Risala* (Paris, 1857). A Hebrew translation was later published by M. Katz, אגרת ר׳ יהודה בן קוריש (Tel-Aviv, 1950). New manuscripts and a discussion as well as an index of the rare words in part two of the *Risala* were published by Allony, "רסאלה", 409-25.

[36]The name of the author of שאלות עתיקות is still unknown. For the latest discussion of the available evidence, see A. Scheiber, "Unknown Leaves from שאלות עתיקות", *HUCA* 27 (1956), 291-94; idem, "Fernere Fragmente," 233-34; E. Fleischer, "לצבירון השאלות העתיקות ולבעית זהות מחברך", *HUCA* 38 (1967), א-יד.

[37]The standard edition of this work is that of J. Rosenthal, "שאלות עתיקות בתנ"ך", *HUCA* 21 (1948), כט-צא. To this edition must now be added the new fragments published by A. Scheiber: "Unknown Leaves," 291-303; and "Fernere Fragmente," 227-59. The chapter הה, which deals with rare biblical words was separately edited by Allony, "שאלות עתיקות", א-יד.

[38]The standard edition of the מחברת is that of Pilipowski, מחברת מנחם. The rare biblical words collected under the entry גלב in the מחברת have been listed together with variants from the different manuscripts by Allony, "מחברת מנחם", 50-54.

[39]The critical edition of the Arabic original of this composition was published by P. Kokovtsov, *Nowiye Materyaly* II (Leningrad, 1916), 1-58, 191-204, with Russian introduction on pp. 1-74 (Russian part). This has now been republished as מספרי הבלשנות בימי הבינים (Jerusalem, 1970), 1-58, 191-204, without the Russian introduction, but with the addition of a new fragment to the כתאב אלנתף published by Allony, "ספר הקרחה", א-מט, which contains a list and discussion of rare biblical words under the commentary to וירדהו אל כפיו (Judg 14:9).

[40]Allony, "הקדמת רס"ג", 241: line one of address: מן מפרדאת אללגה "which are among the isolated (words) in the text (= Bible)." Note that the Arabic verb *farada* means "He, or it, was, or became, single; sole; or one, and no more" (Lane VI, 2363). Note also the variant אלמפרדאת for מן מפרדאת in line one of the address to Saadiah's work quoted above (see Allony, "כתֽאב אלסבעין לפט׳ה", 14). See for the latter the lexicographical term *al-mafrīdat* signifying "What has been transmitted by only one of the lexicologists" (Lane VI, 2364).

[41]See n. 30 above. Note also the usage of this terminology by later medieval commentators such as Rashi and Abraham ibn Ezra as discussed above in n. 23.

[42]This fact was first noted by M. Schloessinger, "Hapax Legomena in Rabbinical Literature," *The Jewish Encyclopedia* VI (New York, 1904), 229, with respect to Saadiah's composition, and was further demonstrated with many examples by S. A. Wertheimer תשעים מלים בודדות, 3-4 (introduction).

[43]A full list of words selected by these authors which qualify as *hapax legomena* according to the definition presented in part three of this chapter will be given in Appendix I.

[44]2 Chr 2:15. Selected by Saadiah, Menaḥem and ibn Quraysh.

[45]Dan 9:24. Selected by Saadiah and Menaḥem.

[46]Prov 29:21. Selected by Saadiah.

[47]Prov 7:16. Selected by Menaḥem.

[48]Ezek 5:1. Selected by Menaḥem and the author of שאלות עתיקות.

[49]Num 6:4. Selected by Menaḥem and the author of שאלות עתיקות.

[50]Lev 21:20. Selected by ibn Quraysh.

[51]Exod 9:31. Selected by ibn Quraysh, author of שאלות עתיקות and ben Ḥayyūj.

[52]Num 6:4. Selected by ibn Quraysh.

[53]Lev 11:30. Selected by the author of שאלות עתיקות.

[54]Deut 14:5. Selected by the author of שאלות עתיקות.

[55]Esth 1:6. Selected by the author of שאלות עתיקות.

[56]Ps 119:69; see also Job 13:4; 14:17. Selected by Saadiah and ibn Quraysh.

[57]Lam 1:3; see also Ps 118:5. Selected by Saadiah and ibn Quraysh.

[58]Job 3:8; see also Isa 27:1; Ps 74:14; 104:26; Job 40:25. Selected by Saadiah and ibn Quraysh.

[59]Deut 8:15; see also 32:13; Isa 50:7; Ps 114:8; Job 28:9. Selected by Menaḥem.

[60]Lev 1:15; see also 5:8. Selected by Menaḥem.

[61]Cant 7:13; see also 2:13, 15. Selected by Menaḥem.

[62]Deut 1:12; see also Isa 1:14; Job 37:11. Selected by ibn Quraysh.

[63]Eccl 1:10; see also 2:12, 16; 3:15; 4:2; 6:10; 9:6, 7. Selected by ibn Quraysh.

[64]1 Kgs 6:18; see also 7:24. Selected by ibn Quraysh.

[65]Amos 5:8; see also Job 9:9; 38:31. Selected by the author of שאלות עתיקות.

[66]Isa 55:13; see also 7:19. Selected by the author of שאלות עתיקות.

[67]Exod 35:22; see also Num 31:50. Selected by the author of שאלות עתיקות.

[68]Cant 5:1; see also Ps 80:13. Selected by ben Ḥayyūj and Saadiah.

[69]See above, nn. 27 and 29.

[70]A. S. Yahuda, "Hapax Legomena im Alten Testament," *JQR* 15 (1903), 698-714.

[71]Ibid., 698-700.

[72]E.g., SHL, III-IV; L. G. Zelson, "Les Hapax Legomena du Pentateuque Hebraique," *RB* 36 (1927), 243-44; "Hapax Legomena," *Enciclopedia Judaica Castellana* V (Mexico, 1949), 268; Allony, "מיכה", 362; Ring, מבוא לספרות התנ"ך, 70-72; J. Blau, "Hapax Legomena," *EncJud* VII, 1318-19.

[73]I. M. Casanowicz, "Hapax Legomena - Biblical Data," *The Jewish Encyclopedia* VI (New York, 1904), 226-28.

[74]Ibid., 226.

[75]Ibid.

[76]Ibid., 226-28.

[77]SHL.

[78]Ibid., IV.

[79]Note that three years later, in a separate study, Zelson published his definition and a list of all *hapax legomena* in the Pentateuch. See Zelson, "Les Hapax Legomena," 243-48.

[80]B. Kirschner, "Hapax Legomena," *Jüdisches Lexikon* II (Berlin, 1928), 1429; H. Torczyner, "Hapax Legomena," *Encyclopedia Judaica* VII (Berlin, 1931), 997-1000; I. Landman, ed., *The Universal Jewish Encyclopedia* V (New York, 1941), 212; "Hapax Legomena," *Enciclopedia Judaica Castellana* V, 268.

[81]See n. 80.

[82]Tur-Sinai later dealt with this subject in volume one of his הלשון והספר (Jerusalem, 1954), 363-92.

[83]See, e.g., H. L. Ginsberg, "Abram's Damascene Steward," *BASOR* 200 (1970), 31-32.

[84]Allony, "מיכה", 362-66; idem, "ישעיהו", 279-88; idem, "ירמיהו", 43-49; H. Rabin, "מלים בודדות", *EM* IV, 1066-70; Ring, מבוא לספרות התנ"ך, 70-72; Blau, "Hapax Legomena," 1318-19.

[85]See, e.g., the references in n. 84.

[86]Rabin, "מלים בודדות", 1066-70.

[87]Ibid., 1067:
לגבי הפרשנות ייחודן של מלים אלו הוא בכך, שהן
מופיעות רק בהקשר אחד ושאין ללמוד על משמעותן
בשיטה הרגילה של השוואת הקשרים שונים.

[88]Ibid.

[89]Casanowicz' "absolute hapax legomena" were termed "בודדות שרש", while his "unique forms" were called "מלים שהן גזורות משרשים ידועים".

[90]Blau, "Hapax Legomena," 1318.

[91]See above, part one of this chapter. Note also the conclusion of Sandys, *Classical Scholarship* I, 144:

> The scholars of Alexandria were (as we have seen) mainly...concerned with the verbal criticism of the Greek poets, primarily with that of Homer....They

were the earliest examples of the professional scholar, and they deserve the gratitude of the modern world for criticising and classifying the literature of the Golden Age of Greece and handing it down to posterity.

[92]See above, section B, part 1.

[93]See above, section B, part 2.

[94]The ל׳ was used to indicate all syntactically and morphologically unique forms or expressions. See above, part two, section A.

[95]Many of the words chosen appear twice or more. See above, section B, part 2.

[96]See above, section B, part 3.

[97]See above, n. 75.

[98]E.g., אכילה (1 Kgs 19:8) "food" from אכל "to eat"; מעמד (Ps 69:3) "place to stand" from עמד "to stand"; תלמיד (1 Chr 25:8) "pupil" from למד "to learn"; קריאה (Jonah 3:2) "proclamation" from קרא "to call, proclaim".

[99]See above, n. 75.

[100]See above, n. 74.

[101]For a collection of these parallel verses, see the extremely useful study of A. Bendavid, *Parallels in the Bible* I-IV (Jerusalem, 1965-69).

[102]E.g., פרת in Gen 49:22.

[103]Homonyms present a special problem of classification. In order for a homonym to be a *hapax legomenon*, it must be strictly a homonym beyond any shadow of a doubt. Special usages of known attested roots would not qualify. For many examples, see the list of homonymic *hapax legomena* in Appendix II.

[104]See n. 77 above.

[105]While Zelson's thesis was never published, an article of his did appear in *RB* (see above, n. 79) which contained his definition as well as a list of all the *hapax legomena* in the Pentateuch. Of all the articles on *hapax legomena* referred to in part two of this chapter, only the article in the *Enciclopedia Judaica Castellana* (see above, n. 72) saw fit to mention Zelson's article in the bibliography.

[106]See n. 87 above.

[107]See n. 90 above.

[108]The use of the "single context" as the key to a definition of the term *hapax legomenon* was already proposed for Old English *hapax legomena* in the thesis of N. O. Waldorf on this subject. See N. O. Waldorf, "The *Hapax Legomena* in the English Vocabulary: A Study Based upon the Bosworth Toller Dictionary" (Unpublished Ph.D. dissertation; Stanford University, 1953), 2.

[109]Here it must be noted that while the definition presented here does not take into account the unique usages of common words by individual biblical authors, this is not meant to imply that such distinctions are invalid. Rather, distinctions based on an individual writer's literary style are too fine to be included within the definition. Such distinctions are extremely important in determining and appreciating the literary style of a particular biblical author, but are so open to subjective interpretation that they would hamper rather than aid the investigation undertaken here.

CHAPTER II

METHODOLOGY

A. The Method Utilized in Previous Studies

Before embarking on a complete description of the method which has guided the present study, a review will be made of the various methodological principles underlying previous biblical *hapax legomena* research from the Middle Ages to the present.

1. The Period of the Early Hebrew Grammarians[1]

The existence of an independent consistent method guiding any of the medieval works dealing with biblical *hapax legomena*[2] is open to serious question. As shown above, the polemical nature of these compositions caused their authors to stretch the definition of *hapax legomenon* to absurd proportions.[3] It would not be surprising therefore to find that their methodological principles were also colored by these same polemical goals. Since only Saadiah and Menaḥem explicitly discuss their methodological principles, and since only these two authors comment on the words which they have isolated, it is with them alone that we will deal.

Saadiah, in the introduction to his work, states several times that his purpose is to explain difficult words in the Bible on the basis of the "popular prosaic spoken language" of the Mishnaic period.[4] Nowhere is there any discussion of the importance of the context in which these words are found. Nor could Saadiah have included this element even if he so desired. For, explaining these rare words on the basis of their respective contexts was precisely the method of Saadiah's arch-enemies, the Karaites (see below). Thus, Saadiaḥ's method was devoid of the major element of contextuality. The following analysis of a few of the interpretations offered by Saadiah should suffice to indicate this methodological shortcoming.[5]

(1) *Lev 25:47* (<u>לעקר</u> משפחת גר). Clearly the substantive עקר must mean "offspring" in this context, and there is now conclusive evidence for this meaning from the Old Aramaic

Sefîre inscriptions.[6] Saadiah, on the other hand, attempted to explain this term on the basis of Mishnaic עיקר "the main thing" citing *Berakot* 6:7.[6a]

(2) *Isa 28:25* (נסמן). While this is admittedly an extremely difficult text for which no completely acceptable translation has yet been offered,[7] the interpretation suggested by Saadiah ignores the context of the verse completely. For נסמן clearly relates in some way to שעורה "barley" and must refer to some agricultural process which is used for growing barley successfully. Saadiah, on the other hand, sought to explain this difficult term on the basis of Mishnaic סימן "sign" citing *Baba Meṣi'a* 2:7.[8]

(3) *Ezek 17:9* (יקוסס). As parallel to ינתק, this verb must mean "to strip off" though clear philological evidence for this meaning is still wanting.[9] Saadiah, however, compared Mishnaic קסס "to be sourish (said of wine)" citing *Baba Batra* 6:2.[10]

(4) *Ps 60:4* (פצמתה). Clearly this verb with ארץ as its direct object must mean "to split open" or the like in this context. Yet Saadiah derived its meaning from Mishnaic פצים "board" citing *Shabbat* 8:7.[11]

Thus while Saadiah did offer several valid interpretations of biblical *hapax legomena* based on cognates in Middle Hebrew,[1] his polemical overzealousness caused him at times to lose sight of the respective contexts in which these words occurred. As a result, several methodologically unsound comparisons were made.

Menaḥem's method is made crystal clear by the following statement in his work:[13]

> ויש בתורה מלין אשר אין להם דמיון אבל עניינם יורה
> עליהם ולולא אחיזתם במהוה ותלייתם מענין לא נודע פתרונם.
>
> For there are words in the Bible which are not attested elsewhere, but their context sheds light upon them. Were it not for their inclusion in a phrase and their dependence upon context, their interpretation would remain unknown.

This method for the treatment of *hapax legomena* is in perfect consonance with the Karaite attitude towards the Bible in general.[14] While Saadiah tried to prove that the Oral Torah and Middle Hebrew were indispensable for a proper understanding of biblical Hebrew, Menaḥem's contention was that the Bible is a self-contained unit which could be completely understood in and of itself, without the need of utilizing any outside sources. Not only was Middle Hebrew invalid for the biblical researcher, but also Aramaic and Arabic, the only other Semitic languages known at the time, could not be used either. Thus, Menaḥem's polemical goals prevented him from making use of one of the biblical researcher's most important tools, the tool of comparison with Middle Hebrew and other Semitic languages. The lack of this tool as a component part of Menaḥem's method caused him to suggest several invalid interpretations for biblical *hapax legomena* as may be seen from the following examples.[15]

(1) *Exod 12:9* (נא). Menaḥem[16] connects the substantive נא with such texts as Num 32:7 (תניאון) and Ps 33:10 (הניא) which clearly must be derived from נוא "to prevent, thwart,"[17] thus ignoring Middle Hebrew נא "raw, half-cooked."[18]

(2) *Ps 80:14* (יכרסמנה). Menaḥem[19] connects this verb with Jer 51:34 (כרשו) ignoring Middle Hebrew קרסם "devour"[20] and the last letter of the verbal root (מ).

Thus, notwithstanding his many valid suggestions concerning biblical *hapax legomena*,[21] Menaḥem's faulty method caused him to operate largely without the use of extrabiblical comparisons, and this omission became the source of several incorrect interpretations on his part.

2. The Modern Period[22]

To my knowledge, no consistent independent method has ever been proposed to deal with biblical *hapax legomena*. In fact, the most recent article on the subject states the following opinion rather emphatically:[23]

> ...the philological treatment of hapax legomena does not differ from that of words occurring more often. The meaning of both is elucidated by comparison with other Semitic languages, which often makes it possible to establish the etymology of the word treated.

To be sure, many scholars have recognized that the occurrence of these words in but one context constitutes a special problem.[24] However, no scholar has attempted to evolve a special method for biblical *hapax legomena* based on that fact. Scholars at one time or another have emphasized comparisons with Arabic[25] and Middle Hebrew[26] when dealing with these words, but no one has presented any methodological principles to govern the comparisons.

B. The Present Method

The key to a proper method for biblical *hapax legomena* lies in the realization that such words occur in but one context, thus eliminating the possibility of utilizing the proven method of inner biblical comparison of the different contexts in which a given word occurs in order to shed light on its meaning. Here it should be made clear that the extant rarity of a given word is by no means any indication as to how well that word was known in ancient times. Surely the many *hapax legomena* which occur in the list of clean and unclean animals in Leviticus 11 and Deuteronomy 14 must have been well understood by the ancient Israelites. No law intending to regulate the daily eating habits of a society could possibly be effective if the average man did not understand which foods he was permitted to eat and which foods were being prohibited. On the other hand, where one or more synonyms occur for the word in question and these synonyms are much more commonly attested, it may well be that the word in question originally belonged to the layer of language known as poetic language, while its synonyms were part of the layer called daily language.[27] Regardless, however, of whether or not an extant *hapax legomenon* was commonly or rarely attested in ancient times, its single contextual occurrence in the extant Hebrew Bible is the major problem it presents to the modern biblical philologist.

Thus, it is necessary for the biblical scholar to rely quite heavily on the only other major tools at his disposal--the ancient versions and translations of the Bible and comparisons with the other Semitic languages.[28] The latter tool, however, cannot be utilized in exactly the same way as it is with words that occur in more than one context.[29] For in the case of such words, the other contexts in which a given word occurs serve as a check against the irresponsible use of this valuable tool. In other words, a biblical word may be truly identified with its alleged etymological equivalent in another Semitic language only if the usage of the biblical word in all its contexts can be shown to correspond to the usage of the proposed etymological equivalent in the other Semitic language. If such is the case, then the biblical word may be said to be both semantically and etymologically equivalent to its counterpart in the other Semitic language and the two words may be considered true cognates. If, however, the usage of the alleged etymological equivalent in the other Semitic language does not correspond to that of its biblical counterpart,[30] and/or if it can be shown that in an interdialectal distribution[31] including the biblical word, a word other than the proposed etymological equivalent must be used for the Semitic language in question, then the comparison is completely invalid.

Since the regular method of checking comparisons with other Semitic languages is invalid in the case of *hapax legomena* because of the latter's existence in but one context, an alternative method must be sought. What is here suggested is that the single context in which the *hapax legomenon* occurs may itself serve as a check on etymological comparisons. For if a proper comparison has been made, then the meaning of the biblical word according to the meaning of its proposed etymological equivalent should be such that *the resultant meaning of the entire contextual phrase should have some parallel in another context*[32] *where the proposed etymological equivalent or its synonym is attested*. This other context could conceivably come from any textual source in any Semitic language, but the similarity in meaning of the key word in this other context to the proposed etymological equivalent would have to be clearly demonstrated unless this key word were the proposed etymological equivalent itself. For such a demonstration, the tool of synonymous parallelism, the notion of semantic development, and the use of interdialectical distributions[33] could well be employed. Once a possible etymological equivalent has been suggested and a corroborative parallel context has been found, one can consider the meaning of the *hapax legomenon* to be reasonably assured. While comparisons from all Semitic languages could be governed by the above method in the case of biblical *hapax legomena*, only Akkadian and Ugaritic comparisons will be considered in detail in this study.[34]

The method proposed in this study is also valid for determining whether a given word is truly a *hapax legomenon*. In several cases, suspected *hapax legomena* have been reduced to unique forms of known biblical roots once having been subjected to the above procedure. Some of these suspect *hapax legomena* are discussed below as an illustration of the method:

(1) *1 Sam 9:7* (תשורה)

ותשורה אין להביא לאיש האלהים

There is no gift to bring to the prophet.

Lie Sar. 78:8

[*t*]*āmartu* kabittu ušamḫiršunūti

I presented them (the gods) with valuable gifts.

That תשורה clearly means "gift" in this context is acknowledged by many commentaries on the Book of Samuel, both ancient[35] and modern.[36] The correct etymology was first suggested by Menaḥem in his מחברת[37] and it is this etymology which may now be confirmed by Akkadian *tāmartu*.[38] תשורה is to be derived from שור "to see" as *tāmartu* is derived from *amāru* "to see."[39] Since *tāmartu* clearly means "gift"[40] and occurs in contexts similar to 1 Sam 9:7 (such as the one quoted above), this etymology may be considered quite plausible.

(2) *Hos 10:7*[41] (קצף)

נדמה שומרון מלכה כקצף על פני מים

Samaria and its king shall perish
like foam on the surface of the water.

Era IV:67-68[42]

ni̲šī ša iṉa l̲ibbišu kī qanê tuḫtaṣṣis
kī *ḫubuš*[43] pān mê ḫuburšina tubtai̇li̇

You broke the population in its (Der's) midst
like a reed; You brought their din to an end
like foam on the surface of the water.

The existence of the simile "like foam on the surface of the water" in an Akkadian text dating from some time between the eleventh and the ninth centuries B.C.E.[44] clearly demonstrates that Hos 10:7 could be translated as above if a suitable etymology could be found for the term קצף. Such an etymology has been found in the substantive קצף "anger" heretofore understood as a homonym of קצף in Hos 10:7.[45] For the semantic range of words denoting "anger" includes the meaning "foam." Examples of words exhibiting this semantic range are Hebrew חמה and its Akkadian etymological equivalent *imtu* which share the common meaning "venom, poison" and which, when taken individually, include the meanings "wrath" and "foam."[46] Furthermore, the Aramaic root רתח is a clear example of a Semitic root denoting both "to be angry" and "to foam, to bubble."[47] The relevance of the latter to our verse is confirmed by the occurrence of רותחא in Targum Jonathan translating קצף in Hos 10:7.[48] Thus, those ancient translations, and scholars both medieval and modern, who translated קצף in our text as "foam"[49] rather than as "splinter or chip of wood,"[50] now appear to be vindicated.[51]

(3) *Ps 93:3* (דכים)

נשאו נהרות ה׳ נשאו נהרות קולם ישאו[52] נהרות דכים

The rivers have lifted, O Yahweh,
The rivers have lifted their "voices,"[53]
The rivers have lifted their waves.

Ps 93:4

מקלות מים רבים[54] אדיר ממשברי ים[55]

Stronger than the "voices" of mighty waters,
Mightier than the waves of the sea...

דכים has been interpreted in many different ways from the Middle Ages[56] to the present.[57] Its understanding in the modern period, however, has been hampered by the persistent comparison with Ugaritic *dkym* which occurs in a completely different context with apparently a completely different meaning.[58] Since דכים is parallel to קולם "their voices" in Ps 93:3, while in Ps 93:4 קלות "voices" is parallel to משברים "waves," the synonymous parallelism in the two verses could certainly be considered as supporting contextual evidence for any valid etymology of *דכי leading to the translation "wave." The derivation of דכים from Hebrew דכה[59] provides just such an etymology. For *דכי "wave" could come from דכה "to crush" just as משבר "wave" is derived from שבר "to break." Such a derivation is further corroborated by the synonomous parallelism of שבר//דכה/דכא.[60]

NOTES

CHAPTER II

[1]See above, Chapter I, section B, part 2.

[2]See above, p. 3.

[3]See above, pp. 3-4.

[4]Allony, "הקדמת רס"ג", 241:11-15, 19-2 with Hebrew translation on p. 244:11-15, 19-2.

[5]A complete analysis of Saadiah's work may be found in S. Kraus, "Saadya's Tafsir of the Seventy Hapax Legomena Explained and Continued," *Saadya Studies* (Manchester, 1943), 47-56. On pp. 57-77 of the same article, Kraus presents a "Glossarium Biblico-Mishnicum" in which he lists Biblical-Mishnaic comparisons. For a proper evaluation of the utilization of Middle Hebrew comparisons in modern biblical research, see E. Y. Kutscher, "Mittelhebräisch und Jüdisch-Aramäisch im neuen Köhler-Baumgartner," VTSup 16 (1967), 158-68.

[6]See J. A. Fitzmyer, *The Aramaic Inscriptions of Sefîre* (Rome, 1967), 12:2, 3 and passim. Note also Fitzmyer's commentary on p. 28 where a complete bibliography is given. Add J. C. L. Gibson, *Textbook of Syrian Semitic Inscriptions* II (Oxford, 1975), 34-35.

[6a]Professor M. Weinfeld suggests that עיקר and עקר may both be derived from a stem whose basic meaning is "root." He compares שרש "root" as well as "offspring" in the Bible and in the Aramaic inscriptions of Sefîre together with the phrase כוס של עיקרים "a cup of root drink." As for עיקר "the main thing," he contends that "עיקר in the sense of 'main' is the figurative of 'root' which means 'basic'/'most important'" (oral communication).

[7]The latest translation may be found in H. L. Ginsberg, *The Book of Isaiah* (Philadelphia, 1973), 62: "in a strip," which fits the context admirably but for which no philological evidence is presented. Professor Ginsberg's commentary to First Isaiah which is soon to be published in the Anchor Bible Series may hopefully shed some light on this crux.

[8]See also Kraus, "Saadya's Tafsir," 48, who further notes that Mishnaic סימן is of Greek origin.

[9]This contextual meaning was already seen in BDB, 890, and the translation there "stripped off" has been adopted by the *NEB*. The rendering of KB I, 845, "make scaly" based on קשקשת "scale (of fish)" has absolutely nothing to recommend it.

[10]See also Kraus, "Saadya's Tafsir," 55.

[11]See ibid., 54.

[12]E.g., Hab 3:17 (ברפתים) on the basis of Mishnaic רפת "stall"; Ps 80:14 (יכרסמנה) on the basis of Mishnaic קרסם "to devour"; 2 Chr 2:15 (צרכך) on the basis of Mishnaic צרך "to need."

[13]מחברת מנחם, 56.

[14]See Allony, "מחברת מנחם", 21-49.

[15]Only two examples are cited here due to the many *hapax legomena* which Menaḥem lists but fails to interpret explicitly. See his comments on, e.g., Gen 41:23 (צנמות); Num 6:4 (מחרצנים); 2 Kgs 4:42 (בצקלונו); Isa 55:13 (הסרפד); Ezek 16:40 (ובתקוך); 39:2 (וששאתיך); Job 21:24 (עטיניו); 41:10 (עטישותיו); Cant 8:5 (מתרפקת); Eccl 10:8 (גומץ); Esth 8:15 (ותכריך בוץ וארגמן); 2 Chr 2:15 (צרכך); 2:15 (רפסדות).

[16]מחברת מנחם, 121. Contrast תשובות דונש, 21.

[17]KB I, 600.

[18]For the relevant passages, see מלון הלשון העברית IV, 3460-61. See also *HALAT*, 620-21.

[19]מחברת מנחם, 110. Contrast תשובות דונש, 33.

[20]E.g., *Pe'ah* 2:7 as noted by Saadiah (see above, n. 12). See also *HALAT*, 475.

[21]Note that for both Ezek 17:9 (יקוסס) and Ps 60:4 (פצמתה), Menaḥem suggests the correct contextual meaning, though of course without offering any corroborative philological evidence. For a brief discussion of these two words and Saadiah's misinterpretation of them, see above.

[22]See above, Chapter I, section B, part 3.

[23]Blau, "Hapax Legomena," 1318.

[24]E.g., Torczyner, "Hapax Legomena," 998; Rabin, "מלים בודדות", 1067; Ring, מבוא לספרות התנ"ך, 70; Blau, "Hapax Legomena," 1318. Note that already in the first quarter of the nineteenth century, W. Gesenius had paid special attention to biblical *hapax legomena* when formulating his methodological principles, but he too claimed that no special treatment of them was necessary. See E. F. Miller, *The Influence of Gesenius on Hebrew Lexicography* (reprint; New York, 1966), 22-23 and the references to Gesenius' works cited there.

[25]E.g., Yahuda, "Hapax Legomena," 698-700.

[26]E.g., Torczyner, "Hapax Legomena," 997-998; Blau, "Hapax Legomena," 1318.

[27]On these two layers which have been designated the A-words and the B-words because of the order in which they occur when parallel to each other in poetic texts, see SUL, 5-8. On this fixed order, see also H. L. Ginsberg, "Ugaritic Studies and the Bible," *BA* 8 (1945), 55-56. Some examples of biblical *hapax legomena* which are also B-words in both Hebrew and Ugaritic are שתע "to fear" (#16 in Chapter III); קבעת "chalice" (#18 in Chapter III); מצץ "to suck" (#19 in Chapter III).

[28]Under Semitic languages, we also include Egyptian since, whether or not Egyptian can in fact be so classified, it does contain a Semitic substratum of borrowed words, many common terms which are equally as common in the Semitic languages, and a similar syntactic structure. As an example of a common term, see the study of A. Piankoff, *Le 'coeur' dans les textes égyptiens* (Paris, 1930). This study clearly shows that Egyptian *'ib* "heart" is the exact equivalent of Hebrew לב, Ugaritic *lb*, and Akkadian *libbu*. On the problem of the relationship between the Hamitic and Semitic languages, see H. J. Polotsky, "Egyptian," *World History of the Jewish People* I (Tel-Aviv, 1964), 122-23; I. M. Diakonoff, *Semito-Hamitic Languages* (Moscow, 1965). For some proposed Egyptian comparisons with biblical words, see A. Erman, "Das Verhältnis des Aegyptischen zu den semitischen Sprachen," *ZDMG* 46 (1892), 93-129; *WAS* VI, 243-44; A. Ember, *Egypto-Semitic Studies* (Leipzig, 1930); T. O. Lambdin, "Egyptian Loan Words in the Old Testament," *JAOS* 73 (1953), 145-55.

[29]Contrast the opinion of J. Blau quoted above in section one, part B.

[30]For this very common problem, often occurring because scholars merely utilize dictionaries instead of referring directly to the original texts in which the word is attested, see L. Kopf, "המילון הערבי כאמצעי עזר לבלשנות העברית", *Leshonenu* 19 (1954), 72-82 (= idem, "Das arabische Wörterbuch als Hilfsmittel für die hebräische Lexikographie," *VT* 6 [1956], 286-302); idem, "Arabische Etymologien und Parallelen zum Bibelwörterbuch," *VT* 8 (1958), 161-215; idem, "Arabische Etymologien und Parallelen zum Bibelwörterbuch," *VT* 9 (1959), 247-87. We have attempted to avoid this problem in the present study by quoting at least one key passage for each etymological equivalent discussed so as to demonstrate its relevant usage.

[31]For the whole matter of interdialectal distribution, see M. Held, "mhṣ/*mḫš in Ugaritic and Other Semitic Languages," *JAOS* 79 (1959), 169 and passim throughout this article. For many additional examples of such distributions, see SUL, passim.

[32]This other context must be quoted and translated. Dictionary definitions or even text citations are unacceptable since the interpretation of any text may be open to dispute. For the pitfalls of utilizing only dictionary meanings in this regard, see n. 30 above and the literature cited there. Note further that this other context is here considered parallel if it employs the same parallelism (or juxtaposition), associates the same terms in a list, or uses the same stock phrases as does the original biblical context.

[33]See above, n. 31.

[34]In Chapter III, twenty-eight biblical *hapax legomena* with their suggested Akkadian and/or Ugaritic comparisons are treated. These words have been chosen to be investigated in detail, because they best illustrate the advantages of the proposed method. Any other suggested comparisons from other Semitic languages for these selected words are also taken into consideration, if at all relevant. In Appendix II, sixty additional *hapax legomena* with Akkadian and/or Ugaritic comparisons are dealt with in less detail. The latter represents, in the author's opinion, all the remaining reasonably certain comparisons for biblical *hapax legomena* from Akkadian and/or Ugaritic. Here too, other relevant comparisons from other Semitic languages are taken into consideration, but again, in considerably less detail. Thus, some eighty-eight biblical *hapax legomena* are dealt with in some detail in this study, and these represent in the opinion of the author *all the biblical hapax legomena which have reasonably certain cognates in Akkadian and/or Ugaritic*.

[35]See the comments of Rashi and Kimchi on this word as well as that of Menaḥem in מחברת מנחם, 180.

[36]See M. Z. Segal, ספרי שמואל (Jerusalem, 1964), 66; S. R. Driver, *Notes on the Hebrew Text and the Topography of the Books of Samuel* (London, 1913), 71.

[37]מחברת מנחם, 180. See also פשוטו של מקרא II, 139-40.

[38]The bearing of Akkadian *tāmartu* on this problem was first suggested to me by my good friend and colleague M. Lichtenstein.

[39]The derivation of *tāmartu* from *amāru* has been accepted by both *CAD*, A/2, 5, and *AHW*, 42.

[40]While it is true that *tāmartu* is most often used in contexts of giving tribute to an overlord (god or man), its synonoms in these contexts are often used in other contexts where the giving of tribute is not implied. See, e.g., *šulmānu* "gift" in TCL 3:54 (tribute context) together with *AnSt* 6 (1956), 150:29 (non-tribute context); *kad/trû* "gift" in OIP 2, 31:67 (tribute context) together with *AnSt* 6 (1956), 152:40 (non-tribute context).

[41]For a detailed analysis of this text by the present author, see C. Cohen, "'Foam' in Hosea 10:7," *JANESCU* 2/1 (1969), 25-29. In the present study, only the highlights of my research on this verse will be given. Some updating and corrections will also be made.

[42]As stated in my original article, the comparison of this text to the metaphor in Hos 10:7 was first suggested by M. Held (oral communication). However, the text was somewhat misquoted by me in my original article. The correct text is presented

here according to the edition of L. Cagni, *L'epopea di Erra* (Rome, 1969), 112:67-68 with translation on p. 113:67-68. The cuneiform text may be found in L. Cagni, *Das Erra-Epos Keilschrifttext* (Rome, 1970), 27.

[43]The substantive *ḫubšu* "foam" occurs again in the broken text Era IIb:11. On this word, see now Cagni, *Erra*, 203-204.

[44]See J. A. Brinkman, *A Political History of Post-Kassite Babylonia* (Rome, 1968), 362, and Cohen, "'Foam' in Hosea 10:7," 29, n. 23. On the whole issue of the dating of this epic, see now Cagni, *Erra*, 37-45, where all previous studies on this question are listed.

[45]See, e.g., KB I, 848.

[46]See Cohen, "'Foam' in Hosea 10:7," 26-28.

[47]Ibid., 28-29.

[48]See A. Sperber, *The Bible in Aramaic* III (Leiden, 1962), 402, and Cohen, "'Foam' in Hosea 10:7," 29, n. 22.

[49]The first medieval commentator to understand our verse correctly was Menaḥem, who explained קצף according to its rendering רותחא in Targum Jonathan (see מחברת מנחם, 158). He erred, however, in associating קצף in Hos 10:7 with קצפה in Joel 1:7. The latter is completely divorced in meaning from the former, and is in fact listed in Appendix II as a homonymic *hapax legomenon*.

[50]These scholars connected קצף in Hos 10:7 to קצפה in Joel 1:7, which however has nothing to do with the case (see n. 49 above).

[51]See Cohen, "'Foam' in Hosea 10:7," 25-26.

[52]The sequence of parallel verbs נשאו-ישאו is a *qtl-yqtl* sequence for which see M. Held, "The YQTL-QTL (QTL-YQTL) Sequence of Identical Verbs in Biblical Hebrew and in Ugaritic," *Studies and Essays in Honor of Abraham A. Neuman* (Leiden, 1962), 281-90. This example is quoted on p. 281.

[53]"Voices" here mean waves as is indicated by the parallelism in the next verse with משבר "wave." As the "voice" of God in the heavens was manifest in thunder (see the usage of קול in, e.g., 2 Sam 22:14 = Ps 18:14), the "voice" of God upon the waters was present in the waves of the sea (see, e.g., Hab 3:10). Needless to say, in the mythopoeic thought of ancient man, the sound of the waves was not distinguished from the waves themselves (see H. Frankfort et al., *Before Philosophy* [Baltimore, 1949], 11-36). Furthermore, waves are referred to in Ancient Near Eastern mythological contexts in order to demonstrate divine power (e.g., En. el. I:108) and are also used as a divine epithet (e.g., Winckler Sammlung 2, 1:6). For the general mythological background of Psalm 93 into which the mythological character of waves as described above fits perfectly, see *MLC*, 771.

[54]For the mythological usage of the term מים רבים, see H. G. May, "Some Cosmic Connotations of Mayim Rabbim, 'Many Waters,'" *JBL* 74 (1955), 9-21.

[55]For MT אדירים משברי ים. This slight emendation is accepted by most scholars; see, e.g., *BHS* on this verse.

[56]Rashi on this verse contends that דכים has to do with "depth and lowness." Kimchi interprets it as having to do with "breaking." Ibn Ezra, on the other hand, states that it clearly means "waves."

[57]C. A. Briggs et al., *The Book of Psalms* II (Edinburgh, 1907), 311, suggests emending דכים to זכרם "their commemoration" claiming textual support from Ps 97:12. Also in favor of emendation, although without any specification, is N. H. Tur-Sinai in פשוטו של מקרא IV/1, 198. M. Dahood, on the other hand, accepts the text as is, rendering "their pounding waves"; see M. Dahood, *Psalms II* (New York, 1968), 341.

[58]See SUL, 221-22, n. 7 for several suggestions to connect דכים in Ps 93:3 to *dkym* in *CTA* 6:5:3. That these two texts have nothing to do with each other has now been seen by both J. C. de Moor and P. J. van Zijl; see *SP*, 227 and P. J. van Zijl, *Baal* (Neukirchen-Vluyn, 1972), 134, n. 7, 213-15. Both of these scholars present differing detailed analyses of the relevant Ugaritic text, but both agree that Ps 93:3 is not relevant. Complete bibliographies are included on this issue in both studies. To be added is Dahood, *Psalms II*, 341, where it is still maintained that the two texts are related, and UHPP I, 336 (#513), where Dahood, without any justification whatsoever, compares the two unclear epithets of the sons of Asherah, *rbm* and *dkym* in *CTA* 6:5:1-3, to the totally unrelated terms רבים and דכים in Ps 93:3-4. Even more extreme and totally unconvincing is the hypothesis advocated by J. L. Benor. Benor, in order to compare Ugaritic *dkym* to Hebrew דכים, assumes that the latter together with the words רבים, קולם and ים in Ps 93:3-4 are all names of Ugaritic gods and that these verses were "adopted" directly from Canaanite poetry! See J. L. Benor, "בעניין 'דכים' (תהל' צ"ג)", *Beth Miqra* 63 (1975), 530-35. For verses following the pattern of three-line staircase parallelism and the importance of realizing that the last word(s) of the first line in such parallelism is often in the vocative state (it was Benor's non-realization of this important point which led him astray), see E. L. Greenstein, "Two Variations of Grammatical Parallelism in Canaanite Poetry and Their Psycholinguistic Background," *JANESCU* 6 (1974), 96-105 and the bibliography cited there; C. Cohen, "Studies in Early Israelite Poetry I: An Unrecognized Case of Three-Line Staircase Parallelism in the Song of the Sea," *JANESCU* 7 (1975), 13-17; S. E. Loewenstamm, "The Expanded Colon, Reconsidered," *UF* 7 (1975), 261-64. On Psalm 93 in general, see now O. Loretz, "Psalmstudien IV," *UF* 6 (1974), 215-17 and the bibliography cited there.

[59]The root דכה occurs only in the Psalms and is simply a by-form of דכא (see Isa 57:15 together with Ps 51:9).

[60]See both Pss 34:19 and 51:9.

CHAPTER III

SELECTED BIBLICAL *HAPAX LEGOMENA*

The following twenty-eight biblical *hapax legomena*, dealt with below in detail, have been selected from the lists in Appendix II because they best illustrate the advantages of the method proposed in this study. While all the Akkadian and Ugaritic comparisons adopted here have been previously suggested, the usage of this new method in determining the correctness of these comparisons has produced two major benefits:

a) In many cases, where different comparisons have been suggested for the same word, only one of these comparisons will satisfy the methodological principles adhered to in this study, and it is that comparison alone which is here suggested as being correct.

b) The comparison of the most relevant context(s) of the proposed etymological equivalent (or a word synonymous to it) with the context of the biblical *hapax legomenon* in question has often led to philological, historical, and literary insights, which further our understanding of the biblical word and its context considerably.

1. *Gen 6:14* (כפר)

וכפרת אתה מבית ומחוץ <u>בכפר</u>

And smear it inside and out with bitumen.

Atraḫasis III:ii:51[1]

[*k*]*upru* babil ipeḫḫi bābšu

Pitch was brought so as to caulk its hatch (?).[2]

The identification of Hebrew כפר with Akkadian *kupru* "bitumen"[3] is certainly the most celebrated lexical correspondence between the Akkadian and Hebrew flood stories.[4] The parallels from Atraḫasis,[5] however, are somewhat closer than those usually cited from the eleventh tablet of the epic of Gilgamesh,[6] since the former demonstrate the use of the bitumen for caulking the boat,[7] obviously what is implied in Gen 6:14 as well. Furthermore, in contexts outside the flood story, Akkadian *kupru* is often used with its denominative verb *kapāru*[8] "to smear"[9] and this too is precisely the case in Gen 6:14.

2. *Gen 28:12* (סלם)

ויחלם והנה סלם מצב ארצה וראשו מגיע השמימה
והנה מלאכי אלהים עלים וירדים בו

He (Jacob) had a dream: a stairway was set upon the earth with its top reaching to the sky; and God's messengers were going up and down on it.

STT I, 28:V:42[10]

īlâ Namtar arkat *simmelat* šamā[mi]

Namtar ascended the long stairway of heaven.

STT I, 28:VI:18[11]

[ūrid Ne]rgal arkat *simmelat* šamāmi

Nergal descended the long stairway of heaven.

סלם was first identified as a metathesis of Akkadian *simmiltu* "ladder, stairway"[12] by B. Landsberger in 1933.[13] While accepted by some,[14] this comparison has not gained universal approval.[15] The Akkadian passages above, however, provide conclusive evidence for the correctness of Landsberger's assertion. These passages and others from the Assyrian version of the myth of Nergal and Ereshkigal,[16] first published in 1957, provide us with a very close Mesopotamian parallel tradition upon which Jacob's dream may even have been ultimately based. The "stairway...with its top reaching to the sky" is equivalent to the *simmelat šamāmi* "stairway of heaven,"[17] while the ascending and descending of God's messengers upon it is paralleled in this Akkadian text by the ascending of Namtar[18] and Nergal[19] from the netherworld to the heavens[20] and the descending of Kaka[21] and Nergal[22] from the heavens to the netherworld. They are all specifically identified as either (divine) "messengers" (*mār šipri*)[23] or relaying a (divine) "message" (*šipru*).[24] In the light of this correspondence, מלאכי אלהים can no longer be understood in this context as winged celestial beings[25] but rather as God's messengers.[26] Both this Akkadian comparison with Hebrew סלם and this important Mesopotamian parallel to Jacob's dream should now be considered as fully established.[27]

3. *Gen 40:11* (שחט)

וכוס פרעה בידי ואקח את הענבים <u>ואשחט</u> אתם
אל כוס פרעה ואתן את הכוס על כף פרעה

With Pharaoh's cup in my hand, I took the grapes, pressed them into Pharaoh's cup, and placed the cup in Pharaoh's hand.

CT 22, 38:7-9[28]

ana muḫḫi...karāni...ša bēlī išpuru'anni
karānu ina panātū'a *ṣaḫit*

With regard to...the wine...concerning which my lord wrote to me, the wine was pressed in my presence.

שחט was equated for the first time with Akkadian *ṣaḫātu* "to press (grapes and other fruit)"[29] by S. Daiches in 1903.[30] שחט is to be derived from an original *צחט,[31] and it is this latter form to which the Akkadian is cognate with *ṭ* > *t* in accordance with the Geers law.[32] Since the שר המשקים "chief cupbearer" is relating his own dream in Gen 40:9-11, it is reasonable to assume that the pressing of grapes was one of his professional responsibilities. The existence in Mesopotamian lexical lists of the *ṣāḫit karāni* "professional wine-presser"[33] provides further evidence for this assumption.

4. *Gen 43:11* (בטנים)

והורידו לאיש מנחה מעט צרי ומעט
דבש נכאת ולט <u>בטנים</u> ושקדים

Bring down a gift for the man (Joseph): some balm and some honey, gum, ladanum,[34] pistachio nuts, and almonds.

Iraq 14, 43:127-39[35]

...100 dišpu (!)[36]...10 imēr kulli ša *buṭnāte*...
10 imēr riqqe ṭābi

...100 (containers with) honey,...10 homers *kulli*[37] of pistachio nuts,...10 homers of sweet smelling balm.[38]

בטנים is to be equated with Akkadian *buṭnu/buṭṭutu* "pistachio nut."[39] Its contextual occurrence with balm and honey is paralleled by the above Akkadian passage which is taken from the menu of a banquet prepared for Aššurnaṣirpal's 69,574 guests on the occasion of the dedication of his palace at Kalḫu.[40] If these foodstuffs and aromatics were in fact utilized for such an occasion in ancient Mesopotamia, they undoubtedly would have been appreciated in the Egyptian court as well.[41]

5. *Exod 35:25*[42] (טוה)

וכל אשה חכמת לב בידיה טוו ויביאו מטוה את
התכלת ואת הארגמן את תולעת השני ואת השש

And all the skilled women spun with their own hands, and brought what they had spun, in blue, purple, and crimson yarns and in fine linen.

Šurpu V-VI:149, 151[43]

sinništi ṭēmi sūnšu ušēšib
šipāte peṣâte šipāte ṣal[māte]
qâ eṣpa ina pilakki *iṭme*

(Ištar) had the skilled woman sit down to her spinner (?);[44] She spun with the spindle a double thread[45] of white and black wool.

טוה was first equated with Akkadian *ṭamû*[46] "to spin" by P. Jensen in 1884.[47] As the passages above show, both Israelite[48] and Mesopotamian[49] societies looked upon women who could spin well as skilled women. The semantic correspondence in these two passages between Akkadian *sinništi ṭēmi* and Hebrew אשה חכמת לב, both denoting "skilled woman" is striking.[50] The cognate relationship between Hebrew טוה and Akkadian *ṭamû* should be considered an established fact.[51]

6. *Lev 14:24*[52] (לג)

ולקח הכהן את כבש האשם ואת לג השמן
והניף אתם הכהן תנופה לפני ה׳

The priest shall take the lamb of guilt offering and the log of oil, and wave them as a wave offering before the Lord.

RS 24.643:21[53]

lg . šmn . rqḥ

A log of scented oil.[54]

לג was first equated with Ugaritic *lg* "log"[55] by Ch. Virolleaud in 1933.[56] Not only is a "log of (scented) oil" referred to in both passages quoted above, but in both passages the oil is being used for ritual purposes.[57] Hebrew לג and Ugaritic *lg* clearly represent the same measure.[58]

7. *Num 23:9* (צרים)

כי מראש צרים אראנו ומגבעות אשורנו

For I see them from the mountain tops,
Gaze upon them from the hilltops.

CTA 4:5:77-78[59]

tblk . *ǵrm* . mid . ksp gbʿm . mḥmd . ḫrṣ

The mountains shall bring thee much silver,
The hills, a treasure of gold.

The identification of Hebrew צרים in Num 23:9 with Ugaritic *ǵr*[60] "mountain" was first proposed by W. F. Albright in 1944.[61] The Ugaritic parallel pair *ǵr//gbʿ*, which corresponds to the Hebrew pair צר//גבעה, shows that this identification is correct. צרים//גבעות is simply the parallel pair in early Israelite poetry[62] corresponding to הרים//גבעות in later biblical poetry.[63]

8. *Num 23:10* (תרבע[ת]!)

מי מנה עפר יעקב ומי[64] ספר תרבע(ת)[65] ישראל

Who can count the dust of Jacob?
And who can number the dustcloud of Israel?

BIN II, 72:16-19[66]

epram pîki *tarbu'am* panîki
saḫlî daqqātim umallû[67] īnīki

With dust (to) your mouth, a dustcloud (to) your face,
They fill your eyes with pulverized cress seeds.[68]

OIP II, 43-44:56-60

kīma tibūt aribi ma'di ša pān šatti mitḫariš ana
epēš tuqmāte tebûni ṣēru'a eper šēpēšunu kīma
imbari kabti...[69] pān šamê rapšūte katim ellamu'a
ina Ḫalule ša kišād Idiglat šitkunū sidirta

One and all, they were arisen against me to offer
battle, like a spring invasion of countless locusts;[70]
With the dust of their feet covering the broad heavens
like a dense fog..., they drew up in battle order
in Halule on the bank of the Tigris in front of me.

OIP II, 37:23-25

šû Maniyê *turbû* šēpē ummānātiya ēmurma Ukku
āl šarrūtišu ēzibma ana rūqêti innabit

That Maniyê saw the dust-clouds of the feet of my
armies, abandoned Ukku, his capital city, and
fled to distant parts.

The emendation of את רבע to [71] תרבע(ת) in Num 23:10 on the basis of Akkadian *tarbu'u/turbû/turbu'tu* "dust-cloud"[72] is perhaps the most celebrated case of an emended biblical *hapax legomenon*.[73] While the Akkadian term was first suggested for comparison by Fr. Delitzsch in 1874,[74] it was not until 1944 that W. F. Albright,[75] utilizing additional evidence,[76] proposed the emendation which is generally accepted today.[77] There has recently been some question, however, with regard to the interpretation of the emended verse. S. Gevirtz rejects here "an allusion to the numerical strength of the people of Israel"[78] and suggests instead, on the basis of Akkadian incantation literature,[79] that "the expression 'to count/number the dust of someone'...must denote a practice, not otherwise known in biblical literature, having magical significance."[80] The main reason for Gevirtz' rejection of the usual interpretation[81] is his contention that in the promises of God to Abraham and Jacob,[82] it is the dust of the earth which is said to be uncountable,[83] not the dust of Abraham or Jacob. Therefore, according to Gevirtz, Num 23:10 must be disassociated from these other verses because it is the dust of the people and not the dust of the earth which is being counted here.[84] The above Akkadian passages demonstrate not only that עפר//תרבע(ת) is a legitimate parallel pair, but that both these terms may be used imagistically to indicate numerical strength. In BIN II, 72:16-19, we find the parallelism of *epram//tarbu'am* exactly equivalent to עפר//תרבע(ת) in Num 23:10, showing that the latter is simply a highly poetic variant of the usual pair עפר//ארץ attested in both Hebrew and Ugaritic.[85] The remaining two Akkadian passages illustrate the imagistic usage of both *epru* and *turbû* for the purpose of indicating numerical strength, thus supporting the similar usage of עפר and תרבע(ת) in Num 23:10. *In both Akkadian passages, it is the dust of human beings (or more literally "the dust of their feet") not the dust of the earth which is used figuratively to express the notion of numerical strength.* In OIP II, 44:56-60, *epru* is used in this way referring to the numerical strength of Sennacherib's enemies, alongside such a common simile as "like a spring invasion of countless locusts"[86] which obviously expresses the same notion. In OIP II, 37:23-25, it is the numerical strength of Sennacherib's armies which causes Maniyê, his enemy, who has seen the "dust clouds" (*turbû*) of their feet, to abandon his capital city and flee. Thus Hebrew תרבע(ת) "dust-cloud" finds its exact equivalent in Akkadian *tarbu'u/turbû/turbu'tu* and its imagistic usage together with עפר finds precise parallels in the annals of the Assyrian kings.[87]

9. *Deut 32:34*[88] (כמס)

הלא הוא כמס עמדי חתום באוצרותי

Lo, I have gathered it all,[89]
Sealed up in my storehouses.

STT I, 38:85-86[90]

Gimil-Ninurta šitta eṣṣūrāti[91] ibāramma
ikmis ana quppimma iktanak kišippiš

Gimil-Ninurta caught two birds,
gathered (them) into a cage
and sealed (it) with a seal.

כמס[92] appears to have been first equated with Akkadian *kamāsu* "to gather"[93] by N. H. Tur-Sinai in 1913.[94] While its meaning has usually been correctly understood contextually, many scholars have seen fit to emend the text to כנס "gathered" on the basis of this reading in the Samaritan recension.[95] The above Akkadian passage from The Poor Man of Nippur, in which *kamāsu* "to gather" is juxtaposed with *kanāku* "to seal"[96] provides a clear parallel to the sequence כמס-חתום "gathered-sealed up" in Deut 32:34.[96a] Neither the equation with Akkadian *kamāsu* nor the correct reading of the MT in this case should any longer be questioned.[97]

10. *Josh 5:12*[98] (עבור הארץ)

וישבת המן ממחרת באכלם מעבור הארץ
ולא היה עוד לבני ישראל מן .
ויאכלו מתבואת ארץ כנען בשנה ההיא

And the manna ceased on the morrow[99] as they were eating from the produce of the land; Thus the Israelites no longer had manna, and they ate from the produce of the land of Canaan during that year.

ARM V, 73:4[100]

ebūr mātim u ēkallim šalim

The produce of the land and of the palace is fine.

עבור[101] seems to have been first equated with Akkadian *ebūru* "harvest, produce"[102] in an article by W. Muss-Arnoldt in 1890.[103] Its correct meaning in Josh 5:11-12 has been known, however, since the time of Menaḥem ben Saruq (tenth century C.E.), who correctly equated עבור הארץ with תבואת הארץ "produce of the land" in Josh 5:12.[104] That both Mesopotamian and Israelite cultures utilized this term in their respective expressions for "the produce of the land" (Akkadian *ebūr māti* = Hebrew עבור הארץ--see the passages above) provides confirmation for the identification of the two terms.[105]

11. *2 Kgs 20:13*[106] (בית נכות)

ויראם את כל בית נכתה את הכסף ואת הזהב ואת הבשמים
ואת השמן הטוב ואת בית כליו ואת כל אשר נמצא באוצרותיו

And he showed them his entire treasury--the silver,
the gold, the spices, the fragrant oil,[107] and his
armoury--all that was found among his treasures.

Streck Asb. 50:132-34

aptēma *bīt nakkamātišu*(*nu*) ša kaspu
ḫurāṣu bušû makkūru nukkumū qerebšun

I opened his treasury wherein silver,
gold, valuables and property were stored.

בית נכות[108] was first equated with Akkadian *bīt nakkamāti* "treasury"[109] by Fr. Delitzsch in 1886.[110] The two passages above both describe the opening of a royal treasury before an alien king. Both are clearly written in annalistic style.[111] בית נכות appears to be a clear case of an Akkadian loanword in biblical Hebrew.[112]

12. *Isa 1:23* (שלמנים)

שריך סוררים וחברי גנבים כלו אהב שחד ורדף
שלמנים יתום לא ישפטו וריב אלמנה לא יבא אליהם

Your rulers are rogues and comrades of thieves;
Each one is avid for presents and pursues gifts.

They do not judge the case of the orphan,
And the cause of the "widow"[113] does not reach them.

BWL 132:97-100

dayyāna ṣalpa mēsera tukallam
māḫir *ṭa'ti* lā muštēšeru tušazbal arna
lā māḫir *ṭa'ti* ṣābit(u) abbūti enše
ṭābi eli Šamaš balāṭa uttar

You cause the crooked[114] judge to experience imprisonment,
You make him who accepts a bribe and does not
provide justice bear[115] (his) punishment;
As for one who does not accept a gift, but
espouses the cause[116] of the weak,
It is pleasing to Samas and he will increase (his) life.

שלמן has been equated with Akkadian *šulmānu* "gift"[117] by many.[118] Others derive this noun from Hebrew שלם "to pay,"[119] while some maintain that both are correct.[120] In fact, *šulmānu* should be considered a primary noun in Akkadian,[120a] and there is no Akkadian term which is both etymologically and semantically equivalent to Hebrew שלם.[121] Therefore, if שלמן is truly identical to Akkadian *šulmānu*, it cannot possibly be derived from שלם. The identity of Hebrew שלמן with Akkadian *šulmānu* may be established on the basis of the above passages and the similar usage of *ṭa'tu* "gift, bribe" (used in the above passage) and *šulmānu*. In the *šulmānu* texts edited by J. J. Finkelstein, *šulmānu* takes the place of *ṭa'tu* in similar texts and clearly means "bribe."[122] Furthermore, *šulmānu* is equated with *ṭa'tu* in lexical lists.[123] Finally, the *šulmānu* given by the poor man of Nippur to his mayor is interpreted by the latter as a bribe.[124] Thus, שלמן is to be equated with Akkadian *šulmānu* and completely disassociated from Hebrew שלם.[125]

13. *Isa 2:16* (שכירות החמדה)

ועל כל אניות תרשיש ועל כל שכירות החמדה
Against all the ships of Tarshish,[126]
And against all the gallant barks.

CTA 84:1-5

anyt . *miḫd*[[127]]
br . tpṭb'[l]
br . d̲mty [ ]
t̲kt . ydln[ ]
t̲kt . t̲ryn[ ]

Ships of Ma'ḫadu:[128]
A *br* ship of Tpṭb'l[129]
A *br* ship of D̲mty[130]
A *t̲kt* ship of Ydln[131]
A *t̲kt* ship of T̲ryn[132]

שכירות[133] was first equated to Ugaritic *t̲kt* "type of ship"[134] by both H. L. Ginsberg and G. R. Driver in 1950.[135] It was, however, already compared to Egyptian *skty* "type of ship,"[136] which is equivalent to Ugaritic *t̲kt*,[137] by J. Begrich in 1931.[138] That שכיות must refer to some kind of ship is indicated by the parallelism אניות//שכיות.[139] That Ugaritic *t̲kt* may well be equivalent to שכיות is demonstrated by the above Ugaritic text which is part of a list of *anyt miḫd* "ships of Ma'ḫadu" specifying *br*[140] ships and *t̲kt* ships and their owners.[141] The relationship of *anyt* to *t̲kt* then is that of a generic term to a corresponding specific term, where the latter is clearly described generically by the former. The parallelism of "generic term//corresponding specific term" is well known in both biblical Hebrew and Ugaritic,[142] and is surely the case in the parallelism of אניות//שכיות.[143]

14. *Isa 19:3* (אטים)

ודרשו אל האלילים ואל <u>האטים</u>
ואל האבות ואל הידענים

They (the Egyptians) will consult the idols
and the spirits of the dead,
And the ghosts and the familiar spirits.[144]

Bab. 12 pl. 3:36[145]

ilāni ukabbit *eṭemmē* aplaḫ

I honored the gods,
revered the spirits of the dead

אטים was first equated with Akkadian *eṭemmu* "spirit of the dead"[146] by A. Jirku in 1912.[147] As the above Akkadian passage shows, the juxtaposition of Hebrew אלילים "false gods" with אטים "spirits of the dead" is in no way different from the Akkadian parallelism *ilāni* "gods"//*eṭemmē* "spirits of the dead."[148] While previous scholars have compared Arabic[149] and Ugaritic[150] roots, only the Akkadian equivalent has the necessary contextual meaning to validate a comparison with Hebrew אטים.[151]

15. *Isa 33:8* (עדים!)

נשמו מסלות שבת עבר ארח הפר ברית
מאס עדים(!)[152] לא חשב אנוש

Highways are desolate,
Wayfarers have ceased.
A covenant has been broken,
A vassal treaty rejected,
...[153] disregarded.

Streck Asb. 12:123-24[154]

eli Tarqû šar Kūsi ana šakān *adê*
u salīme uma''erū rakbêšun

They (the Egyptian kinglets) sent their ambassadors to Tirhaka in order to enter into a vassal treaty and covenant.

Lie Sar. 264-65[155]

adê māmīt ilāni rabûti
ēbukma iklâ tāmartuš

He (Merodachbaladan) repudiated the vassal treaty (secured by) oaths (invoking) the great gods and withheld his tribute from me.

Winckler Sar. pl. 33:79

adê ilāni rabûti ībukma
iklâ tāmartuš

He (Tarḫunazi) repudiated the vassal treaty (invoking) the great gods and withheld his tribute from me.

The reading עדים(!) for ערים in Isa 33:8, now confirmed by IQIs[a],[156] was first suggested by B. Duhm in 1892.[157] It was not until 1958, however, that the correct meaning of עדים "vassal treaty"[158] was discovered by J. A. Fitzmyer[159] through comparison with Sefîre עדן[160] and Akkadian *adû*,[161] both with the same meaning.[162] The Akkadian passages reproduced above demonstrate the validity of this assertion. In the first passage, the hendiadys *adê u salīme* "vassal treaty and covenant"[163] is found which is in no way different from the parallelism עדים//ברית "covenant"//"vassal treaty" in Isa 33:8. In the two remaining Akkadian passages, a contextual parallel to Isa 33:8 occurs, where it is clear that *adê abāku* "to repudiate a vassal treaty"[164] is the semantic equivalent of מאס עדים "reject a vassal treaty." The latter parallel also produces some historical and literary ramifications in that it clearly indicates that the subject of Isa 33:8 is a nation which has rejected its vassal treaty and thereby rebelled against its overlord. Therefore, the prophet must be speaking here of the vassal, Judah, not of the overlord, Assyria.[165] Historically, the usage of the technical term עדים "vassal treaty" in this context tends to corroborate the opinion of those scholars who have dated Isaiah 33 immediately after the subjugation of Judah by Assyria in 701 B.C.E.[166] Those who seek allusions in this chapter to the Persian, Greek, or Maccabean eras will find it rather difficult to explain the occurrence of this technical term in such a late context.[167] While the Akkadian and Aramaic equivalents of עדים "vassal treaty" are shown to be correct,[168] the proposed etymological connection with Hebrew עדות "testimony" and related terms[169] is far from certain.[170] Likewise, the attempt[171] to relate the Canaanite loanword in Egyptian *ʿdt* "conspiracy"[172] should be abandoned.[173]

16. *Isa 41:10*[174] (שתע)

אל תירא כי עמך אני אל <u>תשתע</u> כי אני אלהיך

Fear not for I am with you,
Be not afraid for I am your God.

CTA 5:2:6-7

yraun . aliyn . bʿl *ṯṯʿ* . nn . rkb . ʿrpt

Afraid[175] is Puissant Baal,
Frightened is the rider of the clouds.[176]

The existence of the Hebrew root שתע was already recognized at least[177] some sixty years ago by A. B. Ehrlich.[178] It was first compared to Ugaritic *ṯṯʿ* by H. L. Ginsberg in 1936.[179] The existence of the Ugaritic parallel pair *yrʾ*//*ṯṯʿ*,[180] the exact equivalent of the biblical pair ירא//שתע is decisive proof for this derivation. The verb שתע "to fear" also occurs in the Azitawadda inscription from Karatepe,[181] and has turned up most recently in Ammonite in the new Ammān Citadel Inscription.[182] The abundance of evidence makes this derivation one of the most celebrated and certain examples of Ugaritic-Hebrew philology.[183]

17. *Isa 44:14-15*[184] (ארן)

ויאמץ לו בעצי יער נטע <u>ארן</u> וגשם
יגדל והיה לאדם לבער ויקח מהם
ויחם אף ישיק ואפה לחם אף יפעל אל
וישתחו עשהו פסל ויסגד למו

He secures[185] for himself trees of the forest;
He plants cedar trees, and the rain makes them grow.
All this serves man as fuel: He takes some to warm himself, and he kindles[186] a fire and bakes bread.
He also constructs a god and bows down to it.
He fashions it into an idol and worships it.

Maqlû IX: 39-40[187]

šiptu aṯṯīmannu kaššāptu ša tubtana''ennī
ṣalam bīni ṣalam *erēni*

Incantation: Whoever you are, sorceress,
who keeps seeking me out.[188]
(Prescribed Ritual): An image made of tamarisk wood, an image made of cedar wood.

SBH 144:20[189]

2 kinūnu ša *erēni* ina bīt papāḫi ikkassū

2 braziers full of cedar wood
are set up in the sanctuary.[190]

ארז[191] was first compared to Akkadian *erēnu* "cedar"[192] by Fr. Delitzsch in 1874.[193] The passage quoted above from Isaiah mocks those who fashion their gods (in reality their gods' images)[194] out of the same material which they use as firewood to keep themselves warm. The above Akkadian passages illustrate the usage of *erēnu* both in the manufacturing of images for cultic use[195] and as fuel for the hearth in the sanctuary. In the light of these parallels from the very civilization which is being discussed in the biblical verses quoted above,[196] this Akkadian comparison should surely be accepted.[197]

18. *Isa 51:22*[198] (קבעת)

הנה לקחתי מידך את כוס התרעלה
את קבעת (כוס) חמתי לא תוסיפי לשתותה עוד

Herewith I take from you hand the cup of poison,[199]
The chalice (cup)[200] of my venomous wrath,[200a]
you will never again drink.[201]

CTA 19:IV:215-16[202]

qḥn . wtšqyn . yn qḥ ks . bdy *qbʿt* bymny

Take her and let her give me wine to drink.[203] Place the cup in my hand, the chalice in my right hand.[204]

קבעת[205] was compared for the first time with Ugaritic *qbʿt* "chalice"[206] by Ch. Virolleaud in 1936.[207] The correspondence of the Hebrew parallel pair כוס//קבעת with its Ugaritic counterpart *ks//qbʿt* is conclusive evidence in favor of this comparison. That Ugaritic *qbʿt* is the exact equivalent of Hebrew קבעת should be considered an established fact.[208]

19-20. *Isa 66:11* (מצץ; זיז)

למען תינקו ושבעתם משד תנחמיה
למען תמצו והתענגתם מזיז כבודה

That you may suck from her breast
consolation and be satiated;
That you may draw from her teat
glory and be joyful.

CTA 15:II:25-27[209]

tld . yṣb [.] ǵlm
ynq . ḥlb . a[t̲]rt
mṣṣ . t̲d . btlt̄ . [ʿnt]

She shall bear Yaṣṣib the lad,
Who shall draw the milk of Asherah,
Suck the breasts of the maiden Anath.

Craig ABRT I, 6:r. 8[210]

erbi *zīzēša* ina pīka šaknā
2 tenniq 2 taḫallib ana panīka

Her (Istar's) four teats are placed in your mouth,
You suck at two, and two you milk[211] for yourself.

Isa 66:11 contains two biblical *hapax legomena*, one which has a Ugaritic equivalent and one which has a cognate in Akkadian. מצץ was first compared to Ugaritic *mṣṣ* "to suck, draw milk"[212] by Ch. Virolleaud in 1942-43.[213] This comparison is confirmed by the existence of the biblical parallelism ינק//מצץ "suck// draw milk" in the verse in question and its counterpart in the Ugaritic passage quoted above.[214] זיז[215] was first equated with Akkadian *zīzu* "teat"[216] by S. A. Strong[217] and J. A. Craig[218] independently in 1893. The context of the Akkadian passage makes this comparison virtually certain.[219] Surely the translation "abundance" for זיז, based on an incorrect reading of an Akkadian substantive, must now be abandoned,[220] and replaced, in light of the above comparison, by "teat."

21. *Jer 50:15* (אשיה)

הריעו עליה סביב נתנה ידה
נפלו אשיותיה נהרסו חומותיה

Sound the battle-cry around her on all sides,
She has given in.[221]
Her towers have fallen,
Her walls have been demolished.

AKA 81:27-30

dūršu rabâ u *asayātešu* ša agurri
ana napāli aqbâšumma
ištu uššešu adi gabadibbîšu[222] ippul
ana tīli utîr

Its great wall and its towers of baked bricks,
I ordered him to demolish.
From its foundation to its parapet he demolished (it)
and turned (it) into ruins.

אשיה*[223] seems to have been first compared to Akkadian *asītu* "tower"[224] by H. Zimmern in 1917.[225] The juxtaposition of *dūru* "wall"[226] and *asītu* in the above Akkadian passage corroborates the parallelism of אשיה//חומה "tower//wall" and shows that this pair is in no way different from מגדל//חומה "tower//wall" which occurs in both Hebrew and Ugaritic.[227] In light of this correspondence, the meaning of this *hapax legomenon* is assured.[228]

22. *Ezek 16:30*[229] (לבה)

מה אמלה לבתך נאם אדני ה׳

How am I filled[230] with rage against you, says the Lord.

CCT 4, 2a:26-27[231]

ilum *libbātika* mali

The god is filled with rage against you.

לבתך was first compared to Akkadian *libbātu* "rage"[232] by E. Baneth in 1914.[233] The frequent usage of the Akkadian expression *libbāti malû* "to be filled with rage against" to indicate divine wrath[234] is strong evidence that this comparison is correct. The above Akkadian passage provides a clear contextual and syntactical parallel to its biblical counterpart. In the biblical passage, the God of Israel is furious with Jerusalem, which is here described as an unfaithful wife.[235] In the Akkadian passage, a Mesopotamian god is angry with a Cappadocian merchant for not having delivered the *ikribu* pledge[236] to the temple during his previous voyage.[237] In both passages, the second person accusative suffix is appended to the word for "rage" and takes on the connotation "against you."[238] This Akkadian comparative evidence together with the equally strong Aramaic evidence makes the meaning of this phrase quite certain.[239]

23. *Ezek 19:9*[240] (סוגר)

ויתנהו בסוגר (בחחים)[241] ויבאהו אל מלך בבל

They put him in a neck stock (in restraints)[242]
and brought him to the king of Babylon.

Streck Asb. 66:8-13

ana kullum tanitti Aššur u ilāni rabûti bēlīya
annu kabtu ēmissūma šigāru aškunšūma
itti asi[243] kalbi arkussūma ušanṣiršu abulla qabal Ninua

In order to reveal the glory of Aššur and the great gods my lords, I imposed upon him a severe punishment, put him in a neck-stock, bound him together with a bear and a dog, and made him guard the gate of Nineveh.

סוגר[244] was compared for the first time to Akkadian *šigāru* "neck-stock"[245] by Fr. Delitzsch in 1884.[246] In the above biblical passage, a Judean king[247] is spoken of as a lion who has been captured and brought to Babylon in a neck-stock. The Akkadian passage quoted above shows that Mesopotamian kings did indeed make their prisoners submit to such confinement.[248] There is also iconographic evidence depicting just such a neck-stock.[249] Furthermore, evidence that such a neck-stock was used for lions is provided by a lexical list in which *šigārum ša nēšim* "neck-stock for a lion" is attested.[250] Thus both the metaphor utilized in Ezek 19:9 and its intended meaning are seen to have direct parallels in Mesopotamian literature.

24. *Ezek 27:24*[251] (ברומים)

המה רכליך במכללים
בגלומי תכלת ורקמה
ובגנזי ברומים

They were your traders in choice garments,[252]
In mantles[253] of bluish purple and embroidery,
And in carpets[254] of multi-colored trim.

AfO 18 306:32-34[255]

1 mardutu...ša šipar išpari
birmušu...nišē u umāmāni

1 *mardutu*-carpet[256]...made by the weaver,
its multi-colored trim...men and animals.

ברומים was first compared to Akkadian *birmu* "(multi)-colored (trim)"[257] by J. Oppert in 1869.[258] This comparison is shown to be correct by the Akkadian passage quoted above in which the *birmu* of a certain kind of carpet is specified as representing men and animals.[259] This precise understanding of ברומים as "(multi)-colored (trim)" and the above comparison with Akkadian *birmu* should no longer be ignored by modern biblical scholarship.[260]

25. *Amos 5:11*[261] (שבסכם!)

לכן יען שבסכם![262] על דל
ומשאת בר תקחו ממנו

Therefore, because you collect a (straw) tax from the poor,
And you take a grain tax[263] from him.

ARM III, 17:27-31[264]

ana še'im *šibšim* ša ḫalṣiya [u ana] še'im ša ēkallim
[ina lib]bi Terqa kamāsim aḫam ul nadêku

I have not neglected the collecting in Terqa of the barley, tax for my district, and the barley for the palace.

שבס! was first compared to Akkadian *šabāšu* "to gather; collect a (straw) tax"[265] and its derivative *šibšu* "(straw) tax" by N. H. Tur-Sinai in 1936.[266] While in the Akkadian text quoted above, as in many other passages, the *šibšu* represents a tax on barley, it may also represent a tax on straw, wheat, emmer, sesame and other agricultural produce as well,[267] demonstrating the validity of the parallelism שבסכם!//משאת בר תקחו "you collect a (straw) tax//you take a grain tax" in the above biblical verse. In view of this correspondence, the meaning and origin of this *hapax legomenon* now seem to be established.[268]

26. *Ps 74:6*[269] (כילפות)

...[270] פתחיה[271] יחד בכשיל וכילפות יהלמון

They knocked down (?) all its doors,
They battered with hatchets[272] and axes.

AKA 322:76-77[273]

ana Lāra šadû marṣu ša ana mēteq narkabāti
ummānāti lā šaknu ina *kalabbāte*[274] parzilli akkis
ina akkul(li)[275] erî aqqur narkabāti ummānāti ušēteq

Lāra, the treacherous mountain which was not suitable
for the passage of chariots and troops, I cut up with
iron axes and broke up with bronze hatchets,[276] and
then had the chariots and troops pass through.

כילפות appears to have been first identified with Akkadian *kalappātu* "axes"[277] by W. Muss-Arnoldt in 1905.[278] As can be seen from the above Akkadian parallel, this tool was used for building and tearing down.[279] The pair כשיל וכילפות "hatchets and axes" is matched perfectly by the corresponding parallel pair in the above Akkadian passage *kalabbāte//akkulli* "axes// hatchets." In light of these equivalences, the meaning of Hebrew כילפות should be considered as established.[280]

27. *Job 26:13*[281] (שפרה)

ברוחו שם ים[282] <u>שפרה</u>[283] חללה ידו נחש ברח

By his wind, he put Yam into his net;
His hand slew the serpent slant.[284]

En. el. IV:95[285]

ušparrirma[286] Bēlum *saparrašu* ušalmēši

The Lord (Marduk) spread out his net
and enmeshed her (Tiamat).

*שפר[287] was first compared to Akkadian *saparru* "net"[288] by N. H. Tur-Sinai in 1941.[289] The usage of *saparru* in the above mythological context in which Marduk captures Tiamat, the Mesopotamian equivalent of the Canaanite sea monster Yam,[290] in his net, and then lets loose the "evil wind" against her,[291] provides a clear thematic parallel to the above biblical text, whose provenance is the demythologized battle between God and his rebellious helpers, among whom is Yam.[292] The many Akkadian passages in which *saparru* is used in association with gods[293] and kings[294] provide additional confirmation for this comparison. Although further suggested comparative evidence from Aramaic is highly questionable,[295] the above Akkadian parallel is sufficiently close contextually to its biblical counterpart so that the meaning and origin of שפרה may be considered reasonably assured.[296]

28. *Job 40:20*[297] (בול הרים)

כי בול הרים ישאו לו
וכל חית השדה ישחקו שם

For the wild animals acclaimed him,[298]
And all the beasts of the field rejoiced.[299]

BWL 172:15-16

abrāte mala bašâ ana Nisaba [dullā][300]
būl ṣēri nammaššê šūpâ narb[ēša][301]

All mankind, give praise to Nisaba,
Wild animals, creatures, extol her greatness!

בול הרים was first compared to Akkadian *būl ṣēri* "wild animals"[302] by Fr. Delitzsch in 1886.[303] While the parallelism to חית השדה "beasts of the field" provides confirmation for this comparison, the meaning of the entire verse has remained unclear.[304] According to the above interpretation, Behemoth,[305] who was the foremost of God's creations and who served his creator as sword-bearer,[306] was revered by all creatures because of his important status. Similarly in the Akkadian passage quoted above, all wild animals extol the greatness of Nisaba, the Mesopotamian goddess of grain.[307] The two passages are sufficiently close contextually to make the meaning and origin of this expression as well as the above interpretation of the verse an established fact.[308]

NOTES

CHAPTER III

[1]W. G. Lambert and A. R. Millard, *Atra-Ḫasīs* (London, 1969), 92:51.

[2]For this meaning of *bābu*, see C. Cohen, "Hebrew TBH: Proposed Etymologies," *JANESCU* 4/1 (1972), 43-44.

[3]*CAD*, K, 553-55; *AHW*, 509.

[4]E.g., *CIOT* I, 48-49; H. Zimmern, *The Babylonian and the Hebrew Genesis* (London, 1901), 55; S. R. Driver, *The Book of Genesis* (London, 1911), 87; *AF*, 60, 66; SHL, 3; A. Heidel, *The Gilgamesh Epic and Old Testament Parallels* (Chicago, 1963), 265-67; E. A. Speiser, *Genesis* (New York, 1964), 52; M. D. Cassuto, פרוש על ספר בראשית (Jerusalem, 1965), 42; N. M. Sarna, *Understanding Genesis* (New York, 1966), 45; M. Weinfeld, ספר בראשית (Tel-Aviv, 1975), 35; *HALAT*, 471.

[5]In addition to the text already quoted above, see Atraḫasis III:i:33 (= Lambert and Millard, *Atra-Ḫasīs*, 88:33), Atraḫasis III:ii:13 (= Lambert and Millard, *Atra-Ḫasīs*, 90:13), and Atraḫasis W:3 (= Lambert and Millard, *Atra-Ḫasīs*, 128:3 [restored]).

[6]Gilg. XI:54, 65.

[7]For other passages in which *kupru* is used for caulking boats, see *CAD*, K, 553-55. For the general usage of bitumen in Mesopotamia and ancient Israel, see E. Ebeling, "Erdöl, Erdpech," *RLA* II, 462-63; S. Abramsky, "חמר", *EM* III, 187-90; Z. Yeivin, "Bitumen," *EncJud* IV, 1062.

[8]According to *AHW*, 442-43, *kapāru* II "mit Asphalt übergiessen" is a denominative verb from *kupru* "bitumen" and is to be disassociated from *kapāru* I "abschälen, abwischen." This assertion, however, is disputed by B. Landsberger, *The Date Palm and its By-products According to the Cuneiform Sources* (Graz, 1967), 30-34. Landsberger, now follwed by *CAD*, K, 178-80, shows convincingly that von Soden's *kapāru* I must be divided into *kapāru* I "to trim, clip, strip off" and *kapāru* II "to wipe off" [this division was also proposed independently by B. Levine, "כיפורים", *EI* 9 (1969), 91, n. 20]. Landsberger, however, further contends that von Soden's *kapāru* II cannot be a denominative of *kupru* "bitumen" but rather is to be translated "to smear" and to be classified under *kapāru* II "to wipe off" with *kupru* "bitumen" as its derivative (see also *AF*, 60, n. 2 and *CAD*, K, 179-80). Landsberger's main reason for the latter contention is as follows (Landsberger, *Date Palm*, 32): "...it cannot be a denominative because it occurs also with other substances than *kupru*." He then quotes CT 40, 2:47 (duplicate CT 38, 17:92) where *kapāru* "to smear" is used with *iṭṭû* "(crude) bitumen," *kupru* "(refined) bitumen," *agurru* "kiln-fired bricks,"

gaṣṣu "gypsum," and *qadūtu* "river-sand." However, in both Hebrew and Akkadian, denominative verbs may in fact have objects other than the noun from which they were formed. In biblical Hebrew, the denominative verb המטיר "to rain down" from מטר "rain" is used with such objects as גפרית "sulfurous fire" (Gen 19:24; Ezek 38:22), ברד "hail" (Exod 9:18, 23), לחם "food" (Exod 16:4), מן "manna" (Ps 78:24), and שאר "meat" (Ps 78:27). Likewise, the denominative verb חמר "to smear" which only appears in Exod 2:3, but provides an excellent parallel to Akkadian *kapāru* "to smear," takes both חמר "asphalt" (the noun from which it is derived) and זפת "pitch" as its objects. Similarly in Akkadian, *labānu* II "to mould, form," clearly denominative from *libittu* "air-dried brick" (see *AHW*, 522), is used several times with *agurru* "kiln-fired brick" (for references, see *AHW*, 522 and *CAD*, L, 8-10). Thus, Landsberger's refusal to consider *kapāru* "to smear" as denominative from *kupru* "bitumen" is unjustified, and we must agree with Levine, "כיפורים", 91, n. 20, who simply changes von Soden's *kapāru* II to *kapāru* III. See now also B. A. Levine, *In the Presence of the Lord* (Leiden, 1974), 123-27 and passim.

[9] For text references, see *CAD*, K, 179.

[10] See O. R. Gurney, "The Myth of Nergal and Ereshkigal," *AnSt* 10 (1960), 124:42.

[11] Ibid., 126:18.

[12] *AHW*, 1045.

[13] B. Landsberger, "Zu Meissner, Beiträge zum assyrischen Wörterbuch II," *ZA* 41 (1933), 230-31; idem, "Zu ZA 41, 230," *ZA* 42 (1934), 166; B. Landsberger and H. G. Güterbock, "Das Ideogramm für simmiltu ('Leiter, Treppe')," *AfO* 12 (1937-39), 55-57. Note the much earlier assertion of F. Schwally, "Lexikalische Studien," *ZDMG* 53 (1899), 197: "Assyrische Herkunft des Wortes [סלם] ist sehr warscheinlich." This statement, however, was not supported by any evidence whatsoever, and the relevant Assyrian word was not specified.

[14] E.g., W. Baumgartner, "Das semitische Wort für 'Leiter, Treppe'," *TZ* 7 (1951), 465-67; *AHW*, 1045; S. Moscati et al., *An Introduction to the Comparative Grammar of the Semitic Languages* (Wiesbaden, 1964), 63; H. A. Hoffner, Jr., "Second Millennium Antecedents to the Hebrew *'ÔB*," *JBL* 86 (1967), 397, n. 30.

[15] E.g., Speiser, *Genesis*, 218; G. von Rad, *Genesis* (Philadelphia, 1961), 279. Both of these authors derive סלם from סלל "to heap up" following BDB, 700. The objections of Hoffner to this derivation are to the point. See Hoffner, "Antecedents to Hebrew *'ÔB*," 397, n. 30.

[16] STT I, 28. See also the small fragments belonging to this composition in STT II, 113-14. Until the publication of the Sultantepe Tablets, all that was known of this myth was the very fragmentary Amarna version published by J. A. Knudtzon in

1915 as EA 357 and translated most recently by E. A. Speiser in *ANET*, 103-4. The Amarna version in its extant fragmentary state does not contain the phrase *simmelat šamāmi* "stairway of heaven." For the latest translation of the Sultantepe version of this myth, see the translation of A. K. Grayson in *ANET*, 507-12.

[17]For such heavenly ladders or staircases in other cultures, see *MLC*, 184-87. Note that the phrase *simmelat šamāmi* was also compared to its counterpart in Gen 28:12 independently by M. Weinfeld in 1975. Weinfeld, however, did not go beyond noting the parallel phrase in Akkadian; see Weinfeld, ספר בראשית, 160.

[18]STT I, 28:I:53 (= Gurney, "Nergal and Ereshkigal," 110:53) [partially restored]; STT I, 28:V:13 (= Gurney, "Nergal and Ereshkigal," 122:13).

[19]STT I, 28:IV:26 (= Gurney, "Nergal and Ereshkigal," 118:26) [partially restored].

[20]Note that after ascending the "long stairway of heaven," both Namtar and Nergal arrive at the *bāb Anim Enlil u Ea* "gate of Anum, Enlil, and Ea," i.e., the gate of heaven. See STT I, 28:IV:27 (= Gurney, "Nergal and Ereshkigal," 118:27) and STT I, 28:V:14 (= Gurney, "Nergal and Ereshkigal," 122:14). It is undoubtedly this gate which Jacob refers to in the same dream as שער השמים "the gate of heaven" (Gen 28:17).

[21]STT I, 28:I:16 (= Gurney, "Nergal and Ereshkigal," 108:16) [restored].

[22]See above, n. 11.

[23]Kaka is so described in STT I, 28:I:39 (= Gurney, "Nergal and Ereshkigal," 110:39), while it is said of Namtar in STT I, 28:V:53 (= Gurney, "Nergal and Ereshkigal," 124:53).

[24]Nergal portrays himself to the gatekeeper of the netherworld as the bearer of Anu's message. See STT I, 28:IV:25 (= Gurney, "Nergal and Ereshkigal," 118:25) [restored]. Both the restorations of Gurney and Grayson (*ANET*, 510) establish this point.

[25]The translation "angel" is of course neutral, since the meaning of angel in Greek is simply "messenger."

[26]That this is the original meaning of מלאך is seen from the occurrence of the verb *l'k* "to send" in Ugaritic (*UT* III, #1344), semantically equivalent to Akkadian *šapāru* "to send" (*AHW*, 1170-71) from which *mār šipri* "messenger" is derived (see p. 34 above). In the light of this correspondence, such comments as the following are seen to be completely without foundation (von Rad, *Genesis*, 279): "When we think of the 'ladder to heaven', however, we should not think of an actual ladder, for such a simultaneous mounting and descending of wingless divine messengers on it would not be easily conceivable."

[27]The frequently cited parallel of the Mesopotamian ziggurat should now be replaced by the much closer parallel presented here. Contrast, e.g., Speiser, *Genesis*, 219-20; Sarna, *Understanding Genesis*, 193; L. I. J. Stadelman, *The Hebrew Conception of the World* (Rome, 1970), 55; JPS Torah Notes, 107. Note that the parallel presented here is also much closer than those suggested by Hoffner, "Antecedents to Hebrew *'ÔB*," 390, 397-98. Professor Weinfeld maintains that the ziggurat parallel may still in fact be relevant especially given the similarity in phraseology between Gen 28:12 (וראשו מגיע השמימה) and Gen 11: 4 (וראשו בשמים); see Weinfeld, ספר בראשית, 53, 160.

[28]See E. Ebeling, *Neubabylonische Briefe* (Munich, 1949), #38:7-9. Note also CT 22,38:26-30 (= Ebeling, *Neubab. Briefe*, #38:26-30).

[29]That *ṣaḫātu* means "to press (grapes and other fruit)" may be seen by its congruence in usage with MH סחט. For not only are both used with wine (i.e., grapes) and other fruits (see the passages listed in *CAD*, Ṣ, 60-61 together with those in *OLT* XXVII, 159-61), but both also take "garment" as a direct object. In KAR 198:15-16 (= F. Köcher, *Die babylonisch-assyrische Medizin in Texten und Untersuchungen* III [Berlin, 1964], #222:15-16), the object of *taṣaḫḫat* "you wring out" is an unknown type of woolen garment which is labeled with the *TÚG* (= *lubuštu*) determinative for garments, while in Mikwaot 3:3, we find the phrase הסוחט את כסותו "one who wrings out his garment." Contrast the discussion in *CAD*, Ṣ, 61. Those passages having to do with extracting sesame oil and processing already obtained juice may be explained analogically as specialized usages. Note that *CAD*, K, 203 translates *iṣaḫḫata* in ABL 456: r.2-3 as "produces (lit. presses)" contradicting *CAD*, Ṣ, 61: "The specific translation 'to press' is to be abandoned." See also E. Salonen, *Über das Erwerbsleben im alten Mesopotamien* (Helsinki, 1970), 209, where *ṣaḫātu* is translated "keltern." Most recently, see now *AHW*, 1074, which correctly translates "auspressen" and compares Heb. שחט and Aram. סחט.

[30]S. Daiches, "Lexikalisches," *ZA* 17 (1903), 92. See also F. Küchler, *Beiträge zur Kenntnis der assyrisch-babylonischen Medizin* (Leipzig, 1904), 144; *CAD*, Ṣ, 61; *AHW*, 1074.

[31]Reconstructing a dissimilation of צ to שׂ in the presence of a second emphatic (ט). A clear example of this dissimilation occurs in צחק > שׂחק "to laugh". See P. Jensen apud Küchler, *Medizin*, 144; Y. Kutscher, מלים ותולדותיהן (Jerusalem, 1965), 104-5. Note also the four occurrences of ישׂחק for יצחק (Amos 7:9, 16; Jer 33:26; Ps 105:9). This phenomenon may be considered a partial reflex of the Geers law in Akkadian (see next note). For a similar reflex in certain Aramaic dialects, see H. L. Ginsberg, "Aramaic Dialect Problems, II," *AJSL* 52 (1935-36), 96.

[32]For the Geers law in Akkadian as stated by its author, see F. W. Geers, "The Treatment of Emphatics in Akkadian," *JNES* 4 (1945), 67: "An Akkadian consonantal base does not admit two

different emphatic radicals; wherever the other Semitic languages exhibit two such sounds within a tri-consonantal root, the Akkadian has changed one of them, according to its strength, to the nearest non-emphatic sound." See also *GAG*, §51e.

[33]See the passages listed in *CAD*, Ṣ, 61 and the discussion in Salonen, *Erwerbsleben*, 208-9. Note also the phrase *karānu ṣaḫtu* "(professionally) pressed wine" attested from the Middle Babylonian period on (see *CAD*, Ṣ, 63-64 and Salonen, *Erwerbsleben*, 209).

[34]Here it should be noted that Hebrew לט is to be connected with Akkadian *ladinnu* (*ladunu*, *ladnu*) "ladanum". For references, see Rost Tigl. III, 14:85, and the other references cited in *CAD*, L, 36 and *AHW*, 527. For this relationship as well as a discussion of other cognates, see *CIOT* I, 138-39; *AF*, 58; I. Löw, *Die Flora der Juden* I (reprint; Hildesheim, 1967), 362; *AHW*, 527; *CAD*, L, 36, and the additional bibliography cited there. The objection of M. Zohary, "לט", *EM* IV, 496, that ladanum has a Persian origin and therefore cannot be equated with לט is thus shown to be incorrect. Note also the discussion of M. Weinfeld who compares both Akkadian *ladinnu* and Egyptian *rdny*; see Weinfeld, ספר בראשית, 230. Most recently, see *HALAT*, 501. Contrast M. Elat, קשרי כלכלה בין ארצות המקרא (Jerusalem, 1977), 109 n. 48.

[35]See the edition of this text by D. J. Wiseman, "A New Stela of Aššurnaṣirpal II," *Iraq* 14 (1952), 24-44 and the more up-to-date translation by A. L. Oppenheim in *ANET*, 558-60.

[36]The text has  *AM*^{MEŠ}. However, since this reading makes no sense, the emendation 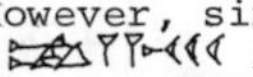 *LÀL*^{MEŠ} has been suggested (see *CAD*, G, 65 and *ANET*, 560) based on haplography of the first wedge (Ť) of the *MEŠ* sign. Since *LÀL* = *dišpu* "honey" (*CAD*, D, 161-63) fits the context so admirably, this emendation should certainly be accepted.

[37]*kullu*, attested only here (*CAD*, K, 508), must be a generic term for "shelled nuts" since it is used to measure both *dukdu* (not **luddu*--see *CAD*, L, 238, contra *AHW*, 561) and pistachio nuts (contra *AHW*, 502, which translates "eine Frucht").

[38]That *riqqu* is semantically similar to Hebrew צרי "balm" is shown by the Canaanite gloss *ṣurwa* (= צרי) to Akkadian *riqqu* in EA 48:8. For this gloss, see *CAD*, Ṣ, 261. On צרי, see now M. Zohary, "צרי", *EM* VI, 770-71.

[39]See most recently *HALAT*, 117. See also *AF*, 54; Löw, *Flora* I, 191-95; *CIOT* II, 218.

[40]See the introduction to this text in Wiseman, "Aššurnaṣirpal," 24-29; see also *ANET*, 560 n. 5.

[41]Note that the balm in EA 48:8 is also apparently being sent to Egypt as a gift; see *EM* VI, 770.

[42]See also Exod 35:26 where טוה is used in the same context.

[43]See the critical edition of this text by E. Reiner, *Šurpu* (reprint; Osnabrück, 1970), 34:149, 151. The parallel Sumerian text may be found in lines 148 and 150. The text of line 149 is largely based on an unpublished copy of K5014 by the late F. W. Geers which is reproduced by Reiner on p. 34. The restoration of *ṣal[māte]* is based on the corresponding *ge*$_6$ in line 150 of the Sumerian version.

[44]See Reiner, *Šurpu*, 58; B. Landsberger, "Über Farben im Sumerisch-Akkadischen," *JCS* 21 (1967), 160 n. 105; *AHW*, 1059; *CAD*, K, 339. While the meaning of *sūnu* II in this context is not at all clear, it must surely be divorced from *sūnu* I "lap". In our text, *sūnu* "designates some as yet unidentified tool used for spinning" (Reiner, *Šurpu*, 58; see also *AHW*, 1059).

[45]For *qû eṣpu* "double thread," see *CAD*, E, 351.

[46]For *w* > *m* in Akkadian, see *GAG*, §21c. For this development between Akkadian and Hebrew, see, e.g., Akkadian *kamānu* "a sweetened cake" (see *CAD*, K, 110-11), which comes into Hebrew as כונים (Jer 7:18; 44:19) and Akkadian *bīt nakkamāti* "treasury" which comes into Hebrew as בית נכות (see word #11 below). For the intransitive use of *ṭamû* to describe symptoms of vertigo and dizziness, see B. Landsberger, "Einige unerkannt gebliebene oder verkannte Nomina des Akkadischen," *WO* 3 (1964), 51-52 n. 27.

[47]P. Jensen, "De Incantamentorum Sumerico-Assyriorum seriei quae Dicitur šurbu Tabula VI, II," *ZK* 2 (1885), 43. See also A. Amiaud, "De la prononciation du פ en assyrien," *ZA* 2 (1887), 205; P. Haupt, "Über den Halbvocal u̯ im Assyrischen," *ZA* 2 (1887), 274; BDB, 467-68; SHL, 74; *HALAT*, 357.

[48]For spinning in Israelite technology, see *EM* IV, 998-1003; *EncJud* XV, 1036-37.

[49]For spinning in the Mesopotamian textile industry, see T. Jacobsen, "On the Textile Industry at Ur under Ibbī Sîn," *Toward the Image of Tammuz and Other Essays on Mesopotamian History and Culture* (Cambridge, 1970), 216-29; H. W. F. Saggs, *Everyday Life in Babylonia and Assyria* (New York, 1965), 129-30; and especially Salonen, *Erwerbsleben*, 247-48.

[50]This semantic correspondence was first seen by M. Lichtenstein, "Psalm 68:7 Revisited," *JANESCU* 4/2 (1972), 108-9, who also rightly compares Prov 31:19 (said of the אשת חיל). Note also M. Weinfeld, *Deuteronomy and the Deuteronomic School* (Oxford, 1972), 254 n. 3, where it is suggested that Akkadian *niklat libbi* is the semantic equivalent of Hebrew חכמת לב. Certainly, both Akkadian expressions may parallel the Hebrew idiom.

[51]Contrast מלון הלשון העברית III, 1857, where Akkadian *ṭamû* is ignored and an assertion is made that only Hebrew טוה means "to spin thread." Note also the doubts cast by *AF*, 28 n. 1, where the relationship is accepted, but with reservations.

[52]See also the same contextual usage of לג in Lev 14:10, 12, 15, 21.

[53]See *Ugaritica* V, 579:21 for the text and p. 582 for transliteration and commentary. See also J. C. de Moor, "Studies in the New Alphabetic Texts from Ras Shamra II," *UF* 2 (1970), 308:21.

[54]For other occurrences of *šmn rqḥ* "scented oil" in Ugaritic literature, see R. E. Whitaker, *A Concordance of the Ugaritic Literature* (Cambridge, 1972), 576. The same expression occurs in Eccl 10:1, for which see H. L. Ginsberg, קהלת (Tel-Aviv, 1961), 119. See also n. 107 below.

[55]Ugaritic *lg* also occurs in *CTA* 23:75 with *yn* "wine." See further *CTA* 158:4 which is broken and the personal names *bn lg* (*PRU* V, 80:10) and *bn lgn* (*CTA* 87:23; *CTA* 118:7). For these two names, see F. Gröndahl, *Die Personennamen der Texte aus Ugarit* (Rome, 1967), 154, 398, to which *CTA* 118:7 should be added. Finally, see the unpublished text referred to in both SUL, 115 and *UT* III, #1354: *ʿšr lg šmn t̲lt̲ lg rqḥ* "ten logs of oil, three logs of perfume."

[56]Ch. Virolleaud, "La naissance des dieux gracieux et beaux," *Syria* 14 (1933), 151. See also, e.g., H. L. Ginsberg, כתבי אוגרית (Jerusalem, 1936), 86, 148; T. H. Gaster, "A Canaanite Ritual Drama," *JAOS* 66 (1946), 57; SUL, 115; *CML*, 158 n. 21; *WUS*, #1445; *CTA*, p. 243 n. 3; *UT* III, #1354. For לג in extra-biblical and Aramaic inscriptions, see D. Diringer, *Le Iscrizioni Antico-Ebraiche Palestinesi* (Firenze, 1934), 286-88; *DISO*, 135. See most recently, *HALAT*, 494.

[57]For the provenance of the Ugaritic text involved, see de Moor, "New Alphabetic Texts II," 306. Whether or not de Moor is correct in claiming that lines 18-22 represent "a list of tithes (?) to be paid when ʿAt̲tartu-of-the-Field enters the royal palace," the commodities listed in these four lines are surely being brought to the *bt mlk* "royal palace" to be used in some divine ritual involving ʿAt̲trt, as is clearly shown by line 18 (see also de Moor, "New Alphabetic Texts II," 310). Note also that aside from the fragmentary lines 13-17, which are written in Hurrian (see *Ugaritica* V, 517-18), the other sections of this tablet all deal with offerings and sacrifices to various gods (de Moor, "New Alphabetic Texts II," 306).

[58]Contrast מלון הלשון העברית, 2620, n. 1. Likewise, contrast R. B. Y. Scott, "Weights and Measures of the Bible," *BA* 22 (1959), 29-30, who ignores Ugaritic *lg* in his discussion of Hebrew לג, and finally E. Steinberg, "Weights and Measures," *EncJud* XVI, 379-81, who does the same.

[59]See also *CTA* 3:3:27-28; *CTA* 4:5:93-95, 100-1; *CTA* 5:6:26-28; *CTA* 6:2:15-17.

[60]That Ugaritic *ǵ* may be reflected in Hebrew orthography by צ is indicated by the following examples: Ugaritic *ǵmʾ* (*UT* III, #1973) = Hebrew צמא "to thirst"; Ugaritic *nǵr* (*UT* III, #1670) = Hebrew נצר "to guard"; Ugaritic *yqǵ* (*UT* III, #1670) = Hebrew יקץ "to awake." See *PEPI*, 57.

[61]W. F. Albright, "The Oracles of Balaam," *JBL* 63 (1944), 212 n. 22. See also *PEPI*, 56-57; W. A. van der Weiden, *Le Livre des Proverbes* (Rome, 1970), 81-82; UHPP, #449.

[62]For characteristics of early Israelite poetry, see *SAYP*, 27-35, and also word #9 above.

[63]See *PEPI*, 56 n. 20 for many examples. Note that Dahood's attempt to find *ǵr* in other alleged Ugaritic-Hebrew parallel pairs is not at all convincing. For alleged pair #450, contrast Dahood, *Psalms II*, 267. See UHPP, ##4, 69, 135, 448, 450, 451, 453.

[64]Reading ומי ספר for MT ומספר. This reading is supported not only by the parallelism ספר//מנה in the Bible (1 Kgs 3:8; 8:5 [= 2 Chr 5:6]), but also by the equivalent parallel pair *spr//mnt* in Ugaritic (*CTA* 24:45-47). Note also that the Septuagint, some Samaritan mss., and Saadiah support this reading. See, e.g., Albright, "Oracles of Balaam," 213 n. 27; *PEPI*, 61-63; M. Held, "The Action-Result (Factitive-Passive) Sequence of Identical Verbs in Biblical Hebrew and Ugaritic," *JBL* 84 (1965), 279-80 n. 35; S. E. Loewenstamm, "הערות לתולדות המליצה המקראית", ספר סגל (Jerusalem, 1964), 183-85; UHPP, #401; G. R. Driver, "Abbreviations in the Massoretic Text," *Textus* 1 (1960), 123. This error is not due to an omission of י as *mater lectionis* as implied by Albright. Albright reconstructed the original text to read מ-מנ assuming that in early Hebrew orthography מי would be written as simply מ (see Albright, "The Oracles of Balaam," 213). However, as pointed out by Loewenstamm, "לתולדות המליצה", 184, the י of מי cannot be a *mater lectionis*, because it is found in the Amarna letters as *miya*, in Ugaritic as *my*, in Phoenician as מי, and in Lachish as מי (see F. M. Cross, Jr. and D. N. Freedman, *Early Hebrew Orthography* [New Haven, 1952], 18 [#41] and 53 [#50]). The correct solution is that which was suggested by Y. N. Epstein, מבוא לנוסח המשנה (Tel-Aviv, 1964), 1218. Epstein demonstrated that in Tannaitic times מי was often combined with the following word with the י dropped. Thus, in Tannaitic times, מי ספר was shortened to מספר and this was subsequently misinterpreted as מִסְפָּר.

[65]Reading תרבע(ת) for MT את רבע (see pp. 38-39 above).

[66]See the treatment of this text by W. von Soden, "Eine alt-babylonische Beschwörung gegen die Dämonin Lamaštum," *Orientalia* 23 (1954), 337-44. S. E. Loewenstamm was the first to cite this text as bearing on Num 23:10; see Loewenstamm, "לתולדות המליצה", 187.

[67]The reading *ú-ma-lu-<u>* was first proposed by B. Landsberger, "Corrections to the Article 'An Old Babylonian Charm against Merḫu,'" *JNES* 17 (1958), 57 n. 7. W. von Soden (see n. 66 above) hăd previously read *ú-ba-lu* as a I/1 present of *abālu* "to dry up, dry out." For the correct reading, see also *CAD*, A/1,31 and *CAD*, D, 107.

[68]For *saḫ̌lû* "cress," see *AHW*, 1009.

[69]The text reads here *kīma imbari kabti sa dunni erīyāti*. For *erīyātu* "icy cold wind (?)," see *CAD*, E, 293 and the bibliography cited there.

[70]For this simile, see also OIP II, 75:91-94; TCL III:256. Note other passages listed in *CAD*, E, 257 and add Piepkorn Asb., 58:46-47. Compare Hebrew ואין (להם) מספר//כארבה לרב "like a multitude of locusts//beyond number" in Judg 6:5; 7:12. In Ugaritic, see *CTA* 14:103-5; 192-94. See the thorough study of this simile in all the Semitic languages by M. Held, "Studies in Comparative Semitic Lexicography," *Studies in Honor of Benno Landsberger on his Seventy-Fifty Birthday* (Chicago, 1965), 400-1.

[71]Since all three forms *tarbu'u*, *turbû* and *turbu'tu* are attested in Akkadian (see passages listed above and in n. 72), the reconstructed biblical form could be with or without a final ה. Contrast Albright, "Oracles of Balaam," 213 n. 28, where it is claimed that *tarbu'tu* was the original form in Aramaic which developed into Akkadian *turbu'tu* as an Aramaic loanword. Certainly the Old Babylonian occurrence of *tarbu'am* cited above effectively refutes Albright's theory (see Loewenstamm, "לתולדות המליצה", 186-87).

[72]Besides the three passages listed above, other passages in which this word occurs with somewhat relevant usage are BBSt., #6:31 (*turbu'tišunu*); SBH 12:21 = Langdon BL. #158:21 (*turbumma* --for this reading, see W. von Soden, *OLZ* 49 [1954], 37 n. 1).

[73]See, e.g., Albright, "Oracles of Balaam," 213 n. 28; *PEPI*, 63-65; Loewenstamm, "לתולדות המליצה", 185-87; JPS Torah Notes, 236-37.

[74]AS, 73. Note that both Gevirtz, *PEPI*, 63 n. 38 and Loewenstamm, "לתולדות המליצה", 185 n. 33, wrongly claim that this comparison was first made by Delitzsch in Fr. Delitzsch, *Assyrische Lesestücke* (Leipzig, 1900), 184. Among those who accepted Delitzsch's comparison, but who did not emend the Hebrew text, were H. L. Ginsberg, "Lexicographical Notes," *ZAW* 51 (1933), 309 [he now accepts the emendation wholeheartedly (oral communication)], and B. Landsberger, *Die Fauna des alten Mesopotamien* (Leipzig, 1934), 123 n. 3.

[75]Albright, "Oracles of Balaam," 213 n. 28.

[76]Albright asserted that the *nota accusativi* את does not belong in early Israelite poetry (note that in the forty-three verses of Deuteronomy 32 [The Song of Moses], את does not occur even once) and that the ת of את should be combined with the word רבע. Albright further noted that את was missing in the Samaritan recension. [Loewenstamm, "לתולדות הצליצה", 186, noting that in the letters of Bar Kosiba, את was often combined with the following word with the initial א omitted (e.g., J. T. Milik, "Une Lettre de Simeon Bar Kokheba," *RB* 60 [1953], 277:3--את שמים = תשמים) has now suggested that this might be the source of the scribal error.] Albright's contention, however, that the original form of the Akkadian word was *turbu'tu* and that the corresponding Hebrew form must be תרבעת is to be rejected (see above, n. 71). Note also the suggested Arabic cognate *rabǵun* "dust" mentioned by Ginsberg in his aforementioned study, where the third radical *ǵ* corresponds to Hebrew ע.

[77]E.g., JPS Torah, 293 (see JPS Torah Notes, 236-37); *RSV*, 140 n. 5; contrast *NEB*, 211.

[78]*PEPI*, 64.

[79]*PEPI*, 64-65. Gevirtz cites his examples from *CAD*, E, 185, and adds W. G. Lambert, "An Incantation of the Maqlû Type," *AfO* 18 (1957-58), 291:21, but does not indicate the significance of the gathering of the dust of one's feet in these texts.

[80]*PEPI*, 64.

[81]See, e.g., JPS Torah, 293, which compares Gen 13:16.

[82]Gen 13:16; 28:14.

[83]For this simile, see EA 16:14; 19:61; 20:52, 55; 26:41-42; 27:106; 29:146, 164; Streck Asb., 165:1, and passages listed in n. 4 there. Note also the similar expressions comparing the number of stars in the sky (Gen 15:5; 22:17; 26:4; Exod 32:13; Deut 1:10; 10:22; 28:62; Nah 3:16; Neh 9:23; 1 Chr 27:23), and for the latter, see M. Held, "A Faithful Lover in an Old Babylonian Dialogue," *JCS* 15 (1961), 9:11-12 and the passages listed in the commentary on p. 24. See also the additional passages listed in *CAD*, K, 48.

[84]*PEPI*, 64. Gevirtz also contends that "the context of the sixth couplet demands that Balaam's question...comment upon the impossibility of harming Israel by (any form of) enchantment" (p. 64). However, the notion of Israel's military strength and security is a major theme throughout the poem, and there is no reason why it should not be included here (see Num 23:9, 22, 24; 24:8, 9, 17, 18, 19). Professor M. Weinfeld also notes that the image of a dust cloud in connection with military strength likewise occurs in Nah 1:3 and Jer 4:13 (oral communication).

[85]See M. D. Cassuto, "ספרות מקראית וספרות כנענית", *Tarbiz* 14 (1942), 1-2, for examples in both Ugaritic and biblical Hebrew. See also UHPP, #67 and the bibliography therein.

[86]For other examples of this simile, see n. 70 above.

[87] This emendation, surprisingly, has not been accepted universally. Contrast A. Guillaume, "A Note on Numbers 23:10," *VT* 12 (1962), 335-37; פשוטו של מקרא I, 175-76; M. Dahood, "Ugaritic Lexicography," *Mélanges Eugène Tisserant* I (Rome, 1964), 99 (by implication); D. W. Goodwin, *Text-Restoration Methods* (Naples, 1969), 105-7; *NEB*, 211. Note also *CPOT*, 270 and 355, where reference is made only to the 1933 article of H. L. Ginsberg (see above, n. 74) and all subsequent research is ignored.

[88]The dating of Deuteronomy 32 is an old problem which has yet to be resolved. There are two basic issues involved. The first is the identification of the historical catastrophe lying behind the poem, while the second requires a philological judgment concerning the poem's archaic elements. Are these elements indicative of the time the poem was written or do they represent intentional archaizing in some later period? While much has been written recently concerning both these issues, no definitive answers have yet been presented. Major studies on this problem include O. Eissfeldt, *Das Lied Moses Deuteronomium 32: 1-43 und das Lehrgedicht Asaphs Psalm 78* (Berlin, 1958); W. F. Albright, "Some Remarks on the Song of Moses in Deuteronomy XXXII," *VT* 9 (1959), 339-46; G. E. Wright, "The Lawsuit of God: A Form-Critical Study of Deuteronomy 32," *Israel's Prophetic Heritage* (London, 1962), 26-67; D. A. Robertson, *Linguistic Evidence in Dating Early Hebrew Poetry* (Montana, 1972), passim. The two dates most frequently mentioned as the time of composition of Deuteronomy 32 are "about 1025 B.C. well after the fall of Shiloh" (*YGC*, 17) and "not...earlier than the ninth century B.C." (*CMHE*, 264 n. 193).

[89]The antecedent of הוא "it" in this verse would appear to be the sins and moral corruption of Israel's enemy. See S. R. Driver, *Deuteronomy* (Edinburgh, 1895), 373, who compares Hos 13:12 and Job 14:17 among other passages.

[90]See Gurney, "Poor Man of Nippur," 154-55. The reading adopted here is that suggested by E. Reiner, "Another Volume of Sultantepe Tablets," *JNES* 26 (1967), 183 n. 7, and noted already in *CAD*, K, 115, 451. That *kanāku* "to seal" and *kišibbu/kišippu* "seal" go together is clear from En. el. IV:122.

[91]The reading *eṣṣūrāti* instead of *iṣṣūrāti* is based on the occurrence of the substantive *ʿṣr* "bird" in Ugaritic. Assuming the etymological identity of these two substantives implies that *e* (reflecting ע) should be read instead of *i* (oral communication from Professor M. Held).

[92]For other suggested etymological equivalents of Hebrew כמס in Syriac, Mandaic, and MH, see *HALAT*, 459. Here it should be noted that the recent attempt of P. J. van Zijl to find this root in Ugaritic (see van Zijl, *Baal*, 193-94) is completely unacceptable. Van Zijl suggests that the form *ktmsm* in *CTA* 6: I:49-52 "may be taken as the Gt-inf. constr. with the adverbial

-m, and related to the Hebrew root *kms* meaning 'conceal, store up'" (von Zijl, *Baal*, 194). However, this suggestion is based on van Zijl's new clause division, according to which *ly'db mrḥ//ktmsm* means "arranges indeed the lance//stores it up." Such a notion of "storing up weapons" is surely alien to this context where the general weakness and ineffectiveness of Baal's future successor is being described. Van Zijl's assumption that within this passage there is an additional thematic element, namely "possible rebellion emerging from the dialogue," is far-fetched, and completely unnecessary. The treatment of this passage by H. L. Ginsberg in *ANET*, 140 (see also *LKK*, 45) is still generally the best available, with the additional possibility of a chiastic parallelism of *dq anm//ktmsm* as first suggested by M. Dahood, "Ugaritic-Hebrew Syntax and Style," *UF* 1 (1969), 24-25 and further developed in *SP*, 202-3 (with complete bibliography), not to be ruled out entirely. Whatever the meaning of *ktmsm* in this context, it should be clear from the above that no connection with Hebrew כמס "to store up" is feasible. Note further that van Zijl completely confuses *kamāsu* A "to gather, collect" and *kamāsu* B "to squat, kneel" in Akkadian (see *CAD*, K, 114-20). It is the latter which had previously been compared to Ugaritic *ktmsm* in *WUS*, #1330 (see now also *SP*, 203), while van Zijl's comparison is with the former (contrast van Zijl, *Baal*, 194 n. 5).

[93]For Akkadian *kamāsu* A "to gather, collect," see *CAD*, K, 114-17 and *AHW*, 431 (*kamāsu* I). Note also the Akkadian passage quoted above sub word #25.

[94]H. Torczyner (= N. H. Tur-Sinai), *Altbabylonische Tempelrechnungen* (Wien, 1913), 119. See also פשוטו של מקרא I, 230; *HALAT*, 459; *AHW*, 431.

[95]In view of the fact demonstrated here that the reading of the MT כמס in this passage is perfectly acceptable, the reading כנס "gathered" in the Samaritan recension should most probably be considered an intentional emendation of a rare Hebrew word at a time when its meaning was no longer remembered. Such an intentional emendation must also be behind the Samaritan reading כסותו for MT סותה in Gen 49:11. The latter is clearly equivalent to Phoenician סות "garment" which is attested in *KAI* 24:8, *KAI* 11, and elsewhere in Phoenician. See *SAYP*, 84 and the bibliography cited there. Many modern scholars have also emended the MT to כנוס "gathered" in Deut 32:34 on the basis of the Samaritan reading. See, e.g., most recently, *BHS* III, 139. Note however the caution exercised by H. L. Ginsberg, "סיום שירת האזינו", *Tarbiz* 24 (1954-55), 1 n. 1. Note finally that A. Hurvitz has shown quite convincingly that the verb כנס in Biblical Hebrew occurs only in the biblical literature of the Second Temple period replacing קבץ and אסף (and less frequently לקט) which are the regular verbs for "to gather" in the biblical literature of the First Temple period. See A. Hurvitz, בין לשון ללשון (Jerusalem, 1972), 175 n. 308 and the works cited there. Hurvitz' analysis clearly demonstrates on the one hand how inappropriate is the emendation of כמס to כנס by modern scholars in a text as early as Deuteronomy

32, and on the other hand how easily explainable is this suggested emendation in a text as late as the Samaritan version of the Pentateuch. [My thanks to Professor M. Weinfeld for calling my attention to Hurvitz' analysis and discussing with me its relevance to the point in question.]

[96]Note that *kanāku* "to seal" is also the regular term used for sealing up material in storehouses. See the many passages listed in *CAD*, K, 136-42.

[96a]Professor M. Weinfeld first compares the usage of חתם "to seal up" together with צרר "to tie up, bind" in Job 14:17 and Isa 8:16 and then especially the parallelism צרר "to tie up, bind"//אסף "to gather" in Prov 30:4. He also notes the usage of צרר in Job 26:8 and that of Akkadian *kaṣāru* for which see M. Weinfeld, "'Rider of the Clouds' and 'Gatherer of the Clouds,'" *JANESCU* 5 (1973), 425-26 [oral communication]. For the usage of the latter verb in Akkadian literature, see also M. Held, "Two Philological Notes on Enūma Eliš," *Kramer Anniversary Volume* (Neukirchen-Vluyn, 1976), 234-36.

[97]Contrast Driver, *Deuteronomy*, 373; BDB, 485; *BHS* III, 139; מלון הלשון העברית III, 2423 n. 1.

[98]See also Josh 5:11, where עבור occurs in the same context.

[99]For the significance of ממחרת in this verse, and the different version of the LXX, see J. A. Soggin, *Joshua* (Philadelphia, 1972), 73-76 and the bibliography cited there. Add Y. Kaufman, ספר יהושע (Jerusalem, 1966), 108.

[100]For *ebūr māti* "produce of the land" in many other Akkadian texts, see *CAD*, E, 17-19 and *AHW*, 183-84.

[101]עבור also occurs in the Aramaic of Elephantine in the phrase עבור ארקתא "produce of the land" (*AD*, #12:6). For discussion and other passages, see *AD*, p. 82; *DISO*, 202. Note further the rendering of Hebrew דגן "grain" by עיבורא in the various Targumim (see Jastrow II, 1066a). This fact was already noted by Ibn Janaḥ (see W. Bacher ed., ספר השורשים [reprint; Jerusalem, 1966], 352--I am grateful to Professor H. L. Ginsberg for this information). Note finally that עבור seems to be attested now on an ostracon from Arad with the meaning "harvest-produce." See Y. Aharoni, "Three Hebrew Ostraca from Arad," *BASOR* 197 (1970), #3:10, with discussion on p. 36 and most recently, idem, כתובות ערד (Jerusalem, 1975), #31:10 with discussion on p. 60.

[102]The major work on Akkadian *ebūru* especially in its secondary meaning "summer" is B. Landsberger, "Jahreszeiten im Sumerisch-Akkadischen," *JNES* 8 (1949), 248-97. See also *AHW*, 183-84; *CAD*, E, 16-20 and the bibliography listed on p. 20. Add A. Salonen, *Agricultura Mesopotamica* (Helsinki, 1968), 258-62.

[103]W. Muss-Arnoldt, "Notes on the Publications Contained in Volume II of E. Schraeder's Keilschriftliche Bibliothek. II. The Inscriptions of Esarhaddon," *Hebraica* 7 (1890-91), 82 n. 3. Note, however, that Muss-Arnoldt assumed that *ebūru* was "an Aramaean loan-word in Assyrian," a view which is refuted by the many Old Babylonian passages in which *ebūru* occurs (e.g., the Mari passage quoted above). On the equation of Hebrew עבור with Akkadian *ebūru*, see also MA I, 10; *AF*, 41; BDB, 721; *FWOT*, 128; מלון הלשון העברית V, 4266; *AD*, p. 82; *AHW*, 183; Aharoni, "Arad," 36; idem, כתובות ערד, 60; *AIA*, 47 and n. 77.

[104]מחברת מנחם, 130. That Menaḥem's interpretation was not generally accepted by the medieval commentators may be clearly seen from the commentary of Qimchi on Josh 5:11.

[105]It has been suggested that Ugaritic *'br* is likewise a cognate of Hebrew עבור. See *AHW*, 183; *UT* III, #19.1807; Salonen, *Argicultura Mesopotamica*, 258; FFM, #86. This proposal is surely incorrect. *'br* occurs in *CTA* 3:6:7-9 and *CTA* 22: B:15. In the first passage, *'br* seems to mean "to travel (from one locality to another)" = Hebrew עבר, and certainly has nothing to do with עבור "produce." See *SP*, 51, 156, for the latest interpretation of this difficult passage. See also the translation of H. L. Ginsberg in *ANET*, 138; ענת, 73; *CML*, 142; *WUS*, #1990. Note that Gordon has apparently changed his mind, for he now translates *'br* in this passage "cross" (C. H. Gordon, *Ugarit and Minoan Crete* [New York, 1966], 57). The second passage is a real crux and there is no satisfactory interpretation for the word *l'brm*. The immediate context (*kksp l'brm...ḫrṣ l'brm* "like silver to *'brm*...gold to *'brm*"), however, clearly eliminates the meaning "harvest, produce" from any consideration. Note that Gordon seems to have changed his mind on this passage as well, for he now translates *'brm* in this passage "merchants" (Gordon, *Ugarit and Minoan Crete*, 142). See also *AIA*, 47 n. 77.

[106]Note the parallel verse in Isa 39:2. The suggestion in KB I, 618, to emend ונות בית to ובית נכת in Ps 68:13 has nothing whatsoever to recommend it. For some other interpretations of this difficult verse, see M. D. Cassuto, "תהלים ס"ח", *Tarbiz* 12 (1940-41), 13-14; W. F. Albright, "A Catalogue of Early Hebrew Lyric Poems (Psalm LXVIII)," *HUCA* 23/1 (1950-51), 13, 21-22, 37; Dahood, *Psalms II*, 131, 141 and the bibliography cited there.

[107]Reading with Isa 39:2 השמן הטוב as opposed to שמן הטוב in 2 Kgs 20:13. See also Ps 133:2 and Eccl 7:1. Both J. A. Montgomery, *The Book of Kings* (Edinburgh, 1951), 513, and J. Gray, *I and II Kings* (Philadelphia, 1970), 702, claim that the reading in 2 Kgs 20:13 is correct and that טוב here is not an adjective, but a noun cognate with Arabic *ṭayb* "perfume." Both find this noun in Jer 6:20 and in Cant 7:10, and Gray also cites Ugaritic *ṭb* in *CTA* 33:12, 15. Actually, שמן טוב is equivalent to Akkadian *šamnu ṭābu* (e.g., Wiseman, "Aššurnaṣirpal," 35:138) "sweet smelling oil" and is in no way different from שמן רקח (Eccl 10:1). For the correct interpretation of

the biblical passages referred to above by both Montgomery and Gray, see Ginsberg, קהלת, 96, 119. For *ṭb* "sweet-smelling" in Ugaritic, see now FMM, #61 and the bibliography there. See also n. 54 above.

[108]For Akkadian words with *m* going into Hebrew with *w*, see above, n. 46. Such being the case, a consonantal *w* must be restored to the Hebrew form resulting in בית נכות. See, e.g., *AF*, 8.

[109]For other passages, see *AHW*, 721-22.

[110]Fr. Delitzsch, *Prolegomena eines neuen hebräisch-aramäischen Wörterbuchs zum Alten Testament* (Leipzig, 1886), 140-42. See also T. Noeldeke, *ZDMG* 40 (1886), 731; Haupt, "Über den Halbvocal u̯," 266; C. F. Burney, *Notes on the Hebrew Text of the Books of Kings* (reprint; New York, 1970), 351; *AF*, 8; BDB, 649; מלון הלשון העברית IV, 3674 n. 1; KB I, 618; *FWOT*, 114; Gray, *I and II Kings*, 702; H. Cohen, "Treasure, Treasury," *EncJud* XV, 1361-62.

[111]See J. A. Montgomery, "Archival Data in the Book of Kings," *JBL* 53 (1934), 46-52, who showed that very often sections containing the phrase בעת ההיא = Akkadian *ina ūmišu* "at that time" include archival data and are written in annalistic style. The classic example of such a section is 2 Kgs 18:14-16, which is missing from Isaiah 36 and is clearly an independent account comprising a tribute list for the temple record. See L. L. Honor, *Sennacherib's Invasion of Palestine* (New York, 1926), 36-37; B. S. Childs, *Isaiah and the Assyrian Crisis* (Illinois, 1967), 69-73. To this section should be compared 2 Kgs 20:12-13 (= Isa 39:1-2), which, while perhaps somewhat reworked editorially, still bears the earmarks of an annalistic introduction to the sequel 2 Kgs 20:14-19 (= Isa 39:3-8).

[112]The native Hebrew term for "treasury" occurs in the phrases אוצרות בית ה׳ "temple treasury" (e.g., 1 Kgs 7:51 = 2 Chr 5:1) and אוצרות בית המלך "palace treasury" (e.g., 1 Kgs 14:26). The other two terms בית נכות and גנזים (Esth 3:9; 4:7) are loanwords from Akkadian and Persian respectively. See Cohen, "Treasure, Treasury," 1361-62; *EM* IV, 1072, 1079; *FWOT*, 57, 114.

[113]אלמנה in the Hebrew Bible often does not denote "widow" in the modern understanding of this term, but rather "a once married woman who has no means of financial support and who is thus in need of special legal protection." This is the connotation of Akkadian *almattu* according to *CAD*, A/1, 364, and this is often the meaning of the terms translated as "widow" in both biblical Hebrew and Egyptian. See H. Cohen, "Widow," *EncJud* XVI, 487-91, and idem, "The Widowed City," *JANESCU* 5 (1973), 75-81.

[114]*ṣalpu* "crooked" (*CAD*, Ṣ, 86) is to be associated with Hebrew סלף "pervert" in, e.g., Exod 23:8 and Deut 16:19 (oral communication from Professor M. Held).

[115]For the semantic range of *zabālu*, whose root meaning is "to transport, carry," see M. Held, "The Root zbl/sbl in Akkadian, Ugaritic and Biblical Hebrew," *JAOS* 88 (1968), 90-96.

[116]For *abbūta ṣabātu* "to espouse a cause," see *CAD*, A/1, 24-25.

[117]For *šulmānu* "gift," see, e.g., En. el. IV:134; TCL III: 54; STT I, 38:29; EA 10:13, 43; 35:10-11, 41-42, 50-53. See also Chapter II, n. 40 above.

[118]*AF*, 10; מלון הלשון העברית VIII, 7188 n. 1; KB I, 981; J. J. Finkelstein, "The Middle Assyrian Šulmānu Texts," *JAOS* 72 (1952), 79; P. Artzi, "ראשית עלייתה של ממלכת אשור לפי מכתבי אל עמרנה", *EI* 9 (1969), 27 n. 43; B. Levine, *In the Presence of the Lord* (Leiden, 1974), 16 n. 35.

[119]E.g., S. D. Luzatto, פרוש על ספר ישעיהו (reprint; Tel-Aviv, 1970), 27-28; S. Kraus, ספר ישעיהו (reprint; Jerusalem, 1969), 4.

[120]KB I, 981.

[120a]Contra *GAG*, §56r; Artzi, "ראשית עלייתה של ממלכת אשור", 27; Levine, *In the Presence of the Lord*, part one. As shown above, the primary meaning of *šulmānu* is "gift," and while this term is used with the meaning "tribute" in international relations in the Ancient Near East (see the aforementioned article of Artzi), this usage in no way differs from that of other synonomous Akkadian terms with the same basic meaning "gift" (see again Chapter II, n. 40 above). Furthermore, Levine's assertion that *šulmānu* is found in cultic contexts also in no way differs from the usage of these other synonomous Akkadian terms (see the "cultic" usage of *igisû*, *ṭa'tu*, *šulmānu*, *kad/trû* and *tāmartu* in passages listed in *CAD*, I/J, 42-43 already referred to by Levine in his aforementioned study). However, Levine's attempt to connect Akkadian *šulmānu* "gift" with the biblical שלמים-sacrifice cannot be accepted for the simple reason that *šulmānu*, *despite its attestation in cultic contexts, never refers to a specific type of sacrifice in Akkadian texts, while* שלמים *never means "gift" in non-cultic biblical contexts*. Furthermore, not a single one of the synonoms of *šulmānu* mentioned above ever refers to a specific type of sacrifice. Nor can the assertion of Artzi that *šulmānu* should be derived from *šulmu* "health, greetings" (also accepted in *GAG*, §56r) be adopted here. Artzi's reasoning is that in international relations the *šulmānu* was given to symbolize covenantal relations of goodwill. He also sees in the *šulmānu* a kind of bribe on the part of a vassal for protection or a commercial partner for commercial "rights." Now such reasoning may indeed be acceptable *for this particular usage of šulmānu in the international sphere*. However, as already stated, the basic meaning of *šulmānu* is "gift," and this basic meaning cannot be semantically connected to terms meaning "health, greetings." The usage of *šulmānu* in the Tale of the Poor Man of Nippur (see above, Chapter II, n. 40) certainly has nothing to do with covenantal

relations, and there is surely no hint of this type of relationship in Isa 1:23 either. Finally, as regards the structure of *šulmānu* as a primary noun, there are many examples of nouns of this form in Akkadian which cannot be derived from any known Akkadian verbal stem (e.g., *almānu*, *arsānu*, *duprānu*, *hašmānu*, *ištānu*, *kirbānu*, *pargānu* and *sagbānu*). Thus, while it is certainly possible structurally to analyze *šulmānu* as equivalent to *šulmu* "health, greeting" + *-ānu* (= suffix of specification) [see *GAG*, §56r and Z. Kallai and H. Tadmor, "בית-נינורתה = בית-חורון", *EI* 9 (1969), 141 and n. 27], this is not the only possibility. Semantic considerations as noted above favor the analysis of *šulmānu* as a primary noun which cannot be derived from any known Akkadian verbal stem.

[121]"To pay" in Akkadian is denoted mainly by *nadānu* and *šaqālu* (literally "to weigh out"). For the former, see *AHW*, 701, and for the latter, see *AHW*, 1178-79. Akkadian *šalāmu* means "to complete, be whole, be healthy" (see *AHW*, 1143-45).

[122]Finkelstein, "MA Šulmānu Texts," 77-80. While Finkelstein may be correct in assuming that the bribe was ostensibly made in order to expedite, rather than necessarily to pervert, the legal process, the distinction here is very fine, and Finkelstein himself notes that this practice may have been responsible for the judges' delaying the hearings concerning the poor and the weak. This too is a perversion of justice and may in fact be one of the perversions implied in the passage from BWL cited above.

[123]LTBA II, #2:276; #3:IV:12; #4:IV:7.

[124]STT I, 38:29. See the interpretation of Gurney, "Poor Man of Nippur," 145.

[125]A comparison with Egyptian *šrmt* has been suggested by both *AF*, 10, and מלון הלשון העברית VII, 7188 n. 1. The latter refers to W. M. Muller, *Asien und Europa* (Leipzig, 1893), 87-88, who however compares Egyptian *ša-ra-mâ-ti* to Hebrew שלמות* not שלמון or שלמונים (see also *AKF*, #871). In fact Egyptian *šrmt* occurs only in Papyrus Anastasi I, 17, 5 (= A. H. Gardiner, *Egyptian Hieratic Texts* I [Leipzig, 1911], 29, with translation on p. 19), and means, according to *WAS* IV, 528:11, "provisions of soldiers." Gardiner's rendering "complimentary gift" is based solely on this alleged comparison and does not fit the context.

[126]For אניות תרשיש, see also 1 Kgs 10:22; 22:49; Isa 23:1, 14; 60:9; Ezek 27:25; Ps 48:8; 2 Chr 9:21; 20:36, 37. Note also Jonah 1:3. For the identification of Tarshish, see W. F. Albright, "New Light on the Early History of Phoenician Colonization," *BASOR* 83 (1941), 21-22; J. M. Myers, *II Chronicles* (New York, 1965), 55, and the bibliography cited there. Add *YGC*, 219 n. 30, and *EncJud* XV, 825. Albright contends that תרשיש was originally a substantive derived from Akkadian *rašāšu* "to glow red, refine (said of glass and copper)" for which see now *AHW*, 960-61 and A. L. Oppenheim et al., *Glass and Glass*

Making in Ancient Mesopotamia (New York, 1970), 73. Albright would translate אניות תרשיש as "refinery fleet." Most recently, see now M. Elat, קשרי כלכלה בין ארצות המקרא (Jerusalem, 1977), 146-53. Elat discusses Albright's theory and other suggestions as well.

127 *miḫd*[ ] was originally restored *miḫd*[*t*] and translated "seized" by Ch. Virolleaud in the original publication of this text. See Ch. Virolleaud, "Textes administratifs de Ras-Shamra," *RA* 37 (1940-41), 33-34, and most recently J. M. Sasson, "Canaanite Maritime Involvement in the Second Millennium B.C.," *JAOS* 86 (1966), 131. The form *miḫdt* was apparently analyzed as a feminine plural passive participle of *ʾḫd* "to seize" in the simple conjugation, for which see *UT* I, 78. However, on the basis of new textual evidence from Ugarit, first M. L. Heltzer and then M. C. Astour succeeded in identifying *miḫd* with the harbor city, Maʾḫadu. Among this evidence were the Akkadian list of personal names, RS 1509, which includes a heading *LÚ*^{MEŠ} ^{URU}*Ma-a-ḫa-di* "people of (the city) Maʾḫadu" where the determinative for cities *URU* appears before the name (*PRU* III, p. 195), and two Ugaritic lists of personal names of *Miḫdym* "Maʾḫadians" where the latter term is a plural gentilic (*PRU* V, 16, 17). This view was strikingly confirmed by the new quadralingual dictionary in which we find Akkadian *kāru* "harbor, trading station, community of merchants" (see *CAD*, K, 231-37) equated with Ugaritic *ma-aḫ-ḫa-*[*du*] (*Ugaritica* V, 137:II:21'). For all this evidence as well as the suggested comparisons with Akkadian *māḫāzu* (*AHW*, 582), Aramaic מחוזא (*DISO*, 147 and Jastrow II, 757) and Hebrew מחוז (Ps 107:30), see M. C. Astour, "Maʾḫadu, the Harbor of Ugarit," *JESHO* 13 (1970), 113-27 with previous literature cited. Add R. Borger, "Weitere ugaritologische Kleinigkeiten," *UF* 1 (1969), 1-3; E. Y. Kutscher, "Ugaritica V בעקבות," *Leshonenu* 34 (1969-70), 5-18; A. F. Rainey, "הערות לווקאבולארים ההברתיים שבאוגרית", *Leshonenu* 34 (1969-70), 183-84; R. Kutscher, "*māḫāzu* המקבילות השומריות של", *Leshonenu* 34 (1969-70), 267-69; and most recently R. R. Stieglitz, "Ugaritic Mḫd--the Harbor of Yabne-Yam?," *JAOS* 94 (1974), 137-38. מחוז "port, harbor" in Ps 107:30 has not been included in this study as a *hapax legomenon* because there is a strong possibility that the term מזח in Isa 23:10 may well be a metathesized by-form of מחוז. On this point, see Ginsberg, *Isaiah*, 55; *BHS* VII, 34; *HALAT*, 535 and the literature cited there. [I wish to thank Professor D. Marcus for kindly calling my attention to this entire matter.]

128 The underscoring of *anyt miḫd* in the original text is here equivalent to a colon after these two words. See the example cited in *UT* I, p. 24, and note further at the beginning of the following texts in which no lines are underscored other than the first one or two: *PRU* II, 32, 34, 36, 42. In each of these cases the underscored line should be interpreted as the heading of a list, which may be properly indicated in translation by placing a colon at the end of the line in question.

129 See Gröndahl, *Personennamen*, 199, 417.

130 Ibid., 124, 382.

[131]Ibid., 124, 391.

[132]Ibid., 313, 418.

[133]Prior to 1950 (see n. 135 below), שכיות was usually interpreted as either "imagery" (from Aramaic סכא "to look, see" which was thought to be the root of משכית "image" in, e.g., Num 33:52) or "watchtowers" (based on the rendering of the Peshitta). A third possibility was the emending of שכיות to ספינות on the basis of Jonah 1:5. On all these possibilities, see, e.g., BDB, 967; G. B. Gray, *The Book of Isaiah I-XXVII* (Edinburgh, 1912), 59; J. Skinner, *Isaiah, Chapters I-XXXIX* (Cambridge, 1915), 22-23; S. Kraus, ספר ישעיהו, 6. See also n. 138 below.

[134]See *UT* III, #2680; *WUS*, #2862; Sasson, "Canaanite Maritime Involvement," 131. Aside from *CTA* 84 which is quoted above, *ṯkt* occurs in a list of boats together with their owners in *PRU* V̄, 85, and in a very obscure passage in *CTA* 4:5:68-69. For the latter, in which *ṯkt* is left untranslated by such an authority as H. L. Ginsberg (*ANET*, 133), see most recently *SP*, 148-51; van Zijl, *Baal*, 110 and the bibliography cited there. Van Zijl's proposal to emend the text to **ṯrt*, assuming a scribal error, and then to translate **ṯrt* "service" equivalent to Hebrew שרת is completely groundless. Not only is the resultant phrase **ṯrt bglṯ* "the service in upstirring" meaningless in this context, but Hebrew שרת has already been correctly identified with *šrd* in *CTA* 14:2:77-79 and *CTA* 14:4:169-71 by M. Held, "סתומה מקראית ומקבילתה באוגריתית", *EI* 3 (1954), 101-3. De Moor's translation, "the time of the *ṯkt*-ship with snow," fares little better contextually.

[135]H. L. Ginsberg apud W. F. Albright, "Baal-Zephon," *Festschrift Alfred Bertholet* (Tübingen, 1950), 4-6 n. 3; G. R. Driver, "Difficult Words in the Hebrew Prophets," *Studies in Old Testament Prophecy* (Edinburgh, 1950), 52-53. See also W. F. Albright, *JBL* 69 (1950), 386; M. Dahood, *Biblica* 43 (1962), 545; idem, *Enciclopedia de la Biblia* VI (Barcelona, 1965), 1128; idem, UHPP II, 8 (#5); *CPOT*, 280-81. As noted by most of these authors, we must read שׂכיות for שׁכיות since the ṯ of *ṯkt* corresponds to שׂ not שׁ.

[136]See *WAS* IV, 315:9, 10; T. Säve-Söderbergh, *The Navy of the Eighteenth Egyptian Dynasty* (Uppsala, 1946), 50-52; A. Alt, "Ägyptisch-Ugaritisches," *AfO* 15 (1945-51), 69-71; R. A. Caminos, *Late Egyptian Miscellanies* (London, 1954), 160.

[137]For this derivation of Ugaritic *ṯkt*, see especially Alt, "Ägyptisch-Ugaritisches," 69-71; Säve-Söderbergh, *Navy*, 50-52; Sasson, "Maritime Involvement," 131. Sasson's Akkadian etymology for both Ugaritic *ṯkt* and Egyptian *skty* is incorrect, however. He relates both terms to Akkadian *siqtum* which occurs in MSL V, 179:347: *GIŠ.MÁ.SIG.GA = siqtum*. This he translates following A. Salonen, *Die Wasserfahrzeuge in Babylonien* (Helsinki, 1939), 45, as a "small light ship." However, in MSL V, 179:346, we find the equation *GIŠ.MÁ.GÍD.DA = ariktum* "long,"

and there is no doubt that in the next line *siqtum* is simply a feminine adjectival form of *sīqu* "narrow," thus having nothing to do with Ugaritic *ṯkt* or Egyptian *skty*. See now *AHW*, 1049.

[138] J. Begrich apud K. Budde, "Zu Jesaja 1-5," *ZAW* 49 (1931), 198. Note that S. Aḥituv still mentions only Egyptian *skty* in his recent treatment of שכיות; see S. Aḥituv, "ספנות", *EM* V, 1073.

[139] Note that the rendering of the LXX also supports the meaning "boats." See Driver, "Difficult Words," 52-53; contrast *CPOT*, 280-81.

[140] Ugaritic *br* is to be equated with Egyptian *br* "type of ship" which is a loanword of Canaanite origin in Egyptian. See *AKF*, #348, *WAS* I, 465:8, 9; Säve-Söderbergh, *Navy*, 50 n. 3; W. Helck, *Die Beziehungen Ägyptens zu Vorderasien im 3. und 2. Jahrtausend v. Chr.* (Wiesbaden, 1971), 511 (#56); Sasson, "Maritime Involvement," 131; Alt, "Ägyptisch-Ugaritisches," 69-71. The Akkadian etymology for this term suggested by Säve-Söderbergh and accepted by both Helck and Sasson is incorrect, however. The relevant Akkadian term *bā'iru* means "fisherman, hunter" (*CAD*, B, 31-33), and while the phrase *elip bā'iri* "boat of a fisherman" does occur in MSL V, 174:274, no derivative of *ba'āru* "to fish, hunt" is used as the name of any kind of boat (see the derivatives of *ba'āru* listed in *CAD*, B, 31). Note that W. Spiegelberg, already in 1896, had compared Egyptian *br* with Greek βαιρι; see W. Spiegelberg, *Rechnungen aus der Zeit Setis I* (Strassburg, 1896), 60. [This information was kindly supplied by Professor J. Schmidt.]

[141] For the correct provenance of *CTA* 84, a broken list of sixteen ships of the *ṯkt* and *br* types together with the names of their owners from Ma'ḫadu, as well as an attempt to identify the harbor city Ma'ḫadu with the settlement at Minet el-Beiḍa, see Astour, "Ma'ḫadu," 117ff. Contrast Sasson, "Maritime Involvement," 131.

[142] See, e.g., the parallelism of עץ//ארז in Ps 104:16 which is equivalent to the Ugaritic pair *'ṣ//arz* "tree//cedar" in *CTA* 4:6:18-19. See Dahood, *Psalms III*, 354, 454, and UHPP, #442.

[143] Note the contrary opinion of N. H. Tur-Sinai who connects שכיות with שכוי in Job 38:36 and translates "high flying birds." See מלון הלשון העברית VIII, 7562; N. H. Tur-Sinai, "A Contribution to the Understanding of Isaiah I-XII," *Studies in the Bible* (Jerusalem, 1961), 159; פשוטו של מקרא III/1, 9; idem, *The Book of Job* (Jerusalem, 1967), 534. The objections of M. Dahood to this interpretation are to the point; see Dahood, *Biblica* 43 (1962), 545. Note finally that C. G. Howie has suggested that the parallelism of אניות//שכיות may also be found in Ezek 27:25, by emending שרותיך to שכיותיך and translating "ships of Tarshish, thy ships of merchandise"; see C. G. Howie, *The Date and Composition of Ezekiel* (Philadelphia, 1950), 60-61. While the meaning of שרותיך is unknown at present, there is no

basis for this emendation whatsoever. Furthermore, to translate שכיותיך מערבך* as "thy ships of merchandise" is to ignore the fact that there are two pronominal suffixes involved rather than one, and that the resulting combination is difficult to understand syntactically. For other suggested interpretations, see W. Zimmerli, *Ezechiel 2* (Neukirchen-Vluyn, 1969), 633; H. J. van Dijk, *Ezekiel's Prophecy on Tyre* (Rome, 1968), 81-82.

[144]For אב(ות) in juxtaposition with ידעני(ם), see also Lev 19:31; 20:6, 27; Deut 18:11; 1 Sam 28:3, 9; 2 Kgs 21:6; 23:24; Isa 8:19; 2 Chr 33:6. Note that the B-word ידעני occurs only in parallelism or juxtaposition with אב, never standing alone. Recently, an etymology has been suggested for Hebrew אוב which embraces similar sounding terms in Akkadian, Sumerian, Ugaritic, and Hittite. See M. Vieyra, "Les noms du 'mundus' en hittite et en assyrien et la pythonisse d'Endor," *RHA* 69 (1961), 47-55; idem, "Ištar de Ninive," *RA* 51 (1957), 100-1; H. Hoffner, Jr., "Second Millennium Antecedents to the Hebrew *'ÔB*," *JBL* 86 (1967), 385-401. See also C. Rabin, "Hittite Words in Hebrew," *Orientalia* 32 (1963), 115-16. We will deal here only briefly with the proposed Akkadian and Ugaritic equivalents. The alleged Akkadian equivalent is *apu* "hole, opening in the ground," which is listed as *apu* B in *CAD*, A/2, 201. While it is true that the few passages in which *apu* B occurs are ritual in nature, at no time does anyone seek, consult, or turn to the *apu* for advice (of the fifteen occurrences of אוב, seven involve the usage of the verbs שאל "to ask," דרש "to consult," and פנה "to turn to"). Conversely, the verbs which are used with Akkadian *apu*, e.g., *tabāku* "to pour into," *alāku ina libbi* "to go into," *karāru ina libbi* "to place into," and *mullû* "to fill," are never used with Hebrew אוב. Furthermore, the suggested semantic development of "pit" > "spirit of the pit" > "spirit" is invalid unless the root meaning, "pit", can be demonstrated internally for Hebrew אוב. Thus, semantically, the two words have nothing to do with each other, and the etymology from Akkadian *apu* must be rejected. The Ugaritic derivation is based on the occurrence of *ib* as a component part of *ilib* and is much more complicated. That Ugaritic *ib* cannot possibly be related to Akkadian *apu* "hole, opening in the ground" however, can be demonstrated by the following:

a) *ilib* occurs mainly as a divine name, and the deity so named was a prominent member of the Semitic pantheon at Ugarit. See J. C. de Moor, "The Semitic Pantheon of Ugarit," *UF* 2 (1970), 190 (#26), 199.

b) *ilib* in its single contextual occurrence as a common noun seems to mean "ancestral spirits" (*CTA* 17:1:27-28, 45-46; *CTA* 17:2:16-17), and this is most probably a semantic development from the major function of the god Ilib, who may well have been "the patron of ancestor worship." See *YGC*, 140-43.

c) *ilib* is equated to Akkadian *DINGER a-bi* in *Ugaritica* V, 18:1. Since *apu* "hole, opening in the ground" is not attested until the Neo-Assyrian period (*CAD*, A/2, 201), the element in this name must refer to something else (perhaps simply "father," i.e., "ancestor"). See de Moor, "Semitic Pantheon," 199; *YGC*, 140-43; IFCM, 78-79 (#7). Thus, while the Ugaritic theophoric element *ib* may in fact be related to Hebrew אוב,

there is really not enough evidence yet to make a final decision. However, in either case, neither Ugaritic *ib* nor Hebrew אוב have anything to do with Akkadian *apu* "hole, opening in the ground." Note finally that the above equation *ilib* = *DINGER a-bi* has also been used by M. Dietrich, O. Loretz and J. Sammartín as evidence against the connection of Ugaritic *ilib* with Hittite *a-a-bi* "sacrificial pit." Their reasoning is that this equation shows a primary connection with Akkadian *abu* "father" (= Ugaritic *ab*) and this must be the ultimate origin of both Ug. *ilib* (< **ilab* through vowel harmony) and Heb. אוב; see M. Dietrich, O. Loretz and J. Sammartín, "Ugaritisch ILIB und hebräisch ʾ(W)B 'Totengeist,'" *UF* 6 (1974), 450-51, together with the additional literature cited there. Despite this most recent attempt, it is the opinion of the present author that the origin of Hebrew אוב has still not been determined with any assurance and that this problem will not be solved until additional evidence comes to light.

[145] For transliteration and translation, see S. Langdon, "The Legend of Etana and the Eagle," *Babyloniaca* 12 (1931), 34-35; see also *ANET*, 117.

[146] See *CAD*, E, 397-401; *AHW*, 263-64.

[147] A. Jirku, *Die Dämonen und ihre Abwehr im Alten Testament* (Leipzig, 1912), 11-12. See also, e.g., idem, "*Eṭimmu* und אטים," *OLZ* 17 (1914), 185; F. Perles, "*Eṭimmu* im Alten Testament und im Talmud," *OLZ* 17 (1914), 108-10; idem, "Noch einmal *eṭimmu* im AT und im Talmud," *OLZ* 17 (1914), 233; *AF*, 69; N. H. Tur-Sinai, "דרישה אל המתים בתקופת המקרא," מנחה לדוד (Jerusalem, 1935), 70, 76; idem, הלשון והספר III (Jerusalem, 1955), 156-57, 162-63; idem, פשוטו של מקרא III/1, 58; *AHW*, 263; *FWOT*, 25; H. Wohlstein, "Zu den altisraelitischen Vorstellungen von Toten und Ahnengeistern," *BZ* 5 (1961), 35-36; S. Aḥituv, "Divination," *EncJud* VI, 114; *HALAT*, 36; *AIA*, 50.

[148] Contrast M. D. Cassuto, "מותו של בעל", *Tarbiz* 12 (1941), 172-73.

[149] See, e.g., מלון הלשון העברית I, 164-65 n. 3; Gray, *Isaiah*, 324; Kraus, ספר ישעיהו, 35; S. Yeivin, "אטים", *EM* I, 237. The Arabic root usually cited was *ʾaṭṭa* "produce, make, give, emit, or utter a sound, noise, voice or cry"; see Lane I, 66.

[150] See, e.g., Cassuto, "מותו של בעל", 172-73; H. L. Ginsberg, "The Rebellion and Death of Baʿlu," *Orientalia* 5 (1936), 186; B. Maisler, "Zur Urgeschichte des phönizisch-hebräischen Alphabets," *JPOS* 18 (1938), 290 n. 62. Cassuto, Ginsberg and Maisler (Mazar) all compare אטים to Ugaritic *uṭm* in *CTA* 5:1:4-6 (see also *CTA* 18:4:3). However, the entire passage *CTA* 5:1:4-6 is so full of obscurities that a philologically justifiable translation is a virtual impossibility. Note that Ginsberg now does not even attempt to translate this passage in *ANET*, 138, and labels the passage *CTA* 5:1:4-6 as "two couplets very obscure." Therefore, Ugaritic *uṭm* must be considered completely obscure in its present context, and no connection with Hebrew אטים can be assumed.

[151]Note that in 1966 O. Eissfeldt was still translating אטים as "Murmeler," obviously still deriving it from the Arabic root mentioned in n. 149 above; see O. Eissfeldt, "Wahrsagung im Alten Testament," *La divination en Mésopotamie ancienne* (Paris, 1966), 141.

[152]The reading עדים "vassal treaty" for MT ערים "cities" is now confirmed by 1QIs^{a}; see below, n. 156.

[153]אנוש "man" in this passage is totally incomprehensible and cannot under any circumstances be considered a valid parallel to ברית "covenant" and עדים "vassal treaty." Note further the objections raised by H. L. Ginsberg, "למילון לשון המקרא", ספר ה. ילון (Jerusalem, 1963), 171. Ginsberg originally thought that both in Isa 33:8 and in Isa 8:1, אנוש should be read !ארשן and be derived from Ugaritic *ušn* "gift" which occurs as a B-word to *ytnt* "gift" in *CTA* 14:3:135-36; 14:5:258-59 (restored); and 14:6:277-78. For this proposal and a discussion of the verb ארש "to give" as an element in Hebrew and Aramaic personal names, see H. L. Ginsberg, "Judah and the Transjordan States from 734 to 582 B.C.E.," *Alexander Marx Jubilee Volume* (New York, 1950), 361 n. 41. Ginsberg translated (!)ארשן as "(a deed of) gift." This proposal, however, is problematic in that Ugaritic *ušn* means simply "gift" and does not have anything to do with written documents or political agreements. The latter concepts seem to be what is called for in both biblical passages, and thus it is no surprise that Ginsberg has now put forth an alternate suggestion, to read אמון or אמנה "covenant; obligation" for the impossible אנוש based on such passages as Neh 10:1 and the common orthographic interchange of ש and מ. For this suggestion, see Ginsberg, "למילון לשון המקרא", 171, and most recently, idem, "First Isaiah," *EncJud* IX, 58; idem, *Isaiah*, 69. Were it not for the connection with Isa 8:1, one might be tempted to return to Ginsberg's first suggestion and read ארשן in Isa 33:8, still deriving it from Ugaritic *ušn* "gift", but translating it "tribute" based on the Akkadian parallels presented here for עדים (see below) and the semantic relationship of the meanings "gift" and "tribute" discussed above on p. 30 n. 40. Here it should be noted that the recent attempt of D. R. Hillers to connect אנוש in Isa 33:8 with Alalaḫ *unuššu*/Ugaritic *unṯ* "real-estate tax (paid to the king)" cannot be correct. The parallelism in Isa 33:8 and the historical background of the verse (see n. 165 below) together require that אנוש refer to some agreement (or symbol of an agreement) which Judah agreed to uphold in favor of her Assyrian overlord, and which she subsequently broke as a sign of rebellion. A real-estate tax payable to the local king hardly suits the context in that case. Hiller's assertion "Even if we could be more exact as to the meaning of *unuššu* in the second milennium B.C., this would not establish exactly what the sense was in Israel at a later time" may well be true, but surely does not help his case. See D. R. Hillers, "A Hebrew Cognate of unuššu/unṯ in Isa. 33:8," *HTR* 64 (1971), 257-59. For a comparison between Ugaritic *unṯ* and Akkadian *ilku* and *pilku* (both real-estate taxes), see A. F. Rainey, "Observations on Ugaritic Grammar," *UF* 3 (1971), 169 and the literature cited there.

[154] See also the duplicate, Streck Asb. 160:38, and note the similar expression *adê u sulummê* "vassal treaty and covenant" in Streck Asb. 130:86-87. Contrast the translation and understanding of this passage in M. Cogan, *Imperialism and Religion: Assyria, Judah and Israel in the Eighth and Seventh Centuries B.C.E.* (Montana, 1974), 43 n. 6. The parallel referred to above in addition to the one added by Cogan himself (Asb B. VIII. 59) should be sufficient to demonstrate that the concluding of a vassal treaty must be the subject of these passages whatever their historical circumstances.

[155] See also the duplicate, Winckler Sar. pl. 34:122-23, and note also Lie Sar. 68-69, where in a very similar context, *mêšu* "to disregard" is used instead of *abāku* "to repudiate."

[156] This reading is noted in Y. Kutscher, הלשון והרקע הלשוני של מגילת ישעיהו השלמה ממגילות ים המלח (Jerusalem, 1959), 203-4, but without a correct understanding of the meaning of עדים.

[157] B. Duhm, *Das Buch Jesaia* (reprint; Göttingen, 1968), 242. Other scholars who advocated this emendation without recognizing the true meaning of עדים include K. Marti, *Das Buch Jesaja* (Tübingen, 1900), 238; O. Procksch, *Jesaia I* (Leipzig, 1930), 420; J. Ziegler, *Isaias* (Würzburg, 1948), 99.

[158] The insistence here on the precise translation "vassal treaty" rather than simply "treaty" is based on the correct meaning of both Aramaic עדן and Akkadian *adû*, for which see n. 162 below. It is this lack of recognition that we are dealing here with a *terminus technicus* that has led many scholars to erroneously assume a connection with Hebrew עדות "testimony" and related terms. See nn. 169-70 below. This is not to say that *adû* always means "vassal treaty," but rather that whenever *adû* refers to a formal treaty between two parties, it is used as the *terminus technicus* for "vassal treaty."

[159] J. A. Fitzmyer, "The Aramaic Suzerainty Treaty from Sefîrē in the Museum of Beirut," *CBQ* 20 (1958), 456. Note, however, that W. F. Albright may have already seen this sometime before 1958; for in his discussion of covenant in 1957, he refers to his discovery of a term "ʿâdîm in hitherto misunderstood passages"; see W. F. Albright, *From the Stone Age to Christianity* (New York, 1957), 16-17. Other scholars who have noted the correct meaning of עדים in Isa 33:8 include H. L. Ginsberg, "למילון לשון המקרא", 171; J. A. Thompson, "Expansions of the עד Root," *JSS* 10 (1965), 239; J. A. Fitzmyer, *The Aramaic Inscriptions of Sefîre* (Rome, 1967), 24; F. O. Garcia-Treto, "Genesis 31:44 and 'Gilead,'" *ZAW* 79 (1967), 13-14; פשוטו של מקרא III/1, 95; B. Volkwein, "Masoretisches ʿēdūt, ʿēdwōt, ʿēdōt--'Zeugnis' oder 'Bundesbestimmungen'?," *BZ* 13 (1969), 37-38; Hillers, "A Hebrew Cognate of unuššu/unṯ in Isa. 33:8," 257-59; M. Weinfeld, "'הברית והחסד'", *Leshonenu* 35 (1972), 102; idem, "Covenant Terminology in the Ancient Near East and its Influence on the West," *JAOS* 93 (1973), 197 n. 99; idem, *Deuteronomy*, 111 n. 1; Ginsberg, *Isaiah*, 69.

[160]On Sefîre עדיא, עדי, עדן see especially Fitzmyer, *Sefîre*, 23-24 and the bibliography listed there. Add *DISO*, 203-4; J. J. Koopmans, *Aramäische Chrestomathie* I (Leiden, 1962), 43; A. Dupont-Sommer, *Les inscriptions araméenes de Sfiré* (Paris, 1958), 21-22; idem, "Ancient Aramaic Monumental Inscriptions," *An Aramaic Handbook* I/2 (Wiesbaden, 1967), 5; J. C. Greenfield, "Stylistic Aspects of the Sefire Treaty Inscriptions," *Acta Orientalia* 29 (1965-66), 9-10; *KAI* II, 242; Volkwein, "Masoretisches ʿēdūt, ʿēdwōt, ʿēdōt," 34-37. Here it should be noted that Professor H. L. Ginsberg has expressed strong phonological reservations concerning the identity of Sefîre עדיא, עדי, עדן with Akkadian *adû*, despite the historical and contextual evidence presented in n. 162 below (oral communication). See now also J. C. L. Gibson, *Textbook of Syrian Semitic Inscriptions* II (Oxford, 1975), 34 (against the comparison); M. Parnas, "'עדֻת', 'עדוֹת', 'עדוות' במקרא על רקע תעודות חיצוניות", *Shnaton* 1 (1975), 239-40, 244-45 (in favor of the comparison).

[161]For Akkadian *adû* "vassal treaty," see *CAD*, A/1, 131-34; *AHW*, 14; D. J. Wiseman, *The Vassal Treaties of Esarhaddon* (London, 1958), 3, 81; K. Deller, "Zur Terminologie neuassyrischer Urkunden," *WZKM* 57 (1961), 31-33; idem, *Orientalia* 34 (1965), 265; I. J. Gelb, *Bibliotheca Orientalis* 19 (1962), 160-62; R. Frankena, "The Vassal Treaties of Esarhaddon and the Dating of Deuteronomy," *OTS* 14 (1965), 134-36; W. von Soden, *OLZ* 61 (1966), 357-58; D. B. Weisberg, *Guild Structure and Political Allegiance in Early Achaemenid Mesopotamia* (New Haven, 1967), 32-40; Volkwein, "Masoretisches ʿēdūt, ʿēdwōt, ʿēdōt," 32-34, and n. 115; Cogan, *Imperialism and Religion*, 42-49, 122-25; Parnas, "'עדֻת', 'עדוֹת', 'עדוות'", 240-44.

[162]Here it must be stressed that Akkadian *adû* and Aramaic עדן are the cognate technical terms for "vassal treaty" in their respective languages. The proof that these two terms are equivalent comes from a comparison of the two vassal treaties between Matîʿel, king of Arpad, and his two overlords. The first, the Aramaic Sefîre inscriptions (for the text, see Fitzmyer, *Sefîre*), represents a vassal treaty of the eighth century B.C.E. between Matîʿel and Bir-Gaʾyah, king of KTK (for the various attempts to identify this location, see Fitzmyer, *Sefîre*, 127-35). The second, an Akkadian document of the eighth century B.C.E., represents a vassal treaty between Matîʿel and Aššurnirari V (754-745 B.C.E.) of Assyria (for the text, see E. F. Weidner, "Der Staatsvertrag Assurniraris VI mit Matiʾilu von Bit-Agusi," *AfO* 8 [1932-33], 17-26). The term *adû* is used consistently in the Akkadian document as a referrent to the vassal treaty involved, while the term עדן is its exact counterpart throughout the Sefîre inscriptions. That Akkadian *adû* (and hence also Aramaic עדן) is not a generic term for "treaty" but rather a technical term for "vassal treaty" has been noted several times on the basis of the contextual evidence from which "...it is clear that *adê* (in plural) or *adû* (in singular) is a pact or agreement imposed by one party upon another and sworn to by the obligated party only. It is not a pact between equals" (Gelb, *Bibliotheca Orientalis* 19 [1962], 161). See

also *CAD*, A/1, 133; Wiseman, *Vassal Treaties*, 81; Frankena, "Vassal Treaties," 134. The source of this misunderstanding would appear to be both von Soden's erroneous translation in *AHW*, 14 ("Eid"), and the unfortunate tendency of some scholars "for convenience" to render *adû* with "treaty" (Wiseman, *Vassal Treaties*, 81 and see also p. 3 where it is stated that *adû* will be "hereafter translated by the general term 'treaty' as an abbreviation of 'vassal-treaty stipulations'"). As a result, in such a standard non-assyriological work as D. J. McCarthy, *Treaty and Covenant* (Rome, 1963), *adû* is translated consistently as "treaty" or "oath" (see especially p. 97: "In the Aramaic treaty from Sfiré the term for the treaty is ʿdy....There is no doubt that *ade* is the regular word for treaty in Assyria"). Most of the comparisons between Akkadian *adû*, Aramaic עדן and Hebrew עדות "testimony" and related terms have been based on this incorrect translation and thus must be abandoned (see nn. 169-70 below).

[163] *salīme/sulummê šakānu* (see n. 154 above) is the Akkadian interdialectal equivalent of Hebrew נתן/שם ברית "to establish a covenant." For references and discussion, see M. Held, "Philological Notes on the Mari Covenant Rituals," *BASOR* 200 (1970), 33 and nn. 9-10. On *salīmu* and *sulummû*, see now *AHW*, 1015-16, 1057. It is difficult to understand why, of the two terms, only *sulummû* is translated "Bündnisvertrag" (among other definitions), while *salīmu* is defined as "Frieden, Freundschaft."

[164] Another parallel to מאס עדים "reject a vassal treaty" in Akkadian is *adê mêšu* "to disregard a vassal treaty" (see n. 155 above).

[165] That the subject of Isa 33:8 is Judah and not Assyria is true despite the fact that it is Assyria which is undoubtedly the subject of Isa 33:1. The prophet is apparently describing in v. 8 the mechanics of a Judean revolt against the Assyrian overlord. The predominant opinion in biblical scholarship that this verse refers to Assyria or some other suzerain (see, e.g., the discussion and bibliography in E. J. Kissane, *The Book of Isaiah* I [Dublin, 1960], 356-57, and B. S. Childs, *Isaiah and the Assyrian Crisis* [Illinois, 1967], 113-17) cannot be correct. Isa 33:7-9 would seem to describe the events of 701 B.C.E., which probably began with Judah (like Merodach Baladan some twenty years before--see J. A. Brinkman, "Merodach Baladan II," *Studies Presented to A. Leo Oppenheim* [Chicago, 1964], 19) rejecting its vassal treaty with Assyria and withholding tribute (see 2 Kgs 18:7)--a sure sign of outright rebellion. We are informed that this rebellion was part of a coordinated effort with Egypt, Judah's ally at the time (see Isa 30:1-7; 31:1-3; and the words of the רבשקה--2 Kgs 18:20-21, 24 = Isa 36:5-6, 9). The revolt was not successful, however, and the result was the ravaging of Judah by the Assyrian army, the effects of which are described in Isa 33:7-9. That the breaking of a vassal treaty and its effects upon Judah should be discussed in these verses is not at all surprising since the background of chaps. 30-31 of "the Book of Ahs" (Isaiah 28-33; 17:12-18:7) "is obviously Judah's negotiations with Egypt for aid in a contemplated or ongoing revolt against Assyria's suzerainty..." (Ginsberg, "First Isaiah," 59).

[166]E.g., Ginsberg, "First Isaiah," 59.

[167]See the bibliographies in the works of Childs and Kissane cited above in n. 165.

[168]See above, n. 162. Those who still do not accept this comparison include KB I, 701; Childs, *Isaiah and the Assyrian Crisis*, 112; *BHS* VII, 50; see also n. 156 above.

[169]Those who relate Akkadian *adû* and Aramaic עדן not only to Hebrew עדים "vassal treaty" in Isa 33:8 but to other similarly written Hebrew substantives (such as עד, עדה, and עדות) as well, include Fitzmyer, *Sefîre*, 23-24; Albright, *From the Stone Age to Christianity*, 16-17; Thompson, "Expansions of the עד Root," 237-38; Garcia-Treto, "Genesis 31:44 and 'Gilead,'" 13-17; Volkwein, "Masoretisches ʿēdūt, ʿēdwōt, ʿēdōt," 18-40; Weinfeld, "'הברית והחסד'", 87-88; idem, "Covenant Terminology," 191; idem, *Deuteronomy*, 65, 86-87. Those who do not compare *adû* and עדן to עדים in Isa 33:8, but who nevertheless relate them to other Hebrew substantives, may be found listed in both Fitzmyer, *Sefîre*, 23-24, and Volkwein, "Masoretisches ʿēdūt, ʿēdwōt, ʿēdōt," 18-40, esp. 36-37. Add Wiseman, *Vassal Treaties*, 81; Greenfield, "Sefire Treaty Inscriptions," 9; Koopmans, *Aramäische Chrestomathie*, 43; *CMHE*, 267; Weisberg, *Guild Structure*, 32-34; Parnas, "'עדֻת', 'עדוֹת', 'עדוות'", 239-45; Artzi, "ראשית עלייתה של ממלכת אשור", 23 n. 5א.

[170]The case for connecting Akkadian *adû* and Aramaic עדן with Masoretic *ʿēdūt*, *ʿēdwōt*, and *ʿēdōt* has been made most recently and most persuasively by Volkwein, "Masoretisches ʿēdūt, ʿēdwōt, ʿēdōt," 18-40. His major arguments may be summed up as follows (note also now the similar arguments put forth by Parnas, "'עדֻת', 'עדוֹת', 'עדוות'", 235-46, who adds, however, a detailed analysis of the parallel usage of Akkadian *adû* and Hebrew עדֻת, עדוֹת and עדוות):

1. *ʿēdūt*, usually translated "testimony" and analyzed as the abstract form of *ʿēd* "witness" (*ʿēd* + *ūt*), and its related forms *ʿēdwōt* and *ʿēdōt*, must be translated "treaty" or "treaty stipulations" in many of their occurrences in the Bible especially in the following cases:

a) *According to parallelism or juxtaposition especially in Deuteronomic texts*--*ʿēdwōt*/*ʿēdōt*//חקים, משפטים --Deut 4:45; 6:20. //חקים, מצות--Deut 6:17; 2 Kgs 23:3 = 2 Chr 34:31; 1 Chr 29:19. //ברית--Ps 25:10; 132:12. //משפטים, מצות, חקים--1 Kgs 2:3. //חקים, ברית--2 Kgs 17:15. //חקת, תורה--Jer 44:23. //מצות--Neh 9:34. *ʿēdūt*//תורה--Ps 19:8; 78:5. //חק, משפט--Ps 81:6.

b) *In Priestly texts*--The phrase ארון העדות occurs very often in P and other priestly texts, and here *ʿēdūt* surely refers to the contents of the ark. The decisive occurrence, however, is Exod 31:18 (note also Exod 34:29) where the phrase לוחות העדות is found. This must be compared to such verses as Deut 9:9, 15, where the similar phrase לוחות הברית occurs, showing here that *ʿēdūt* must be identical in meaning with ברית "treaty."

2. Philologically, if *ʿādōt* (plural) is read in all the above cases (compare *ʿādîm* in Isa 33:8), it may then be considered cognate to Akkadian *adû* and Aramaic עדן (both in the plural) and thereby obtain the required meaning "treaty (stipulations)."
3. The occurrence of the forms *ʿēdūt*, *ʿēdwōt*, and *ʿēdōt* in the Masoretic vocalization must be due to a confusion between *ʿādōt* "treaty (stipulations)" and *ʿēdūt* "judgment, testimony." The latter, which is formed with the late abstract ending *-ūt*, is known independently from Ben Sirah (e.g., 36:20), and this explains the source of the confusion in later times.

Against these arguments, the following must be stated:
1. Akkadian *adû* and Aramaic עדן are *technical terms* meaning "vassal treaty" in their respective languages. They are not generic terms for "treaty" like Hebrew ברית (see n. 162 above).
2. As correctly noted by S. Loewenstamm, "עדות", *EM* VI, 89, *ʿēdūt* is not used in a single context where an actual treaty is established between two parties (contra Greenfield, "Sefire Treaty Inscriptions," 9).
3. There is absolutely no justification for the assumption that *ʿēdūt* "testimony" must be a late word (i.e., Aramaism) because of its construction with the abstract ending *-ūt*. While this ending is common in Aramaic, it is just as common in Akkadian (*-ūtu*) where not only many of the concepts which are attested with this ending in Hebrew occur (e.g., Heb. מלכות--Akk. *šarrūtu* "kingship"; Heb. עבדות--Akk. *ardūtu* "slavery"), but many are also cognate (e.g., Heb. רפאות--Akk. *ripūtu* [Amarna] "health"; Heb. אלמנות--Akk. *almānūtu* "'widowhood'" [see n. 113 above]; Heb. כבדות--Akk. *kabtūtu* "heaviness, majesty"). Therefore, the occurrence of *šībūtu* (= *šību* "witness" + *-ūtu*) as the regular word for "testimony" in Akkadian (*AHW*, 1229-30) clearly demonstrates that Hebrew *ʿēdūt* "testimony" should indeed be analyzed as *ʿēd* "witness" + *-ūt*, and that there is no valid reason for considering either this word or its construction as late due to Aramaic influence.
4. As for Volkwein's contextual evidence (his argument #1 above), there can be no doubt that *ʿēdūt* and *ʿēdwōt*/*ʿēdōt* must approach the meanings "treaty" and "treaty stipulations" in the passages he cites. This, however, has been noted before, and has been generally explained as a semantic development of *ʿēdūt* "testimony." Since the treaties and laws are by definition testified (i.e., sworn) to, they may themselves be called *ʿēdūt* or *ʿēdōt*/*ʿēdwōt* as "a testimony of God" [i.e., treaty] or "of laws as divine testimonies or solemn charges" [i.e., "treaty stipulations"] (see BDB, 730). Evidence for this development comes from the usage of שבועה "oath". For just as ברית "treaty" can alternate freely with *ʿēdūt* "testimony" (see Volkwein's argument 1b above), so it can also alternate with שבועה "oath" (compare e.g., Gen 26:3 [והקמתי את השבועה] with Gen 17:7 [והקמתי את בריתי] and Exod 6:4 [וגם הקמתי את בריתי] where both ברית and שבועה must be taken to mean "treaty"). Just as שבועה can mean "treaty" by extension because it is sworn to, so *ʿēdūt* can mean "treaty" because it is testified to (compare also the usage and semantic range of *māmītu* "oath" in Akkadian treaty contexts).

[171] K. A. Kitchen, *Ancient Orient and Old Testament* (Chicago, 1968), 108.

[172]The Canaanite loanword *ʿdt* (*WAS* I, 237:8) occurs in Papyrus Turin IV, 5, for which see A. de Buck, "The Judicial Papyrus of Turin," *JEA* 23 (1937), 154; J. H. Breasted, *Ancient Records of Egypt* IV (New York, 1906), 215; and most recently for historical background, R. O. Faulkner, "Egypt: From the Inception of the Nineteenth Dynasty to the Death of Ramesses III," *Cambridge Ancient History*, fasc. #52 (Cambridge, 1966), 32, with the bibliography referred to there. The substantive *ʿdt* is translated "Verschwörung" in *WAS* I, 237:8; *AKF*, #300; and W. Helck, *Die Beziehung Ägyptens zu Vorderasien im 3 und 2 Jahrtausend v. Chr.* (Wiesbaden, 1971), 510, #46.

[173]The claim that the generally accepted meaning "conspiracy" is a "secondary nuance...derived from the idea of covenant or agreement on terms" (Kitchen, *Ancient Orient and Old Testament*, 108) is without any factual basis. In the Semitic languages, words for "conspiracy" are normally derived from roots meaning "to tie" (e.g., Heb. קשר "to conspire"; Akkadian *kaṣāru* "to plot"). There is no example in the Semitic languages to my knowledge of a word having a secondary meaning "conspiracy" whose primary meaning is "treaty." Note also the objections of Volkwein, "Masoretisches ʿēdūt, ʿēdwōt, ʿēdōt," 32.

[174]See also Isa 41:23 where the verbs ירא and שתע both appear in the same context, and where the vocalization indicates that the Masoretes also derived this form from שתע not שעה. Here ונרא must be vocalized וְנִרָא "and we will fear" standing for ונירא. For the confusion between ירא "to fear" and ראה "to see", see J. C. Greenfield, "Lexicographical Notes I," *HUCA* 29 (1958), 228 n. 18. Note that M. Dahood originally disassociated Isa 41:23 from Isa 41:10 claiming that the reading of 1QIs[a], ונשמעה ונראה יחדו, and the expression in Isa 40:5 (וראו כל בשר יחדו) supported his translation of יחדו as "his face" (derived from Ugaritic *ḥdy* "to gaze, see"), and therefore the two verbs in Isa 41:23 ונשמעה ונֹרא were "verbs of perception and not of emotion"; see M. J. Dahood, "Some Ambiguous Texts in Isaias," *CBQ* 20 (1958), 46-49. Against this interpretation, note that Ugaritic *ḥdy* = Hebrew חזה, the second radical being *ḏ* which is often represented in Ugaritic by *d*, and is always represented in Hebrew as ז (e.g., Ug. *dbḥ* = Heb. זבח "to sacrifice"). There is absolutely no reason to expect Ugaritic *ḥdy* to come into Hebrew with a ד, especially since it already exists in Hebrew with a ז. On this whole issue, see H. L. Ginsberg, "Lexicographical Notes," VTSup 16 (1967), 71-73 and the bibliography cited there. For the reading of 1QIs[a], see Greenfield, "Lexicographical Notes I," 228, and Kutscher, מגילת ישעיהו, 220 (#213). Dahood has apparently changed his stand on this issue, for he now lists Isa 41:23 together with Isa 41:10 when discussing this pair in Ugaritic and biblical Hebrew; see UHPP, #254.

[175]On the problem of the verbal form *yraun*, see most recently J. C. de Moor, "Frustula Ugaritica," *JNES* 24 (1965), 358-59 and the bibliography cited there. While de Moor's solution is possible, the positing of a new *n* suffix (as an

alternative to *h*) for which there are no other Ugaritic examples is problematic. His objections to previous attempts at parsing this form are well taken however.

[176]On *rkb ʿrpt* = רכב בערבת (Ps 68:5), see most recently M. Weinfeld, "'Rider of the Clouds' and 'Gatherer of the Clouds,'" *JANESCU* 5 (1973), 421-26 with bibliography.

[177]Note that the existence of the root שתע may have already been seen by Menaḥem ben Saruq. מחברת מנחם, 183 lists the root שתע as an entry and states the following: "השרש הזה יש ברשימה ואיננו בתוך המחבר׳" "this root is in the list, but is not in the מחברת itself."

[178]A. B. Ehrlich, *Randglossen zur hebräischen Bibel* IV (Leipzig, 1912), 150 (on Isa 41:10). Contrast idem, מקרא כפשוטו III (reprint; New York, 1969), 89 (on Isa 41:10), where תשתע is derived from שעה. Others who posited the existence of this root prior to its discovery in Ugaritic (see n. 179) include Y. Grasovsky and D. Yellin, המלון העברי (Tel-Aviv, 1919) [contrast D. Yellin, חקרי מקרא, ישעיהו (Jerusalem, 1939), 43-44, where שתע is not mentioned]; I. Eitan, *A Contribution to Biblical Lexicography* (New York, 1924), 8.

[179]H. L. Ginsberg, "חדשות אפיגרפיות מאוגרית", *BJPES* 3 (1935-36), 55-56; idem, "The Rebellion and Death of Baʿlu," 170 n. 1; idem, כתבי אוגרית, 49; idem, "Ugaritico-Phoenicia," *JANESCU* 5 (1973), 134 n. 19. See also, e.g., Greenfield, "Lexicographical Notes I," 226-28; ענת, 27; M. Held, "עוד זוגות מלים מקבילות במקרא ובכתבי אוגרית", *Leshonenu* 18 (1953), 150 n. 13; idem, "The Action-Result Sequence," 282 n. 67; idem, "Mari Covenant Rituals," 37 and n. 52; *CPOT*, 294-95; פשוטו של מקרא III/1, 111-12; UHPP, #254.

[180]*CTA* 5:2:6-7; *CTA* 6:6:30-31.

[181]*KAI* 26A:II:3-5. See, e.g., A. Alt, "Die phönikischen Inschriften von Karatepe," *WO* 1 (1948), 281; *DISO*, 322. Virtually all scholars who have dealt with this pair since 1948 have made reference to this attestation of שתע in Azitawadda. See above, n. 179.

[182]See S. H. Horn, "The Ammān Citadel Inscription," *BASOR* 193 (1969), 12-13; R. Kutscher, "כתובת חדשה מרבת עמון", *Qadmoniot* 17 (1972), 28; H. L. Ginsberg, "Ugaritico-Phoenicia," 134 n. 19. Contrast W. F. Albright, "Some Comments on the Ammān Citadel Inscription," *BASOR* 198 (1970), 38, 40.

[183]Note that J. L. McKenzie in 1968 was still translating אל תשתע in Isa 41:10 "do not look about anxiously"; see J. L. McKenzie, *Second Isaiah* (New York, 1968), 29. Even more surprising is the following assertion made by F. M. Cross, Jr., "Epigraphic Notes on the Ammān Citadel Inscription," *BASOR* 193 (1969), 19 n. 16:

> There are two roots *ṯʿy* (> *šʿy*) in Canaanite. One means "to gaze," Gt "to look about (anxiously), to fear." The other means "to offer (a sacrifice, gift)." Both roots

> appear in Ugaritic and Hebrew....It is possible to read here [Ammān Citadel Inscription, line 6] "...you are feared תשתע amongst the gods." In this case we should have to posit a secondary root *št'* from which a passive is developed. The alternative is easier, to read a Gt form (regular in Old Hebrew, in Phoenician, and in Moabite) of *š'y* "to offer."

Note that S. H. Horn, after correctly understanding תשתע in the Ammān Citadel Inscription as coming from שתע "to fear," defers to the above interpretation of F. M. Cross, Jr.; see Horn, "The Ammān Citadel Inscription," 13 n. 28. See the valid criticism of Cross' contention in *SP*, 179.

[184]See also the sequel, Isa 44:16-17.

[185]For ויאמץ לו "He secured for himself," see Ps 80:16, 18, and note the parallelism in v. 16: אמצת לך "you secured for yourself"//נטעת ימינך "your right hand planted," which is similar to the parallelism in Isa 44:14: נטע "he planted"//ויאמץ לו "he secured for himself"; see also BDB, 55.

[186]That השיק means "to kindle a fire" is beyond any doubt in view of its usage with בער "to burn" and אש "fire" in Ezek 39:9. Note also the nifʿal usage with אש in Ps 78:21.

[187]For other images made of *erēnu* which are used in rituals, see, e.g., Maqlû IV:39-41.

[188]*tubta''enni* is here taken as a II/3 present of *bu''û* "to look for" (*CAD*, B, 360). See *GAG*, §106u and paradigm 34c.

[189]See also BRM 4, 25:26-27 for a similar passage.

[190]For *bīt papāḫi* "sanctuary," see *AHW*, 823.

[191]Note that ארן is written with a small *nun*. For large and small letters in the MT, see most recently A. Dotan, "Masorah," *EncJud* XVI, 1408-9 and the bibliography cited on pp. 1479-80. Undoubtedly the small *nun* in this case is due to the potential confusion with ארז, the regular Hebrew word for "cedar" which also occurs in this verse. The closeness of ארן and ארז in writing, meaning, and proximity in this verse is the source of that confusion.

[192]See *CAD*, E, 274-79; *AHW*, 237.

[193]*AS*, 16. See also, e.g., B. Teloni, "Appunti intorno all'iscrizione di Nabonid V.R. 65.," *ZA* 3 (1888), 297-98 and the bibliography cited there; *CIOT* II, 104; BDB, 75; *AF*, 53; Löw, *Flora* II, 120-23; M. Zohary, "ארן", *EM* I, 596-97; C. R. North, *The Second Isaiah* (Oxford, 1964), 138; S. M. Paul, "Deutero-Isaiah and Cuneiform Royal Inscriptions," *JAOS* 88 (1968), 183 n. 27.

[194]For the basic Israelite misunderstanding of the representative function of images in pagan religion, see Y. Kaufman, תולדות האמונה הישראלית II (Tel-Aviv, 1964), 255-85. The

Israelites, according to Kaufman, equated these images with the gods themselves, and the worship of these idols was to them the essence of pagan religion.

[195]For the fashioning of images (*ṣalmu*), see E. D. van Buren, "The *ṣalmê* in Mesopotamian Art and Religion," *Orientalia* 10 (1941), 65-92. For *erēnu* used in the making of ritual figurines, see F. Thureau-Dangin, *Rituels accadiens* (Paris, 1921), 201-2 [on this text in comparison to sections of the Priestly Code, see C. Cohen, "Was the P Document Secret?," *JANESCU* 1/2 (1969), 39-44]. See also the passages listed in *CAD*, E, 276. There is, however, no extant passage to my knowledge in which *erēnu* is used in the making of a divine image or idol. Divine images were often made in the temple workshop known as the *bīt mummi*. Various rituals such as the "washing of the mouth" were performed there to transform the lifeless image into a receptacle of the god. On the *bīt mummi*, see A. Heidel, "The Meaning of *mummu* in Akkadian Literature," *JNES* 7 (1948), 102-5. On the rituals and work performed there, see, e.g., A. L. Oppenheim, *Ancient Mesopotamia* (Chicago, 1964), 185-86 with bibliography listed on pp. 364-65 n. 10; H. W. F. Saggs, *The Greatness that was Babylon* (New York, 1962), 340-41. On the fashioning of divine images for the Akītu festival, see S. A. Pallis, *The Babylonian Akītu Festival* (København, 1926), 136-39. The most complete description of the materials used in the making of divine images may be found in Borger Esarh., 83-84:27-44. See also BBSt., 123:IV:12-28. The absence of *erēnu* from these texts may simply be due to the paucity of extant sources concerning the manufacturing of divine images. The usage of *erēnu* in the fashioning of all other kinds of cultic images leads one to strongly suspect that this material was used in the carving of divine images as well.

[196]The mocking of these idols goes hand in hand with such statements as Isa 42:8:

אני ה׳ הוא שמי וכבודי לאחר לא אתן ותהלתי לפסילים

I am the Lord, that is My name; I will not yield
My glory to another, nor My renown to idols.

See also, e.g., Isa 42:17; 44:9. It is suggested here that the "glory" and "renown" referred to in these passages is the bringing of Cyrus to conquer Babylon (Isa 45:1-8). Now a counterclaim was made in the Cyrus Cylinder (see *ANET*, 315-16) that it was Marduk, chief god of Babylon, who himself had brought Cyrus to liberate Babylon. The prophet's prediction of captivity and exile for בל (i.e., Marduk) and נבו (i.e., Nabû) after Cyrus' conquest of Babylon (Isa 46:1-2), the only place in the Bible where these two Mesopotamian gods are mentioned together, may be contrasted with the conflicting statement in the Cyrus Cylinder concerning Cyrus' fervent prayer that all the gods that he has resettled in their sanctuaries should daily ask Bel and Nabû for a long life for him (F. H. Weissbach, *Die Keilinschriften der Achameniden* [Leipzig, 1911], 6:34-35 and *ANET*, 316). These conflicting beliefs concerning the fate of Bel and Nabû are clearly symptomatic of the major polemical debate which was undoubtedly taking place in Babylon during the time of Second Isaiah with regard to Cyrus' conquest of the city. The Israelites, in Babylonian exile, saw in Cyrus the vehicle by which the God of Israel would free them from their captivity. The influential Babylonian priesthood, the authors of the Cyrus Cylinder, saw in Cyrus the means by which Marduk would exert his will, and restore himself and them to their proper role in Babylonian society. For the historical background to this debate, see the excellent article by H. Tadmor, "הרקע ההסטורי להצהרת כורש", ספר בן-גוריון (Jerusalem, 1964), 450-73.

[197]Contrast A. Büchler, "Zu Sachaus aramäischen Papyrus aus Elephantine," *OLZ* 15 (1912), 126-27; Löw, *Flora* II, 120-23; Zohary, "ארן", 596-97; *HALAT*, 87. All these authors equate biblical ארן with Mishnaic ארנים and translate it as "lauris nobilis" on the basis of the Amoraic explanation of the term ארנים in Para 3:8 (see Baba Batra, 81a and Rosh HaShanah, 23a). Surely, the usage of Akkadian *erēnu* in the land concerning which the prophet is speaking is more vital to the understanding of this term than the amoraic interpretation of Mishnaic ארנים.

[198]See also Isa 51:17, where the parallelism כוס//קבעת is found in the same context. For the general comparison of Isa 51:17-18, 22 with *CTA* 17:I:31-32; II:5-6, 19-20, see now IFCM, 79-80 (#8) and the bibliography listed there.

[199]That תרעלה is some kind of poison and should not be translated "reeling" (from Aramaic רעל) is seen from its parallelism with חמה in Isa 51:17, 22, and by comparing its usage with יין "wine" in Ps 60:5 to the usage of חמה in Deut 32:33. On this whole issue, see H. Cohen, "Poison," *EncJud* XIII, 703.

[200]The second occurrence of כוס in this verse, as in Isa 51:17, must be understood as an explanatory gloss to קבעת. See already H. L. Ginsberg, "The Ugaritic Texts and Textual Criticism," *JBL* 62 (1943), 111 and n. 3. It seems apparent that this gloss was inserted sometime after the second half of the sixth century B.C.E., when the text was first written (see idem, *Isaiah*, 18-21) and before approximately the first century B.C.E., when 1QIs^{a}, which already contains the gloss, was produced (see Kutscher, מגילת ישעיהו, 53-54). Another explanatory gloss may be found in Jonah 2:4 where מצולה "the deep" is explained by בלבב ימים "in the midst of the seas." Here the gloss was probably inserted sometime in post-exilic times when Jonah 1:1-2:2 and 2:11-4:11 were first written and the much older psalm, Jonah 2:3-10, was incorporated into the book. For the dating of Jonah 1:1-2:2 and 2:11-4:11, see now H. L. Ginsberg, *The Five Megilloth and Jonah* (Philadelphia, 1969), 114. For the dating and incorporation of Jonah 2:3-10, see Y. Licht, "יונה", *EM* III, 609. That the second occurrence of כוס in both Isa 51:17, 22 is a gloss was already suggested in BDB, 867. Note however that M. Dahood's comparison of this gloss to the Canaanite glosses in the Amarna letters is not completely appropriate. The latter were inserted by Canaanite scribes in their native language to explain Akkadian terms which they themselves had just used, and with which they were not yet

completely familiar, while the former was not inserted by the original author, but by a later scribe, at a time when readers of the text no longer understood the term in question. Contrast UHPP, #296.

[200a]For the semantic range of חמה which includes both "wrath" and "poison" and the employment of this term in Isa 51: 17, 22 (as well as in many other passages) in order to evoke a *double entendre* based on its two-fold meaning, see p. 25 above and especially this author's article cited on p. 31 n. 46.

[201]The clause "the chalice (cup) of my venomous wrath, you will never again drink" is a classic example of a casus pendens in biblical Hebrew, with the accusative introduced by את and placed in the primary position, and with a clear resumptive pronominal suffix on לשתותה "to drink it." It thus serves as an excellent parallel to the immediately preceding clause, as may be seen from the above translation.

[202]See also *CTA* 19:IV:216-18.

[203]For the difference in usage between *šqy* and its *š* form *ššqy*, see Held, "The Action-Result Sequence," 280-81 n. 45 and the literature cited there.

[204]For the parallelism of יד//ימין in biblical Hebrew and its counterpart in Ugaritic, see UHPP, #218 and the bibliography cited there.

[205]קבעת has been connected with גביע "goblet" and both have been labeled as loanwords from Egyptian *ḳbḥw* "libation vessel" (*WAS* V, 27:13) by L. Koehler, "Hebräische Etymologien," *JBL* 59 (1940), 36. This theory has now been perpetuated by *HALAT*, 166 albeit with a question mark, and by *AHW*, 890 with hesitation whatsoever. Now Egyptian *ḳbḥw* is written with the determinative  (*WAS* V, 27:13), the name of which is the *ḳbḥ* sign (*WAS* V, 26:4). Therefore there is no doubt that *ḳbḥw* is derived from the root *ḳbḥ*, the relevant meaning of which is "to offer a libation" (*WAS* V, 27:3, 4). That *ḳbḥw* is specifically a libation vessel and not a drinking cup may be seen from the pictorial representation of this vessel on such paintings as that from the tomb of Rekh-m'i-Rē' (fifteenth century B.C.E.) which depicts rites before Osiris, and upon which a lector priest is shown pouring water from a  vessel onto the neck of a newly slaughtered bull. See N. Davies, *The Tomb of Rekh-m'i-Rē' at Thebes* (New York, 1943), pl. 83, and H. G. Fischer, "The Butcher Pḥ-r-nṯr," *Orientalia* 29 (1960), 177 n. 3. Therefore, Egyptian *ḳbḥw* "libation vessel" is to be completely disassociated from קבעת "chalice." As for the alleged relationship between קבעת and גביע "goblet," the following brief remarks will have to suffice:

a) גביע has a specialized artistic usage in Exod 25:31, 33, 34; 37:17; which is not attested for קבעת.

b) In Jer 35:5, גביע is used in addition to כוס and seems to mean "pitcher" (see J. Bright, *Jeremiah* [New York, 1965], 187).

c) There is no positive evidence whatsoever for equating קבעת and גביע.
On גביע in general, see A. M. Honeyman, "The Pottery Vessels of the Old Testament," *PEQ* (1939), 80; J. L. Kelso, *The Ceramic Vocabulary of the Old Testament* (New Haven, 1948), 17; L. Y. Raḥman, "גביע", *EM* II, 401-2; *HALAT*, 166.

[206]The translation "chalice" is preferred here to the usual translation "goblet" for both Ugaritic *qbʿt* and Hebrew קבעת because "goblet" has been traditionally used for גביע, and the view has been expounded here that there is no demonstrable connection between these two substantives (see previous note).

[207]Ch. Virolleaud, *La légende phénicienne de Danel* (Paris, 1936), 182. See also, e.g., M. D. Cassuto, "ספרות מקראית וספרות כנענית", *Tarbiz* 14 (1943), 5; ענת, 26; *PEPI*, 9; Held, "Action-Result Sequence," 275 and 281 n. 61; M. Dahood, "Hebrew-Ugaritic Lexicography IX," *Biblica* 52 (1971), 341-42; UHPP, #296; *WUS*, #2385; *AHW*, 890; A. Salonen, *Die Hausgeräte der alten Mesopotamier* II (Helsinki, 1966), 120; KB I, 820.

[208]Akkadian *qabūtu* which is some kind of cup may well be related to קבעת as was first suggested some 100 years ago by E. Schrader, *CIOT* I, 199 n. +. On the usage of *qabūtu*, see *AHW*, 890 and especially Salonen, *Hausgeräte* II, 120-22. It has not been formally included in the above discussion because its relationship to Akkadian *kāsu* "cup" (= Hebrew כוס) is not completely clear. While *qabūtu* and *kāsu* share many common usages (see Salonen, *Hausgeräte* II, 114-22, where all the passages are conveniently assembled), *kāsu* is never equated or associated with *qabūtu* in the lexical lists, while at the same time, *kāsu* is equated or associated in these lists with no less than ten other terms (see *CAD*, K, 253, and Salonen, *Hausgeräte* II, 122-23). Furthermore, *kāsu* and *qabūtu* never appear together in literary texts, in parallelism, or otherwise. Nevertheless, the close congruence in many usages of these two terms is a strong indication that the above negative factors may simply be due to the accident of discovery, and the question of relationship should be left open for the time being. For a bibliography concerning the relationship between Akkadian *qabūtu* and Hebrew קבעת, see Salonen, *Hausgeräte* II, 122-23. Add *CIOT* I, 199 n. +; BDB, 867; Honeyman, "Pottery Vessels," 89; *CML*, 144 n. 11 (comparing Ug. *qbʿt* to Akk. *qabūtu* without referring to Heb. קבעת); *WUS*, #2385; *AHW*, 890.

[209]Sucking milk from the breasts of goddesses is a common theme in the descriptions of the birth and rearing of gods and kings in the ancient Near East as well as Egypt. For a biblical parallel, see Isa 60:16, and note on this theme in general, C. H. Gordon, "Homer and Bible," *HUCA* 26 (1955), 64-65, and FFM, #52. For Akkadian parallels, see *LKK*, 41, and note the relevant passages quoted in *CAD*, E, 165-66.

[210]Note that the sign  = *en* in *te-en-ni-iq* was accidentally omitted here by Craig. For this correction, see Craig ABRT II, IX. This text was first published by S. A. Strong,

"A Prayer of Aššurbanipal," *Transactions of the Ninth International Congress of Orientalists* II (1893), 199-208, and by J. A. Craig, "Prayer of the Assyrian King Asurbanipal," *Hebraica* 10 (1893), 75-87. See also Streck Asb., 342-51; KB VI/2, 136-41; A. Falkenstein and W. von Soden, *Sumerische und akkadische Hymnen und Gebete* (Zürich, 1953), 292-94; J. Pinckert, *Hymnen und Gebete an Nebo* (Leipzig, 1920), 16-22.

[211]For *ḫalāb/pu* "to milk" and *ḫilpu* "milk," see H. Zimmern, "Kleine Mitteilungen und Anzeigen," *ZA* 36 (1925), 85 n. 1; G. Meier, "Ritual für das Reisen über Land," *AfO* 12 (1937-39), 142 n. 33a; *CAD*, Ḫ, 36, 187; W. von Soden, "Gibt es ein Zeugnis dafür, dass die Babylonier an die Wiederauferstehung Marduks geglaubt haben?," *ZA* 51 (1955), 146; AW I, 11 (#53); *AHW*, 309, 345. Both *ḫilpu* and its denominative verb *ḫalāb/pu* may possibly be loanwords from Northwest Semitic *ḥlb* "milk." This would explain the *ḥ-ḫ* correspondence and the fact that *ḫilpu* and *ḫalāb/pu* occur only a few times in the Neo-Assyrian period alongside the regular Akkadian word for milk, *šizbu*. That *ḫilpu* is a synonom of *šizbu* is also shown by the plant list Ūruanna II: 50, 451, where the adjectives *ḫilabānu* and *šizbānu* "milk-yielding" are equated (see *CAD*, Ḫ, 184 and *AHW*, 345). Note also the opinion of B. Landsberger concerning the denominative verb *ḫalāb/pu* "to milk": "*ḫalābu* 'to milk' (*CAD*, Ḫ, 36; *AHW*, 309) is late and probably not genuine." See B. Landsberger, *The Date Palm and its By-Products according to the Cuneiform Sources* (Graz, 1967), 15 n. 42.

[212]Although Ug. *mṣṣ* occurs only here, the parallelism with *ynq* "to suck" makes the translation "to draw milk, suck" quite certain.

[213]Ch. Virolleaud, "Le mariage du roi Kéret," *Syria* 23 (1942-43), 148.

[214]See ענת, 28; Held, "עוד זוגות מלים", 148; UHPP, #251. Contrast *HALAT*, 590.

[215]It is possible that Ugaritic *zd* belongs here. However, *zd* occurs only in *CTA* 23:24:

ynqm . bap . zd . aṯrt
Who suck at the breasts of Asherah.

This line is repeated in *CTA* 23:61 with the substitutes of *št* "lady" for *aṯrt* and *ḏd* for *zd*:

ynqm . bap . ḏd . št
Who suck at the breasts of the Lady.

If *ḏd* and *zd* are in fact phonetic variants of the same word, it is impossible to know for certain what that original word was (note that the regular Ugaritic word for "breast" is *ṯd* which could also be related). Therefore, any comparison between Ug. *zd* and Heb. זיז must be labeled as uncertain at present for phonological reasons. Contrast *UT* III, #818; *HALAT*, 257.

[216]See *CAD*, Z, 149.

[217]Strong, "A Prayer of Aššurbanipal," 208 n. 34.

[218]Craig, "Prayer of the Assyrian King Asurbanipal," 85.

[219]See also H. Holma, *Die Namen der Körperteile im Assyrisch-Babylonischen* (Helsinki, 1911), 48; E. Dhorme, *L'emploi metaphorique des noms de parties du corps en hêbreu et en akkadien* (reprint; Paris, 1963), 107.

[220]Contrast Delitzsch, *Prolegomena*, 67-68 n. 2; BDB, 265; *RSV*, 661; Kissane, *Isaiah* II, 318, 325; *NEB*, 1057; Ginsberg, *Isaiah*, 115 n. e. This incorrect interpretation, first suggested by Delitzsch in 1886, was based on an alleged Akkadian **zāzu* "abundance" (most recently listed in C. Bezold, *Babylonisch-Assyrisches Glossar* [Heidelberg, 1926], 110). The signs originally read **zāzu* are in reality, however, the logogram *ḪÉ.NUN* which is simply to be read *nuḫšu* "abundance." See *CAD*, Ž, 76, and *AHW*, 801. Thus, **zāzu* "abundance" does not exist in Akkadian.

[221]For נתן יד "to submit," see 1 Chr 29:24; 2 Chr 30:8. See also Bright, *Jeremiah*, 354. Finally, note Targum Jonathan: אתמסרת בידהון "she has surrender herself into their hands."

[222]For *gabadibbû* "parapet," see W. Baumgartner, "Untersuchungen zu den akkadischen Bauausdrücken," *ZA* 36 (1924-25), 219-25; *AHW*, 271; *CAD*, G, 1. Concerning the phrase *ištu uššēšu adi gabadibbîšu*, Professor M. Weinfeld has kindly called my attention to the similar phrase in 1 Kgs 7:9--וממסד עד הטפחות for which see now *HALAT*, 362.

[223]Read אשׂיותיה for MT אשׁיותיה in light of the Akkadian comparison presented here. Note that the writing *a-sa-ya-te*^{MEŠ}*-šu* in AKA 81:27 corresponds exactly to the form אשיותיה in Jer 50:15. For the suggested Aramaic and Arabic equivalents of Hebrew אשיה* and Akkadian *asītu*, see *HALAT*, 91 and *AIA*, 37 and n. 32. Here it should be noted that the commonly held view that Hebrew שׂ corresponds *only* to Akkadian *š* (e.g., S. Moscati, *An Introduction to the Comparative Grammar of the Semitic Languages* [Wiesbaden, 1964], 34) is incorrect. While the majority of cases do conform to this rule, there are several clear examples which show that Hebrew שׂ may correspond to Akkadian *s* as well. The clearest example is the correspondence between Heb. בשר "to report" and its derivatives בשורה "tidings" and מבשר "messenger," with Akk. *bussuru* "to report" and its derivatives *bussurtu* "tidings" and *mubassiru* "messenger." That these verbs are identical is shown not only by the similar forms and the similar contexts in which they occur, but also by the fact that both roots refer almost exclusively to the reporting of *good* tidings and only exceptionally to bad news. For the use of this verb in the Bible for the reporting of bad news, see 1 Sam 4:17. For the parallel Akkadian usage, see YOS 10, 25:35; *bussurat lumnim ana bīt(i) awīlim iṭeḫḫi'a* "Bad news will reach the man's house." For other Akkadian references, especially with respect to the bringing of good tidings, see *CAD*, B, 346-48; *AHW*, 142, 665. Other examples in which Heb. שׂ corresponds to Akk. *s* include Heb. משור (Isa 10:15)--Akk. *massāru* (*AHW*, 619) "saw"; Heb. כבשה, כבש--Akk. *kabsu*, *kabsatu* (*CAD*, K, 23;

AHW, 418) "young male sheep," "young ewe." The complexity of the situation with regard to this correspondence may be best underscored by noting that the Ugaritic cognate of Hebrew בשר is *bšr* "to bring tidings" (*UT* III, #535) despite Akkadian *bussuru*. For another example where שׂ should probably be read for Masoretic שׁ so as to conform to an Akkadian cognate with *s*, see *hapax legomenon* #27 above.

[224]See Baumgartner, "Bauausdrücken," 229-33; *AHW*, 74; *CAD*, A/2, 332-33.

[225]*AF*, 14. Before 1917, *asītu* was often read as **asīdu* and compared to Hebrew יסוד "foundation"; see Delitzsch, *Prolegomena*, 46 n. 1; MA I, 74. Others who later equated *אשיה correctly with *asītu* include BDB, 78; Baumgartner, "Bauausdrücken," 233; *AHW*, 74; *FWOT*, 41; *HALAT*, 91; *AIA*, 37 and n. 32.

[226]Akkadian *dūru* "wall" is the interdialectal equivalent of Hebrew חומה "wall" as is demonstrated by the gloss in EA 141:44: *dūrši* ⟨ *ḫumītu*. *ḫumītu* "wall" is the older form of Hebrew חומה which also occurs in Prov 1:21 (read חמיות "walls" with the LXX) as well as in Phoenician (*KAI* 26:1:13, 17), Moabite (*KAI* 181:21) and Ugaritic (see next note).

[227]See UHPP, #343, where all relevant passages are cited.

[228]Contrast *FWOT*, 41, where the translation "sloping glacis" is suggested; Bright, *Jeremiah*, 354. Contrast also the statement in *AIA*, 37 n. 32: "the meaning of the Biblical Hebrew term is uncertain."

[229]For recent commentaries on this verse, see W. Zimmerli, *Ezechiel 1* (Neukirchen-Vluyn, 1969), 338; W. Eichrodt, *Ezekiel* (Philadelphia, 1970), 200.

[230]אֻמְלָה is taken here as a puʾal imperfect of מלא "to fill" with the shift of א to ה which is common in ל"א verbs (GKC, §75qq). Note that the same shift occurs in this very expression in Aramaic in *AP* 37:11: מלין לבתכם "full of wrath against you." See G. R. Driver, "Studies in the Vocabulary of the Old Testament III," *JTS* 32 (1930-31), 366. Contrast F. Stummer, "אמלה (EZ XVI 30A)," *VT* 4 (1954), 34-40; Zimmerli, *Ezechiel 1*, 338; Eichrodt, *Ezekiel*, 200.

[231]For transliteration, translation, and commentary, see P. Garelli, *Les Assyriens en Cappadoce* (Paris, 1963), 254-55.

[232]See *CAD*, L, 163-64; *AHW*, 548-49.

[233]E. Baneth apud D. H. Baneth, "Bemerkungen zu den Achikarpapyri," *OLZ* 17 (1914), 251 n. 1; idem apud D. H. Baneth, "Zu den aramäischen Brief aus der Zeit Assurbanipals," *OLZ* 22 (1919), 58. See also BDB, 525; *AP*, p. 134; Driver, "Vocabulary of the OT III," 366 (contrast idem, "Some Hebrew Words," *JTS* 29 [1928], 393); G. A. Cooke, *The Book of Ezekiel* (Edinburgh, 1936), 173; R. A. Bowman apud L. Waterman, RCAE IV,

282; *HALAT*, 491; J. A. Fitzmyer, "A Note on Ezek. 16:30," *CBQ* 23 (1961), 460-62; פשוטו של מקרא III/2, 304; *KAI* II, 286; *CPOT*, 329; N. Waldman, "A Note on Canticles 4:9," *JBL* 89 (1970), 215 n. 11; B. Porten and J. C. Greenfield, "The Aramaic Papyri from Hermopolis," *ZAW* 80 (1968), 228; *AIA*, 66.

[234]See, e.g., Gilg. XI:171-72//*ītezìz* "became furious" and EA 7:15, 32, as well as the many other passages listed in *CAD*, L, 164, and *AHW*, 540. Note that this same phrase occurs several times in Official Aramaic, especially in the Elephantine Papyri; see Fitzmyer, "A Note on Ezek. 16:30," 460-62, and the bibliography cited there. Add *DISO*, 134; *KAI* II, 286; *AIA*, 66 and n. 177.

[235]See, e.g., Eichrodt, *Ezekiel*, 206-13.

[236]For *ikribu* with the meaning "money or goods pledged by a vow to a deity," see *CAD*, I/J, 64-65 and the discussion on p. 66.

[237]See Garelli, *Les Assyriens*, 254-55.

[238]See also *AP*, 41:4: הוית מלא לבתך "I was filled with wrath against you."

[239]Contrast Stummer, "אמלה", 34-40; Eichrodt, *Ezekiel*, 200. Note the comment of Zimmerli, *Ezechiel 1*, 338: "Doch bleibt die Deutung unsicher."

[240]For recent commentaries on this verse, see Zimmerli, *Ezechiel 1*, 419, 426-27; Eichrodt, *Ezekiel*, 250.

[241]בחחים is here taken as an explanatory gloss of בסוגר inserted under the influence of Ezek. 19:4. See, e.g., Landsberger, *Fauna*, 81 n. 3; Cooke, *Ezekiel*, 208; E. Vogt, "Ioiakîn collari ligneo vinctus (Ez 19,9)," *Biblica* 37 (1956), 389; Zimmerli, *Ezechiel 1*, 419. Contrast Eichrodt, *Ezekiel*, 250.

[242]See M. Held, "Pits and Pitfalls in Akkadian and Biblical Hebrew," *JANESCU* 5 (1973), 183-84. Held rightly compares Ezek. 19:4, 9 to Jer 39:7 and 2 Chr 36:6 on the one hand, showing that חחים should mean something like נחשתים "fetters" according to biblical contextual parallels, and Ezek 19:9 to the Akkadian pair of *erinnu* "neckstock" (a synonym of *šigāru*) and *birītu* "fetters" on the other hand, showing that Akkadian contextual evidence also points to this meaning for חחים. The occurrence of חחים together with נחשתים "fetters" in 2 Chr 33:11 is further evidence in this direction.

[243]For *asu* "bear", see Landsberger, *Fauna*, 80-82; *AHW*, 76; *CAD*, A/2, 344.

[244]The ס in סוגר which corresponds to the *š* in Akkadian *šigāru* must be explained. Firstly, Akkadian *šigāru* seems to occur as an Akkadian loanword in Sumerian *SI.GAR*. Secondly, *sigāru* "neck-stock" does occur at least once (Langdon, Tammuz

III iii 17; see *AHW*, 1230), while at the same time *šigāru* in its other meaning "lock" is often written *sigāru* (e.g., MSL VI, 30:294-95a). Therefore, since *s* and *š* seem to interchange with respect to this word in Mesopotamia itself, the ס in סוגר should not be surprising. For *šigāru/sigāru* > Sumerian *SI.GAR* "lock," see A. Salonen, *Die Türen des alten Mesopotamien* (Helsinki, 1961), 86-88; *AHW*, 1230-31; B. Landsberger apud E. Weidner, "Die Feldzüge und Bauten Tiglatpilesers I.," *AfO* 18 (1957-58), 346 n. 19.

[245]Akkadian *šigāru* was first thought to mean "cage," and this meaning was transferred to Hebrew סוגר (see all the references in the next note prior to 1934). It was also thought to occur as a loanword in Egyptian *šgr* "verschliessbarer Kasten" (*WAS* IV, 550:10). See *AKF*, #890; *ESO*, 61; Helck, *Beziehungen*, 521 (#230). However, in 1934, Landsberger showed conclusively that *šigāru* could not mean "cage" because it is often placed on the *kišādu* "neck." He suggested the translation "collar" (Landsberger, *Fauna*, 81). In 1956, E. I. Gordon proposed the translation "neckstock," based on the occurrence of the determinative *GIŠ* in front of this substantive showing that it was a wooden object, the other meaning of *šigāru* "lock (of a door)," and new iconographic evidence indicating that Mesopotamian kings did in fact put their prisoners in neckstocks; see E. I. Gordon, "Of Princes and Foxes: The Neck-Stock in the Newly Discovered Agade Period Stela," *Sumer* 12 (1956), 80-84; idem, *Sumerian Proverbs* (Philadelphia, 1959), 224 n. 3. While this meaning fits the context in which Hebrew סוגר is found perfectly (see above), the comparison with Egyptian *šgr* is no longer valid and must be abandoned. Contrast KB I, 651.

[246]Fr. Delitzsch apud S. Baer, *Liber Ezechielis* (Leipzig, 1884), XV. Contrast *AS*, 46-47 n. 2. See also, e.g., P. Haupt, "Wateh-Ben-Hazael," *Hebraica* 1 (1884-85), 226; P. Jensen, "Hymnen auf das Wiedererscheinen der drei grossen Lichtgötter II," *ZA* 2 (1887), 198; F. Praetorius, "Zur äthiopischen Grammatik und Etymologie," BASS 1 (1890), 372 n. **; J. Barth, *Die Nominalbildung in den semitischen Sprachen* (Leipzig, 1894), 22; BDB, 689; Streck Asb., 67 n. 8; *AF*, 15; Landsberger, *Fauna*, 81 n. 3; Cooke, *Ezekiel*, 208, 212; Vogt, "Ioiakîn collari," 388-89; Zimmerli, *Ezechiel 1*, 426-27; Eichrodt, *Ezekiel*, 250; Held, "Pits and Pitfalls in Akkadian and Biblical Hebrew," 184-85, especially n. 84; *AHW*, 1230 (with the incorrect translation of Hebrew סוגר as "Käfig?"!).

[247]For the identification of the Judean king involved, see most recently Zimmerli, *Ezechiel 1*, 426-28; Eichrodt, *Ezekiel*, 253-56.

[248]For this practice, see especially H. Hirsch, "Die Inschriften der Könige von Agade," *AfO* 20 (1963), 34-35:20-28.

[249]F. Basmachi, "An Akkadian Stela," *Sumer* 10 (1954), 116-19 and pls. I-II. Basmachi has shown that this stela dates from the Old Akkadian dynasty of Agade, and Gordon has suggested that it may in fact be a pictorial representation of Sargon's

confinement of his prisoners in neck-stocks which is specifically referred to in the text cited in the previous note; see Gordon, "Neck-Stock," 82-84.

[250]S. Langdon, "Miscellanea Assyriaca," *Babyloniaca* 7 (1914), pl. VII (K2057):21. For modern parallels, see Gordon, "Neck-Stock," 82 n. 18.

[251]On this verse, see most recently W. Zimmerli, *Ezechiel 2* (Neukirchen-Vluyn, 1969), 632 and the bibliography on p. 624. Add H. J. van Dijk, *Ezekiel's Prophecy on Tyre* (Rome, 1968), 81; A. Shalit, "חבשים וארזים במרכלתך", *Leshonenu* 7 (1935-36), 131-35.

[252]For מכלל as a garment, see Ezek 23:12; 38:4. See also Zimmerli, *Ezechiel 2*, 632; *HALAT*, 549.

[253]For גלם "to wrap around," see 2 Kgs 2:8. Note that *גלום is undoubtedly equivalent to Aramaic גלימא "mantle" and both are probably cognate with Akkadian *gulēnu* "a coat." See *CAD*, G, 127 and the bibliography listed there; *AHW*, 296; *HALAT*, 185; C. G. Howie, *The Date and Composition of Ezekiel* (Philadelphia, 1950), 52 (#8).

[254]This homonymic *hapax legomenon* is to be translated "carpet" on the basis of its occurrence in the targum to Esth 1:3. See *HALAT*, 191; Zimmerli, *Ezechiel 2*, 632.

[255]F. Köcher, "Ein Inventartext aus Kār-Tukulti-Ninurta," *AfO* 18 (1957-58), 306:32-34.

[256]For *marda/ātu/mardutu* "type of carpet," see K. F. Müller, "Das assyrische Ritual I," MVAG 41/3 (1937), 41; Köcher, "Inventartext," 312; *AHW*, 611. Von Soden compares Ugaritic *mrdt*, for which see *PRU* II, 112:4, 6.

[257]*CAD*, B, 257-58; *AHW*, 129. On Akkadian *birmu* and its derivatives, see now B. Landsberger, "Über Farben im Sumerisch-Akkadischen," *JCS* 21 (1967), 140, 141-42 nn. 13 and 15, and esp. 160-61 n. 106. Landsberger shows quite convincingly that while *birmu* most often refers to "multi-colored trim," it at times may refer to an entire garment, covering or carpet, and at times it may also refer to but a single color as in the case of a robe made out of expensive (perhaps purple) colored wool. Finally, for the commercial importation and use of this type of garment in the Neo-Assyrian empire, see M. Elat, קשרי כלכלה בין ארצות המקרא (Jerusalem, 1977), 83-85.

[258]J. Oppert, *Mémoire sur les rapports de l'Égypte et de l'Assyrie dans l'antiquité* (Paris, 1869), 601, 609. Although no discussion is presented, Oppert translates *birme* here as "berom." See also, e.g., *AS*, 113; *CIOT* I, 207 n. ***; BDB, 140; MA I, 191 and the bibliography cited there; *AF*, 37; Cooke, *Ezekiel*, 311; *ANET*, 275 n. 6; *HALAT*, 154-55; פשוטו של מקרא III/2, 336; Elat, קשרי כלכלה, 83 n. 3.

[259]For this interpretation, see *CAD*, B, 257, where it is stated, however, that the *birmu* "represents gods, men and animals." As can be seen from the above text, no "gods (*ilī*)" are mentioned.

[260]Contrast Zimmerli, *Ezechiel 2*, 632. Zimmerli here ignores Akkadian *birmu* and translates ברומים "zweifarbige" on the basis of Arabic *barīm* which means among other things "anything in which are two colors mixed together" said of such things as an amulet, a garment, the liver and hump of a camel, water, tears, people, an army, and sheep and goats. See Lane I, 195.

[261]On this verse, see most recently R. S. Cripps, *A Critical and Exegetical Commentary on the Book of Amos* (Cambridge, 1960), 187-88; E. Hammershaimb, *The Book of Amos* (Oxford, 1970), 83; H. W. Wolff, *Dodekapropheton 2* (Neukirchen-Vluyn, 1969), 270, 290-91 and the bibliography cited on p. 267.

[262]Read שבסכם for MT בושסכם based on Akkadian *šabāšu* as demonstrated here. Note that in 1946 H. L. Ginsberg, in *LKK*, 49, claimed that *CTA* 16:VI:48 and Amos 5:11a "are destined to elucidate one another, though they have not yet become quite clear to me." The Ugaritic phrase *ṯšm ʿl dl* "those who prey (?) upon the poor" appeared to him to be parallel to Amos 5:11a especially in that the indirect object "upon the poor" (Ugaritic *ʿl dl* = Hebrew על דל) occurs in both cases (see, however, n. 265 below). However, the identification of Hebrew בושסכם with Ugaritic *ṯšm* is problematic in that the first phoneme of the Hebrew root is missing in the Ugaritic verb. Recently, an attempt has been made by T. L. Fenton to overcome this difficulty by assuming that the ב in בושסכם is not a root letter, but rather a prefixed preposition. Fenton also reads עול "child" in both the Ugaritic and biblical passages, and translates Amos 5:11a "therefore because of your despoiling the child of the poor"; see T. L. Fenton, "Ugaritica-Biblica," *UF* 1 (1969), 65-66. The understanding of the ב in בושסכם as a prefixed preposition, however, creates the syntactically impossible combination יען ב... which does not exist in biblical Hebrew except in such passages as Ezek 20:16, 24, where the ב clearly goes with what follows, not with what precedes. Thus, Fenton's first assumption forces him to further assume that "at some stage in the history of the text the preposition *b* was glossed *yaʿan*." No precedent is given for this second assumption, and its only *raison d'être* would appear to be the existence of the first assumption. Fenton's claim that "the preposition *b* was glossed *yaʿan* as a result, no doubt, of its comparatively rare nuance of meaning 'because of.' 'on account of'" is clearly contradicted by the twenty-six occurrences of ב with this meaning listed in BDB, 90. The rendering of the Targum חלף ב... is an indication not that "the translator may have guessed the true meaning and not troubled too much about the double representation of 'because of,'" but rather that he rendered what he considered impossible biblical Hebrew with equally impossible Aramaic. Note that Professor Ginsberg now suggests (oral communication) that the *m* in Ug. *ṯšm* be taken as a root letter, and then relates this root to Akk. *šbš/s* through metathesis and the phonological change *w* > *m* > *b* (see n. 46 above and cf., e.g., Akk. *lawû* > *lamû* > *labû* "to surround"--*CAD*, L, 69-77).

[263]For משאת "tax," see Ezek 20:40; 2 Chr 24:6, 9. See also *DISO*, 169.

[264]See also the similar usage in F. R. Kraus, *Ein Edikt des Königs Ammi-ṣaduqa von Babylon* (Leiden, 1958), 36 (§12). Note the unpublished University of Chicago letter A7695:19 quoted by Kraus, *Edikt*, 130 and *CAD*, Ḫ, 61: *šibši ša ēkallim elīya iddi* "He accused me with regard to the rent (payments) due to the palace." The closest parallels to Amos 5:11, however, may well be the many Neo-Assyrian passages cited by Postgate in which *šibšu* "(straw) tax" occurs together with *nusāḫē* "(corn) tax" (see the following note). It may be just these two taxes that appear in parallelism in Amos 5:11.

[265]For the Akkadian root *šabāšu* and its derivative *šibšu*, see Kraus, *Edikt*, 126-32; J. N. Postgate, *Neo-Assyrian Royal Grants and Decrees* (Rome, 1969), 14; idem, *Taxation and Conscription in the Assyrian Empire* (Rome, 1974), 174-99; *AHW*, 1119, 1227-28; M. de J. Ellis, "Taxation in Ancient Mesopotamia: the History of the Term *miksu*," *JCS* 26 (1974), 234-46 and her two other works referred to in n. 100. We must here reckon with the different final radicals of שבס and *šabāšu*. In Old Akkadian, *šibšu* occurs a total of four times in the forms *ši-ib-ši-im*, *si-ib-su-um* and *si-ib-šum* (see MAD 3, 263 for the references, all of which have now been published in MAD 1 and MAD 4). In BMS 12:55 (= Ebeling, Handerhebung, 78:55), *šabsu* occurs replacing *išbušu* (see Kraus, *Edikt*, 126-27, the translation and discussion of this passage in *PEPI*, 65 with relevant bibliography, and the new variant *šab-šú* published by von Soden in *Iraq* 31, 87, 55 for which see *AHW*, 1119). Finally, Postgate lists one occurrence of *ši-ib-si* in the well-attested Neo-Assyrian phrase *lā šibši lā nusāḫē* "without straw tax, without corn tax" (see Postgate, *Taxation*, 175, 187). From all this evidence, it is clear that while the original form of the Akkadian root is presently unknown, there is some indication that the third radical may have had an alternate form of *s*. As regards the meaning of the root *šabāšu*, it would appear that the original meaning is indeed "to gather" (see *AHW*, 1119). Under the influence of its specialized derivative *šibšu* "(straw) tax," *šabāšu* also took on the specialized meaning "to collect a (straw) tax" (it seems to me a bit artificial to "...distinguish two verbs *šabāšum*: one primary, and one as a denominative verb from *šibšum*..." as suggested in Postgate, *Taxation*, 187). As for *šibšu* "(straw) tax," the summary by Postgate based on Kraus' work, but with many new insights, is quite useful. According to Postgate, "...*šibšu*...could (and in Babylonia did) apply to a variety of crops, but in fact its alternation with *tibnu* ["straw"] in nA texts is strong cause to suppose that it was [mainly] a tax on straw....Excellent confirmation of this is now provided by the texts 1.9.1-3, where the straw is liable to *šibšu* and the corn to *nusāḫē*. Hence we may say as a rule *šibšu* was the government tax on straw and *nusāḫē* on corn" (Postgate, *Taxation*, 188). Note further that, while it is true that Akkadian *šabāšu* is not construed with *eli* "upon, against" as might be expected in view of the usage of על "upon, against" in Amos 5:11 (compare, however, *šibša elīya nadû* "I was accused

with regard to the rent" in the unpublished letter quoted in the previous note), this does not invalidate the suggested comparison. For among the Hebrew verbs which are consistently construed with על and which have recognized cognates in Akkadian, there are some whose Akkadian counterparts are rarely if ever construed with *eli*. A case in point is Heb. רכב--Akk. *rakābu* "to ride, mount." רכב על "to ride upon" occurs more than thirty-five times in the MT, while רכב without על is relatively rare. In Akkadian, *rakābu (ina)* "to ride aboard" is the norm, while *rakābu eli* "to ride upon" is extremely rare (the only examples of *rakābu eli* in the I/1 cited by *AHW*, 944-45 have to do with parts of the body, in which cases *rakābu eli* has the nuance "obenliegen" [*AHW*, 945]). This situation is best exemplified by the rendering of "to ride a donkey" in both languages. In the MT, רכב על חמור occurs in Exod 4:20; 1 Sam 25:20, 42; 2 Sam 19:27; 1 Kgs 13:13; Zech 9:9, while *רכב חמור never occurs. In Akkadian, neither *AHW*, 944-45 nor *CAD*, I/J, 110-14 list a single case of **eli imēri rakābu* "to ride upon a donkey," but *imēra rakābu* is quite common. The clear inference from the above example is that otherwise acceptable Hebrew-Akkadian comparisons of verbal roots should not be abandoned as a result of non-identical usages of על-*eli* with the verbs in question.

[266]N. H. Tur-Sinai (Torczyner), "Presidential Address," *JPOS* 16 (1936), 6-7; פשוטו של מקרא III/2, 463. See also *HALAT*, 158; Wolff, *Dodekapropheton 2*, 270, 290. Note here that both *HALAT* and Wolff refer to *šabāsu šibsa* as if this were the regular form. This is surely not so. Tur-Sinai's comparison was with *šibša šabāšu* "to exact rent." All the evidence for *šabāsu* as an alternate form of *šabāšu* is cited in the previous note.

[267]See *AHW*, 1227-28 and the works listed at the beginning of n. 265. Note, however, Postgate's important summary of this usage cited above in n. 265.

[268]Contrast, e.g., W. R. Harper, *Amos and Hosea* (Edinburgh, 1905), 120; Hammershaimb, *Amos*, 83; K. W. Neubauer, "Erwägungen zu Amos 5:4-15," *ZAW* 78 (1966), 313 n. 5.

[269]For recent commentaries on this verse, see Dahood, *Psalms II*, 202; H.-J. Kraus, *Psalmen 64-150* (Neukirchen-Vluyn, 1972), 513.

[270]MT reads here ועת which is completely incomprehensible. What is required here is a parallel verb to הלם "to batter" such as מחץ "to strike" (Judg 5:26) or possibly כתת "to beat" (Isa 24:12). Contrast פשוטו של מקרא IV/1, 159.

[271]Read פתחיה "its doors" with LXX as against MT פתוחיה "its carvings." See Dahood, *Psalms II*, 202; Kraus, *Psalmen 64-150*, 513.

[272]כשיל "hatchet" occurs only here, but is clearly derived from כשל "to fall, stumble" just as הפיל, the causative of נפל "to fall," is used for "to fell (a tree)" in 2 Kgs 3:19, 25,

and "to throw down (a wall)" in 2 Sam 20:15. Note that כשיל is used in the Targum to render קרדם "axe" in Jer 46:22. Contrast now *HALAT*, 478, where the derivation of כשיל from כשל is labeled with a question mark.

[273]See also AKA 230:11-13 and 330-31:95-96.

[274]Note that both *kalappu* and *kalabbu* are attested. See *CAD*, K, 66.

[275]Corrected on the basis of AKA 230:12.

[276]For *akkullu* "hatchet," see *CAD*, A/1, 276-77 and the bibliography cited there; *AHW*, 30.

[277]For *kalappu* "axe," see *CAD*, K, 66; *AHW*, 424; J. Lewy, "Studies in Old Assyrian Grammar and Lexicography," *Orientalia* 19 (1950), 20 n. 3. For the occurrence of this word in the various Aramaic dialects, see *AIA*, 61. Note that Kaufman's statement that *kalappu* "is limited to Assyrian and that it occurs in Hittite" is now shown to be incorrect by *CAD*, K, 66, where passages are also listed from Nuzi and the Neo-Babylonian period. For this word in Hittite, see Rabin, "Hittite Words in Hebrew," 124.

[278]MA I, 390. See also BDB, 476; *AF*, 12; Lewy, "Old Assyrian Grammar and Lexicography," 20-21 n. 3; Z. Chayes, ספר תהלים (reprint; Jerusalem, 1970), 162; *HALAT*, 450; Rabin, "Hittite Words in Hebrew," 124; *AIA*, 61.

[279]Here it should be noted that the question of whether כשיל and כילפות were used for building and tearing down or as weapons was part of the polemical dispute between Dunash and Menaḥem (see above, Chapters I and II). Menaḥem contended that they were weapons (מחברת מנחם, 106), while Dunash, rightly citing the occurrence of כשיל in the Targum translating קרדם "axe" (see above, n. 272), contended they were tools to cut down trees (תשובות דונש, 34). On this dispute, see מלון הלשון העברית III, 2409 n. 2.

[280]Note that in neither of the two recent commentaries on Psalms cited in n. 269 above is this comparison mentioned.

[281]For recent commentaries on this verse, see Tur-Sinai, *Job*, 383-4, and M. H. Pope, *Job* (New York, 1973), 185-86. The latter also deals with the translation of this verse in the recently published Targum from Qumran.

[282]Read שָׂם יָם "he put Yam" for MT שָׁמַיִם "heavens."

[283]Read שִׂפְרֹה "his net" for MT שִׁפְרָה "brightness," based on the Akkadian comparison presented here. For the correspondence of Hebrew שׂ with Akkadian *s*, see n. 223 above.

[284]For נחש ברח "serpent slant," see Isa 27:1//נחש עקלתון "serpent tortuous," and in Ugaritic, *CTA* 5:1:1, 28: *bṯn brḥ*// *bṯn ʿqltn* "serpent slant//serpent tortuous." The translation

"serpent slant" is based on the parallelism with נחש עקלתון "serpent tortuous" and is the one adopted by H. L. Ginsberg in *ANET*, 138. See also *MLC*, 575-77.

[285]See also En. el. IV:41, 44; V:64; VI:83. Note also *saparriš* "in the net" in En. el. IV:112.

[286]III/l preterit of *šuparruru* "to spread out (a net)." See A. Heidel, *The System of the Quadriliteral Verb in Akkadian* (Chicago, 1940), 30-31. For *saparra šuparruru* "to spread a net," see also the bilingual hymn to Šamaš in P. A. Schollmeyer, *Sumerisch-babylonische Hymnen und Gebete an Šamaš* (Paderborn, 1912), 33:46.

[287]Read with שׂ rather than שׁ (see n. 283 above) because the only evidence for š here is the variant *ša-par-ri-ya* listed in Borger Esarh., 58:18 (apparatus). See *AHW*, 1026. The other alleged evidence from Aramaic involving the substantive שפיר "membraneous bag, sac of a foetus" is dealt with in n. 295 below, and is shown to be invalid.

[288]*AHW*, 1026; E. Salonen, *Die Waffen der alten Mesopotamier* (Helsinki, 1965), 97. That *saparru* is equivalent to Sumerian *SA.PAR* and that both mean "net" is indicated by the lexical equation *SA.PAR = saparru = šētum* (MSL VI, 78:26), where *šētu* is the regular Akkadian term for "net."

[289]N. H. Tur-Sinai, ספר איוב II (Jerusalem, 1941), 314. See also idem, הלשון והספר III, 200-1; idem, *Job*, 383-84; פשוטו של מקרא IV/2, 65; מלון הלשון העברית VIII, 7411; *MLC*, 796; Pope, *Job*, 185-86.

[290]For all the comparative material on this major motif, see *MLC*, 575-77.

[291]En. el. IV:96.

[292]See M. D. Cassuto "שירת העלילה בישראל", *Knesset* 8 (1943), 121-42; T. H. Gaster, *Thespis* (New York, 1961), 142-48; Sarna, *Understanding Genesis*, 2, 21-23.

[293]E.g., the above cited passage and the passages referred to in n. 285 above.

[294]E.g., the epithet *sapar nakirī* "net of the enemies" said of Ḫammurabi in CH II:68. See Seux, *Épithètes royales*, 260.

[295]The Aramaic comparative evidence presented by Tur-Sinai (see n. 287 above) is the usage of the substantive שפיר which is defined as "membraneous bag, sac of a foetus" in Jastrow II, 1616. Never is this word used for "net" or anything similar. Its usage is limited strictly to gynecological contexts and it is never found together with or in the place of מצידתא which is the regular Aramaic word for "net." Similarly, Tur-Sinai's proposal to connect ספרתך in Ps 56:9 with שפרה is highly unlikely. For in Ps 56:9, ספרה is parallel to נאד which clearly means "waterskin" and has nothing to do with "net."

[296]Contrast *NEB*, 703; A. van Selms, "A Systematic Approach to CTA 5,1,1-8," *UF* 7 (1975), 479.

[297]For recent commentaries on this verse, see Tur-Sinai, *Job*, 560-61; Pope, *Job*, 325-26.

[298]The correct understanding of ישאו לו is the key to a proper understanding of this verse. This expression is taken here as an ellipsis of ישאו לו קולם "they acclaim him," which is often the connotation of נשא קול "to lift the voice" when it is not used as an introductory formulaic expression immediately preceding speech or crying. For the latter in Hebrew and Ugaritic, see ענת, 32-33. The former, which is the usage relevant to Job 40:20, may be found in Isa 24:14; 52:8. Crucial is the occurrence of the same ellipsis posited here in Isa 42:11. That acclamation is intended in this case is clear from the next verse, Isa 42:12, in which כבוד "glory" is ascribed to God (see also Isa 24:15). Contrast the interpretation suggested in Tur-Sinai, *Job*, 560-61; Pope, *Job*, 325-26.

[299]The parallelism ישחקו שם//ישאו לו is perfectly valid in light of the interpretation of ישאו לו suggested above and the similar parallelism in Isa 24:14; 42:11; 52:8, where in each case, this same expression is parallel to ירנ(נ)ו "they shout (for joy)." That שחק can mean the same is seen by its parallelism with רנה "(joyful) shouting" in Ps 126:2, and with שמחה "happiness" in Eccl 2:2. Thus, there is no need to emend the text in Job 40:20 as suggested in Pope, *Job*, 325-26.

[300]This restoration is based on such passages as BWL 60: 42, and is already suggested in *CAD*, A/1, 62.

[301]Restored in BWL 172:16. For *dalālu//narbâ šūpû*, see the many relevant passages listed in *CAD*, A/2, 202.

[302]See *CAD*, B, 315-16; *AHW*, 137; A. L. Oppenheim, "Mesopotamian Mythology II," *Orientalia* 17 (1948), 53 n. 7; W. H. P. Römer, *Sumerische Königshymnen der Isin-Zeit* (Leiden, 1965), 170-71.

[303]Delitzsch, *Prolegomena*, 68 n. 2. See also H. Torczyner (Tur-Sinai), *Das Buch Hiob* (Wien and Berlin, 1920), 316; idem, ספר איוב II (Jerusalem, 1941), 467; idem, *Job*, 560; פשוטו של מקרא IV/2, 109; Pope, *Job*, 325-26; *HALAT*, 111. Contrast, e.g., S. R. Driver and G. B. Gray, *The Book of Job* (Edinburgh, 1921), part I: 356-57; part II: 329-30.

[304]Against Tur-Sinai's interpretation (Tur-Sinai, *Job*, 560-61), see the comments of Pope, *Job*, 325-26. Pope's own interpretation, however, involves the totally unwarranted emendation of ישאו לו to ישליו "they are at ease," and he, too, misses the point of the verse.

[305]For the identification of this mythological creature, see most recently Pope, *Job*, 320-22.

[306]Job 40:19. That דרך here refers to the creations of God is clear from the parallelism in Prov 8:22 where דרך is parallel to מפעל "creative act" (all verbs in biblical Hebrew meaning "to do, make" also mean "to create"--see, e.g., Gen 14: 22 vs. Ps 146:6 and note also Deut 32:6).

[307]For the background of this fable, see BWL, 168.

[308]Note, however, that Tur-Sinai now sees this same term in the phrase בול עץ in Isa 44:19, which he would understand as an animal figurine made out of wood; see פשוטו של מקרא III/1, 119. This suggestion is very fanciful and must be rejected.

APPENDIX I

COMPOSITE LIST OF BIBLICAL *HAPAX LEGOMENA* ISOLATED IN THE MIDDLE AGES

The purpose of the following list is to augment the discussion in Chapters I and II concerning the five works written in the medieval period which deal specifically with biblical *hapax legomena*. This list includes each biblical *hapax legomenon* (as defined in Chapter I, section C) isolated by any of these five authors together with the name(s) of the medieval author(s) who succeeded in isolating it. The abbreviations utilized are as follows (for complete references, see Chapter I, section B, part 2): H = Judah ben Ḥayyūj
Q = Judah ibn Qụraysh
SA = Unknown Author of שאלות עתיקות
M = Menaḥem ibn Saruq
S = Saadiah Gaon

Gen	6:14	גפר	M, SA
Gen	26:20	התעשקו	M, Q
Gen	30:20	זבדני...זבד	M, SA
Gen	30:37	לוז	SA
Gen	30:37,38	ויפצל...פצלות; פצל	M
Gen	36:24	הימם	SA
Gen	40:11	ראשחט	M
Gen	41:23	צנמות	M, SA
Gen	43:11	בטנים	SA
Exod	9:31	גבעל	Q, SA, H
Exod	13:16//Deut 6:8//11:18	טטפת	S, Q, H
Exod	16:14	מחספס	SA
Exod	16:31	צפיחת	SA
Exod	21:10	ענתה	S, Q
Exod	30:34	שחלת	SA
Exod	32:16	חרות	M
Lev	11:22	סלעם	SA
Lev	11:22	חרגל	SA
Lev	11:29	חלד	SA
Lev	11:29	צב	SA
Lev	11:30	אנקה	SA
Lev	11:30	כח	SA

Lev	11:30	לטאה	SA
Lev	11:30	חמט	SA
Lev	19:10	פרט	Q
Lev	19:20	בקרת	S
Lev	21:20	אשך	Q
Lev	25:47	עקר משפחת גר	S
Num	6:3	משרת ענבים	S, Q
Num	6:4	חרצנים	M, SA
Num	6:4	זג	Q
Num	24:3,15	שתם העין	S, M
Num	25:8	קבה	SA
Deut	14:5	אקו	SA
Deut	14:5	דישן	SA
Deut	32:15	כשית	Q
Deut	32:34	כמס	M
Deut	33:22	יזנק	M, SA
Judg	3:16	גמד	M
Judg	3:22	פרשדנה	SA
Judg	7:13	צלול לחם שערים	SA
1 Sam	13:21	פצירה	SA
1 Sam	13:21	פים	SA
1 Sam	15:33	וישסף	SA
2 Sam	1:9	שבץ	SA
2 Sam	6:19//1 Chr 16:3	אשפר	M
2 Sam	17:29	שפות בקר	SA
2 Sam	21:16	קינו	SA
2 Sam	22:46!//Ps 18:46	ויחרגו	M
1 Kgs	7:33	חשריהם	SA
1 Kgs	7:50	פתות	S, SA
1 Kgs	18:46	וישנס	M, SA
1 Kgs	20:33	ויחלטוה!	M
2 Kgs	4:42	בצקלנו	M, SA
2 Kgs	19:29//Isa 37:30	שחיס--סחיש	M
Isa	1:22	מהול	M
Isa	3:16	משקרות	M
Isa	3:24	פתיגיל	SA
Isa	5:2	ויעזקהו	M
Isa	13:21	אחים	SA

Isa	14:23	וטאטאתיה במטאטא	S
Isa	17:6	גרגרים	Q
Isa	18:5	התז	S, M, Q
Isa	28:25	נסמן	S
Isa	38:21	וימרחו	S, M
Isa	44:13	שרד	SA
Isa	44:14	תרזה	SA
Isa	48:9	אחטם	Q
Isa	51:8	סס	M
Isa	54:12	אקדח	SA
Isa	55:13	סרפד	M, SA
Isa	57:20	רפש	M
Isa	63:1	חמוץ בגדים	Q
Jer	2:22	נכתם	S
Jer	2:23	משרכת	M
Jer	14:9	נדהם	M
Jer	29:26	צינק	M, SA
Jer	47:3	שעטת פרסות אביריו	M, SA
Jer	51:34	כרשו	M, Q
Jer	51:38	נערו	H
Ezek	2:6	סרבים	M
Ezek	4:15	צפיעי הבקר	SA
Ezek	5:1	גלבים	M, SA
Ezek	7:25	קפדה	Q
Ezek	16:40	ובתקוך	M, SA
Ezek	17:9	יקוסס	S, M, SA
Ezek	26:9	קבלו	SA
Ezek	27:15	הבנים	SA
Ezek	27:24	ברמים	SA
Ezek	37:6, 8	וקרמתי; ויקרם	M, Q
Ezek	39:2	וששאתיך	M
Ezek	44:20	כסום יכסמו	M
Joel	1:8	אלי	Q
Joel	1:17	עבשו	S
Joel	2:20	צחנתו	M
Amos	6:11	רסיסים	S
Amos	7:14	בולס שקמים	SA
Hab	2:11	כפיס	S

Hab	3:17	רפתים	S
Zech	11:8	בחלה	M
Ps	50:20	דפי	Q
Ps	60:4	פצמתה	S, M
Ps	63:2	כמה	M, SA
Ps	68:17	תרצדון	M
Ps	72:6	זרזיף	M, SA
Ps	74:6	כילפות	SA
Ps	78:47	חנמל	SA
Ps	80:14	יכרסמנה	S
Ps	90:5	זרמתם	M
Ps	139:8	אסק	M
Ps	139:16	גלמי	S, M
Ps	140:11	מהמרות	SA
Prov	7:16	אטון מצרים	M
Prov	12:27	יחרך	M, SA
Prov	25:13	צנת שלג	S
Prov	29:21	מפנק	S
Prov	30:15	עלוקה	SA
Prov	30:28	שממית	SA
Prov	30:31	זרזיר	M, SA
Job	2:8	להתגרד	S, M
Job	6:10	ואסלדה	M, SA
Job	9:26	יטוש	M
Job	15:12	ירזמון	Q, SA
Job	15:27	פימה	SA
Job	16:15	גלדי	M
Job	17:1	נזעכו	SA
Job	18:2	קנצי	M
Job	21:24	עטיניו	M
Job	33:20	וזהמתו	M, Q
Job	39:5	ערוד	M
Job	40:17	פחדו	SA
Job	40:18	מטיל ברזל	Q
Job	40:31	צלצל דגים	SA
Job	41:10	עטישתיו	M, Q, SA
Job	41:21	תותח	SA
Cant	2:11	סתו	M

Cant	2:13	פגיה	M, Q
Cant	3:9	אפריון	M, SA
Cant	4:1//6:5	גלשו	M
Cant	5:3	אטנפם	S, M, Q
Cant	8:5	מתרפקת	M, SA
Ruth	1:13	תעגנה	S
Lam	4:8	צפד	SA
Eccl	10:8	גומץ	M
Eccl	12:5	אביונה	S
Esth	1:6	בהט	SA
Esth	7:4	נזק המלך	Q
Esth	8:10	רמכים	SA
Esth	8:15	תכריך בוץ וארגמן	M, Q
Dan	9:24	נחתך	S, M
2 Chr	2:15	צרכך	S, M, Q
2 Chr	2:15	רפסדות	M, SA

APPENDIX II

ANNOTATED BIBLICAL *HAPAX LEGOMENA* LISTS

The following two lists of biblical *hapax legomena* (as defined in Chapter I, section III) are meant to update the lists compiled by Casanowicz, Rabin, Ring and Zelson in their respective works (see Chapter I, section II.C for the exact references). Both of these lists should be considered as provisional in nature, since many of the included words are based on emendations which may now seem correct, but which may be proven incorrect in the future. Other listed words may be shown in the future to require emendation, and they would then (if the root of the emended form were attested elsewhere) acquire the status of "ghost" words (see Chapter I, section B.3) and be removed from these lists.* In the first list, all biblical *hapax legomena* are included which appear to be derived from a non-homonymic root. In the second, only bonafide *hapax legomena* which are unquestionably to be derived from a clearly homonymic root are listed. For all biblical *hapax legomena* in both lists which have reasonably certain cognates in Akkadian and/or Ugaritic, these cognates are presented together with the suggested meaning for the biblical word in question. In the notes, either reference is made to the detailed discussion of the word in Chapter III above, or a brief discussion is presented including a short bibliography for the suggested

---

*Presently known "ghost" words which would otherwise be *hapax legomena* include 1 Sam 15:9 (נמבזה--read !נבזה "despised" and see H. P. Smith, *The Books of Samuel* [Edinburgh, 1899], 135; S. R. Driver, *Notes on the Hebrew Text and the Topography of the Books of Samuel* [Oxford, 1913], 124); Isa 14:4 (מדהבה--read !מרהבה "oppression" with 1QIs[a] and see Kutscher, מגילת ישעיהו, 197; H. L. Ginsberg, "Reflexes of Sargon in Isaiah after 715 B.C.E.," *JAOS* 88 [1968], 53 n. 38; idem, *Isaiah*, 44); Isa 33:1 (כנלתך--read !ככלתך "when you have finished" with 1QIs[a] and see Kutscher, מגילת ישעיהו, 187); Ps 72:17 (Qr. ינון/Kt. ינין--read !יכון "be established" and see J. C. Greenfield, "Scripture and Inscription," *Near Eastern Studies in Honor of William Foxwell Albright* [Baltimore, 1971], 267; S. M. Paul, "Psalm 72:5--A Traditional Blessing for the Long Life of the King," *JNES* 31 [1972], 354-55); Job 33:25 (רטפש--read טפש "to be fat" as a result of dittography with the previous word and see Tur-Sinai, *Job*, 473; contra Pope, *Job*, 252).

comparison. Words which are not dealt with in Chapter III, but for which cognates, suggested meaning, and discussion are provided in these lists, represent those biblical *hapax legomena* which apparently have valid Akkadian and/or Ugaritic cognates, but which the author has chosen not to deal with in detail for the following reasons:

1. The correct meaning of the biblical *hapax legomenon* was well known despite its single contextual attestation long before the decipherment of Akkadian and Ugaritic, and the comparison of the relevant Akkadian and/or Ugaritic contexts results in nothing more than what was previously known (e.g., Isa 56:10 [לנבח] "bark").

2. Comparison between the biblical *hapax legomenon* and its cognate(s) in Akkadian and/or Ugaritic has led to the correct meaning of the word in question or a better understanding of it, but the present author has nothing to add to this successful effort (e.g., Prov 26:23 [ספסיגים!] "glaze").

3. Reasonably certain Akkadian and/or Ugaritic cognates have been suggested, but the author has not been able to locate these cognates or their synonoms in contexts comparable to that of the biblical word. Therefore, according to the methodology suggested in Chapter II above, the resultant meaning of the biblical *hapax legomenon* in question must be considered less than certain, and in need of more contextual evidence (e.g., most of the fauna *hapax legomena* in Leviticus 11 and Deuteronomy 14).

A. NON-HOMONYMIC *HAPAX LEGOMENA*

Gen 21:16	<u>מטחוי</u> קשת	
Gen 24:63	לשוח	
Gen 25:30	הלעיטני	
Gen 26:20	התעשקו	
Gen 28:12	סלם	"stairway, ladder"[1]--Akk. *simmiltu*

[1] See above, Chapter III, #2.

Gen 30:20	זבדני...זבד
Gen 30:37,38	ויפצל...פצלות; פצל

Gen 40:11 — ראשחט — "to press (grapes and other fruit)"[2]--Akk. *ṣaḫātu*

[2] See above, Chapter III, #3.

Gen 41:23 — צנמות

Gen 41:43 — אברך

Gen 47:13 — ותלה

Gen 49:17 — שפיפן — "(kind of) snake"[3]--Akk. *šibbu/šippu*

[3] See KB I, 1004. That *šibbu/šippu* is a kind of snake is clear from its inclusion in the lexical snake list Ḫḫ XIV: 11,12 (= MSL VIII/2, 7:11-12). The term is also used in epithets of various gods: *šibbu galtu* "terrifying š. snake"; *šibbu ezzu* "raging š. snake"; *šibbu lā āniḫu* "restless š. snake". For references, see Tallqvist, *Götterepitheta*, 220. For other occurrences and discussion, see Landsberger, *Fauna*, 58-59; *AHW*, 1226. Note especially AKA 45 ii 76-77 in which the quickness of the Assyrian king advancing against his enemies is compared to that of a š. snake, the same comparison which seems to occur in Gen 49:17:

> kīma šibbi erḫēkūma ina gišillāt šadî pašqāte šalṭiš ētetiq
>
> I, myself, being as quick as a š. snake, triumphantly advanced along the narrow mountain ledges.

Compare also Tn.--Epic iii 42 where the same simile is employed. For other possible Semitic cognates, see KB I, 1004.

Exod 9:9,10 — אבעבעת — "boils"[4]--Akk. *bubu'tu*

[4] See *HALAT*, 9. For references to *bubu'tu*, see *CAD*, B, 300-1 and *AHW*, 135. Note the variant *buḫbuḫtu*, which could reflect the two ע's in the Hebrew word, and the lexical equation with *ibītu* (*CAD*, I/J, 4), which might reflect the prosthetic א. For other Semitic cognates, see *HALAT*, 9.

Exod 9:31 — גבעל

Exod 13:16//Deut 6:8//11:18 — טוטפת

Exod 16:14 — מחספס

Exod 16:33 — צנצנת

Exod 27:5//38:4 — <u>כרכב</u> המזבח; כרכבו

Exod 28:19//39:12 — לשם

Exod 28:28//39:21 — יזח

Exod 28:32//39:23 — תחרא

Exod 32:16 — חרות

Exod 35:25,26 — טוו...מטוה; טוו — "to spin"[5]--Akk. *ṭamû*

[5] See above, Chapter III, #5.

Lev 11:6//Deut 14:7 ארנבת "hare"[6]--Akk. *arnabu*

[6]See *HALAT*, 87. For Akkadian references, see *CAD*, A/2, 294 and *AHW*, 70. For other Semitic cognates, see *HALAT*, 87. Eliminate Ug. *anhb* (*UT* III, #244) which Ginsberg translates "ambergris" in *ANET* for all its occurrences. Note that the comparison with Ug. *arnbt* suggested in FFM, #22 is also invalid because it is based only on a personal name.

Lev 11:13//Deut 14:12 עזניה

Lev 11:16//Deut 14:15 שחף

Lev 11:19//Deut 14:18 דוכיפת

Lev 11:22 סלעם

Lev 11:22 חרגל "(kind of) locust"[7]--Akk. *ergilu*

[7]See *HALAT*, 336. That *ergilu* is a kind of locust is clear from its inclusion in the lexical locust list, Ḫḫ XIV:239 (= MSL VIII/2, 26:239). The reading with *e* (*AHW*, 240) rather than *i* (*CAD*, I/J, 176) reflecting the ח of חרגל would seem to be preferable in light of this comparison (for a similar case, see above, Chapter III, n. 91). *CAD*, I/J, 177 lists a phonetic variant *irgiṣu* which likewise should be read *ergiṣu* (*AHW*, 240). For discussion, see Landsberger, *Fauna*, 123. For other Semitic cognates, see *HALAT*, 336.

Lev 11:30 לטאה

Lev 11:30 חמט

Lev 13:39 בהק

Lev 14:10,12,15, 21, 24 לג; לג (ה)שמן "log"[8]--Ug. *lg*

[8]See above, Chapter III, #6.

Lev 19:28 קעקע

Lev 21:20 אשך "testicle"[9]--Akk. *išku*; Ug. *ušk*

[9]See *HALAT*, 92. For Akkadian *išku*, see *CAD*, I/J, 250-51 and *AHW*, 396. For Ugaritic *ušk*, see *CTA* 11:2 where the *k*, read by Virolleaud in his original edition of the text, was no longer visible for Herdner in 1963, and as a result is restored there (see *CTA*, p. 52, n. 1). This restoration, in any case however, is quite certain (see *ANET*, 142 for translation of *CTA* 11:1-2). For other Semitic cognates, see *HALAT*, 92.

Num 6:4 חרצנים

Num 6:4 זג

Num 11:5 בצלים

Num 11:5 שומים "garlic"[10]--Akk. *šūmu*

[10]See KB I, 955 and *AF*, 58. For this term in Samalian Aramaic, see *KAI* 214:6. In general, see Löw, *Flora* II, 138-49, where other Semitic cognates are also listed.

Num 11:8 לשד השמן

Num 11:20 זרא

Num 24:3,15 שתם העין

Deut 14:5 אקו

Deut 14:5 דישן "bison"[11]--Akk. *ditānu*

[11]See *HALAT*, 212 and *AHW*, 173-74. That *ditānu* means "bison" is clear from its association in lexical lists with *kusarikku*, the regular word for "bison" which is well attested in literary texts (e.g., En. el. I:143; II:29; III:33, 91; for many other references, see *CAD*, K, 584-85 and *AHW*, 514). According to *CAD*, A/1, 349: "The bison as an animal is called *ditānu* (q.v.) and *karšānu*, while in mythological contexts *ALIM*, *GUD.ALIM*, *alimbû* and *kusarikku* are used." For the *t-š* interchange between Akkadian and biblical Hebrew, see the discussion in Landsberger, *Fauna*, 92-94, and now note the Akkadian-Hittite equation where Akkadian *karšānu* ("big-bellied") is rendered in Hittite by the hapax *ti-ša-nu-uš* (MSL III, 64:11), which according to *CAD*, D, 165, "points definitely to Heb. *dīšōn*."

Deut 25:18 נחשלים

Deut 27:9 הסכת "to keep silent"[12]--Akk. *sakātu*

[12]See KB I, 658 and *AHW*, 1011-12. For *sakātu*, see for example BWL, 146:1'-6' where the opposite of *sakātu* is *pâ epēšu* "to open the mouth (to speak)." For other examples, see *AHW*, 1011-12. Note that Arabic *sakata* "He was, or became silent, mute, or speechless" (Lane IV, 1389-90) is likewise cognate, as may be seen, e.g., from Saadiah's rendering of ידמו "they will be still" with יסכתון in Exod 15:16.

Deut 28:57 שליתה

Deut 32:15 כשית

Deut 32:24 מזי רעב

Deut 32:34 כמס "to gather"[13]--Akk. *kamāsu*

[13]See above, Chapter III, #9.

Deut 33:3 חבב

Deut 33:3 תכו

Deut 33:22 יזנק

Judg 3:16 גמד

Judg 3:22 פרשדנה

Judg 4:18 שמיכה

Judg 5:10 צחרות

Judg 5:28 ותיבב

Judg 16:16 ותאלצהו

1 Sam 5:9 וישתרו

1 Sam 15:33 וישסף

1 Sam 21:9 נחוץ

2 Sam 5:23,24//1 Chr 14:14,15 בכאים

2 Sam 22:37//Ps 18:37 קרסלי "lower leg"[14]--Akk. *kursinnu*

[14] See KB I, 857 (which refers however to Akk. *qursinnu*!); H. Holma, *Die Namen der Körperteile im Assyrisch-Babylonischen* (Helsinki, 1911), 148-49; *AHW*, 511. For the phonetic interchange between *l* and *n* as a regular feature of the consonants *lmnr*, see S. Moscati, *An Introduction to the Comparative Grammar of the Semitic Languages* (Wiesbaden, 1964), 32; *GAG*, §34b; idem, *Ergänzungen zu GAG* (Rome, 1969), 7 (to §33i and §34b). For examples of *kursinnu* as the lower leg of human beings, see *CAD*, K, 566 and *AHW*, 511. For other Semitic cognates, see KB I, 857.

2 Sam 22:46!//Ps 18:46 ויחרגו

1 Kgs 5:3 ברברים

1 Kgs 6:8 לולים

1 Kgs 10:22//2 Chr 9:21 קפים "monkey"[15]--Akk. *uqūpu*

[15] See KB I, 833; Landsberger, *Fauna*, 87, and note the variant *qūpum* cited in idem, *Fauna*, 80 n. 5. For monkeys in Mesopotamia, see *RLA* I, 41-42, and most recently, R. D. Barnett, "Monkey Business," *JANESCU* 5 (1973), 1-5. Note finally that W. F. Albright has identified Egyptian *g'if/gf* (*WAS* V, 158:12-16) with Hebrew קוף and this identification has been accepted in *WAS* itself (ibid.). See W. F. Albright, *Archaeology and the Religion of Israel* (New York, 1969), 212-13 n. 16. For other suggested cognates, see KB I, 833.

1 Kgs 10:22//2 Chr 9:21 שנהבים

1 Kgs 10:22//2 Chr 9:21 תוכיים

1 Kgs 18:46 וישנס

1 Kgs 20:33 ויחלטוה!

2 Kgs 4:42 בצקלנו "corn stalk"[16]--Ug. *bṣql*

[16] See U. Cassuto, *Biblical and Oriental Studies* II (Jerusalem, 1975), 197; ענת, 39; *HALAT*, 142; FFM, #26 and the literature cited there. For *bṣql*, see *CTA* 19:2:61-67 where it occurs five times. The meaning "corn stalk" is

based on the occurrence of *šblt* (= Hebrew שבולת "ear of corn") instead of *bṣql* five times in the otherwise almost identical passage *CTA* 19:2:68-74, the fact that the hero Dnil gathers both the *bṣql* and the *šblt* and places them both in the *asm* (= Hebrew אסם "granary"--see *CTA* 19:2:66-67, 73-74) and the occurrence of בצקל together with שעורים "barley" in 2 Kgs 4:42 (note the interchanging of שערים "barley" and שבלים "ears of corn" in Ruth 1:22; 2:2-3). Contrast the treatments of J. Gray, *I and II Kings* (Philadelphia, 1970), 501-2, and *CPOT*, 26, 294, neither of whom compare the parallel passage with *šblt* or note that both the *bṣql* and the *šblt* are placed in the *asm*. The former translates *bṣql* "plant" while the latter remarks (p. 294) "we know that in Ugaritic *bṣql* is a kind of vegetation, the growth of which is highly esteemed and desired, and that it is of value for food"! Most recently, note the discussion of *bṣql* by M. Dijkstra and J. C. de Moor and their attempt to derive the latter term from the root *bṣq* "to swell". They then translate *bṣql* "shoot", asserting "it is not a specific term for a green stalk or an ear of grain"; see M. Dijkstra and J. C. de Moor, "Problematical Passages in the Legend of Aqhâtu," *UF* 7 (1975), 203-4. These two authors likewise, however, ignore the evidence of the parallel passage with *šblt* "ear of corn" and the fact that both *bṣql* and *šblt* are placed in the *asm* "granary" as stated above. Note finally that *bṣql* is also restored in *CTA* 160:4; 161:3; *PRU* II, 127:5.

2 Kgs 19:29//Isa 37:30	שחיס - סחיש	
2 Kgs 20:13//Isa 39:2	בית <u>נכתה</u>	"treasury"[17]--Akk. *bīt nakkamāti*

[17]See above, Chapter III, #11.

Isa 1:22	מהול	
Isa 1:23	שלמנים	"gift"[18]--Akk. *šulmānu*

[18]See above, Chapter III, #12.

Isa 2:20	חפו ־רות!	
Isa 3:16	משקרות	
Isa 3:24	פתיגיל	
Isa 5:2	ויעזקהו	
Isa 9:4	סאון סאן	"sandal"[19]--Akk. *šēnu*

[19]See KB I, 646 and II, 173, 219; G. B. Gray, *The Book of Isaiah I-XXVII* (Edinburgh, 1912), 170-71, 175; E. Stern, "נעל", *EM* V, 888; *AHW*, 1213-14. *šēnu* is the regular term for "sandal" in Akkadian and has been studied quite thoroughly in A. Salonen, *Die Fussbekleidung der alten Mesopotamier* (Helsinki, 1969), 15-30 and passim. For a list of different types of sandals, all designated *šēnu* and further qualified, see Ḫḫ XI:121-28 (= MSL VII, 129: 121-28) and the detailed commentary in Salonen, *Die*

Fussbekleidung, 16-19. For graphic representations of sandals and other footwear in the ancient Near East and Egypt, see plates I-XLVI of the last mentioned work. Note that this comparison is considerably strengthened by the fact that both *šēnu* and סאון have denominative verbs associated with them (as is the case with the biblical *hapax legomenon* discussed above in Chapter III, #1). For *šēna šênu* "to put on, fasten a sandal", see *AHW*, 1214, and note especially Gilg. XII:22: *šēnī ana šēpēka lā tešên(i)*! "You shall not fasten sandals to your feet." For other suggested cognates of both סאון and its denominative verb סאן, see KB I, 646 and *AHW*, 1213-14.

Isa 9:17 ויתאבכו

Isa 11:8 הדה

Isa 11:15 עים רוחו

Isa 14:23 וטאטאתיה במטאטא

Isa 18:2,7 בזאו

Isa 18:5 זלזלים

Isa 18:5 התז

Isa 19:17 חגא

Isa 22:5 מקרקר

Isa 27:8 סאסאה

Isa 28:25 נסמן

Isa 33:20 יצען

Isa 34:15 קפוז

Isa 41:10,23 תשתע; ונשתעה "to fear"[20]--Ug. *ṯtʿ*

[20] See above, Chapter III, #16.

Isa 41:24 אפע

Isa 44:14 תרזה

Isa 47:13 הברי שמים

Isa 48:9 אחטם

Isa 51:8 סס "moth"[21]--Akk. *sāsu*

[21] See KB I, 662; *AHW*, 1032-33; *AF*, 52. For *sāsu*, see the discussion in Landsberger, *Fauna*, 134, and the additional references in *AHW*, 1032-33. Note the occurrence of the Aramaic cognate ססא in *KAI* 222A:31 (Sefire) and *AP*, 218: 184, 186.

Isa 55:13 סרפד

Isa 56:10 לנבח "to bark"[22]--Akk. *nabāḫu*

[22] See *HALAT*, 624; *AHW*, 694. That *nabāḫu* means "to bark" is especially clear from an incantation text in which various animals are listed with the sounds they make;

see S. Langdon, "An Incantation for Expelling Demons from a House," *ZA* 36 (1924-25), 210:11: *lū ša kīma kalbi inabbuhu* "Be it one (a demon) who barks like a dog." For other passages, see *AHW*, 694. Note finally the occurrence of *nabāḫu* in the following popular proverb which occurs in an Akkadian letter (ABL 403, obv. 4-7--see BWL, 281 for text and discussion) and in the Syriac and Arabic versions of Aḥiqar (F. C. Conybeare et al., *The Story of Aḥikar* [Cambridge, 1913], 69:#17 [Syriac text with translation on p. 125], 29:#14 [Arabic text with translation on p. 158]):

ina tēlte ša pī nišī šakin
umma kalbu ša paḫḫāri
ina libbi utūni kī īrubu
ana libbi paḫḫāri unambaḫ

The proverb which is popular among the people
states: "When the potter's dog
enters the (warm) kiln,
it barks at the potter."

Isa 56:10	הזים	
Isa 57:20	רפש	"(muddy) foam, mire"[23]--Akk. *rupuštu*

[23]See KB I, 905; B. Landsberger and J. V. Kinnier-Wilson, "The Fifth Tablet of Enūma Eliš," *JNES* 20 (1961), 175; *AHW*, 994. Note especially the occurrence in En. el. V: 47 of *rupuštu ša Tiamat* "the spittle (foam) of Tiamat," which albeit in a mythological context, is still reminiscent of Isa 57:20, as correctly seen by Landsberger and Kinnier-Wilson in the article cited above. For other references, see *AHW*, 994; for other possible Semitic cognates, see KB I, 905.

Isa 59:10	נגששה	
Isa 64:1	המסים	
Isa 66:11	תמצו	"to suck, draw milk"[24]--Ug. *mṣṣ*

[24]See above, Chapter III, #19-20.

Jer 5:8	מיזנים	
Jer 5:8	משכים	
Jer 6:9	סלסלות	
Jer 14:9	נדהם	
Jer 29:26	צינק	
Jer 36:18	דיו	
Jer 39:3,13	רב-מג	"a high official"[25]--Akk. *rab mugi*

[25]See E. Klauber, *Assyrisches Beamtentum* (Leipzig, 1910), 52-53 n. 2; *AF*, 6; *HALAT*, 515 and the literature cited there; *FWOT*, 151; *AHW*, 667; D. Sperling, "Rab-Saris and

Rab-Mag," *EncJud* XIII, 1481. For references to *rab mugi*, see *AHW*, 667. For the occurrence of Aramaic רבמגא in an Aramaic-Greek bilingual text, see *HALAT*, 515 and the bibliography to this text cited there.

Jer 43:10 שפרירו

Jer 47:3 שעטת פרסות אביריו

Jer 49:24 רטט

Jer 50:15 אשויתיה "tower"[26]--Akk. *asītu*

[26]See above, Chapter III, #21.

Jer 51:34 כרשו "belly"[27]--Akk. *karšu*

[27]See *HALAT*, 476; Holma, *Körperteile*, 74-75; *AHW*, 450-51. For references to *karšu*, see *CAD*, K, 223-25 and *AHW*, 450-51. Note especially the references to *karšu* with *malû* "to be full", which are parallel to מלא כרשו in Jer 51:34, e.g., BWL 144:19:

ša amēli muttaprašš idi mali karassu

As for the stalking man, his belly is full.

For other Semitic cognates, see *HALAT*, 476. The comparison with Ugaritic *krs* should be eliminated from the last mentioned work, since Ugaritic *krs* occurs but once in *CTA* 5:1: 4-6 which has been left untranslated by such an authority as H. L. Ginsberg and labeled by him as "two cuplets very obscure" (*ANET*, 138).

Ezek 1:14 בזק

Ezek 2:6 סרבים

Ezek 4:9 דחן "millet"[28]--Akk. *duḫnu*

[28]See *HALAT*, 210; *AF*, 55; Löw, *Flora* I, 738-40; *CAD*, D, 171; *AHW*, 174; Zimmerli, *Ezechiel 1*, 123. For references to *duḫnu* (*tuḫnu*), see *CAD*, D, 171 and *AHW*, 174. In general, see Löw, *Flora* I, 738-40, where other Semitic cognates are also discussed. For the Aramaic cognates, see also C. G. Howie, *The Date and Composition of Ezekiel* (Philadelphia, 1950), 53 (#10).

Ezek 7:11 נה

Ezek 9:2,3,11 קסת הספר; קסת

Ezek 16:4 משעי

Ezek 16:40 ובתקוך "to cut off/through"[29]--
Akk. *batāqu/buttuqu*

[29]See *HALAT*, 160; J. C. Greenfield, "Lexicographical Notes I," *HUCA* 29 (1958), 220-22; *AHW*, 114-15; *AIA*, 41 n. 52. For references to *batāqu/buttuqu*, see *CAD*, B, 161-65 and *AHW*, 114-15. Note especially En. el. IV:101-2:

issuk mulmulla iḫtepi karassa
qerbīša ubattiqa ušalliṭ libba

He (Marduk) shot the arrow and ripped her (Tiamat's) belly.
It cut through her insides, it slit the inner parts.

For the relationship between בתק and בדק in biblical Hebrew and their cognates in other Semitic languages, see the aforementioned study of Greenfield; *AIA*, 41 n. 51; *HALAT*, 106, 160.

Ezek 17:9 יקוסס

Ezek 23:40 כחלת "to paint the eyes with antimony (?)"[30]--Akk. *guḫlu*

[30]See *HALAT*, 447; *AF*, 61; Howie, *Ezekiel*, 55 (#21); *AHW*, 296. For references to *guḫlu* in general and as eye paint, see *CAD*, G, 125, and *AHW*, 296. For the usage of *guḫlu* and lexically related terms in ancient Mesopotamian glassmaking, see A. L. Oppenheim, "The Cuneiform Texts," *Glass and Glassmaking in Ancient Mesopotamia* (New York, 1970), 20-21, 78-80. For כוחלא in the Talmud, see *EncJud* XI, 1436. While the relationship between these terms is beyond any reasonable doubt, the translation "antimony" for Akkadian *guḫlu* has recently been questioned by a professional chemist. The following remarks are quoted from R. H. Brill, "The Chemical Interpretation of the Texts," *Glass and Glassmaking*, 116:

> As far as Professor Oppenheim has been able to ascertain, the only evidence behind the translation of *guḫlu* as "antimony" (or more properly an antimony-containing substance) is that *guḫlu* was used as kohl, the well-known eye cosmetic. This is where the difficulty arises. If that identification was made purely on the basis that "everyone knows that kohl was stibnite or antimony sulfide," then the whole argument appears to fall apart, for it has been pointed out that this generalization is not really true. More specifically, it is not true for Egypt and may not be true for Mesopotamia. We might repeat here the origin of this persistent misunderstanding which has led to the belief that all kohl was stibnite (Sb_2S_3), even though its fallacy has been amply pointed out by several authors. The chemical symbol for antimony, Sb, is derived from the Latin *stibium* which apparently did refer correctly to stibnite which was used for kohl in Roman times - but possibly not until Roman times.

Brill proceeds to present the evidence for these remarks, which consists of analyses of some seventy-four specimens of ancient Egyptian kohl, the contents of four cosmetic containers from ancient Mesopotamia, and a sample of kohl removed from a cockle shell found in the "Plano-Convex Building" at Kish. Of the seventy-four Egyptian specimens, "only one was found which appears to be antimony sulfide. The analyses showed instead that the specimens consisted mainly of galena, pyrolusite, brown ochre or malachite." No antimony was detected in any of the ancient Mesopotamian samples, whose metallic components consisted mainly of manganese, sulfur, copper, zinc and lead sulfide. Note finally that the attempt in *HALAT*, 300-1, 447 to derive חכלילות and חכלילי from the root כחל is surely incorrect since both חכלילי and חכלילות are to be compared with Akkadian *ekēlu* "to be dark" which certainly has no connection with Akkadian *guḫlu* or Hebrew כחל (for the phrase *bīt ekleti* "dark house," see n. 78A below).

Ezek 27:15 הבנים "ebony"[31]--Ug. *hbn*

[31]*HALAT*, 227; *UHP*, 56; H. J. van Dijk, *Ezekiel's Prophecy on Tyre* (Rome, 1968), 78; FFM, #46. Both Ugaritic *hbn* (*PRU* V, 102:6) and Hebrew הבנים appear to be loanwords from Egyptian *hbny* "ebony" (*WAS* II, 487:7-12). For discussion, see T. O. Lambdin, "Egyptian Loanwords in the Old Testament," *JAOS* 73 (1953), 149. For another example of an Egyptian loanword having penetrated both Ugaritic and biblical Hebrew, see above, Chapter III, #13.

Ezek 27:17 פנג "(type of) cake or meal"[32]--Akk. *pannigu/pennigu*

[32]*AF*, 38-39; G. A. Cooke, *The Book of Ezekiel* (Edinburgh, 1936), 303; Howie, *Ezekiel*, 57 (#35); R. Borger, *Die Inschriften Asarhaddons Königs von Assyrien* (reprint; Osnabrück, 1967), 94 (commentary to line 26); C. Rabin, "פנג", *EM* VI, 509; *AHW*, 818. For references to *pannigu/pennigu*, see *AHW*, 818. That this term is a food commodity is shown both by its occurrence in a lexical list as a synonom of *akalu* "food" (for this equation, see *AHW*, 818 and *CAD*, A/1, 238), and its occurrence with the determinative *ŠE* for types of grain or meal (Borger Esarh., 94:26). That it is cognate with פנג is demonstrated by its occurrence in a list of food commodities together with *dišpu* "honey" in Borger Esarh., 94:25-27, which parallels the sequence ופנג ודבש in Ezek 27:17. The following comment by R. Borger concerning the importance of this Akkadian passage for the understanding of פנג is quoted from his commentary to the passage cited above:

> Der Umstand, dass *pinigu* in unserem Texte und פנג in Hesek. 27:17 zusammen mit *dišpu* bzw. דבש "Honig" genannt werden, spricht für die von Zimmern vorgeschlagene Gleichstellung und gegen die Konjecturen, mit denen man פנג zu eliminieren versucht hat.

Contrast M. Elat, קשרי כלכלה בין ארצות המקרא (Jerusalem, 1977), 154.

Ezek 27:24 ברמים "(multi)-colored (trim)"[33]--Akk. *birmu*

[33]See above, Chapter III, #24.

Ezek 37:6,8 וקרמתי; ויקרם

Ezek 39:2 ורששאתיך

Ezek 41:16 שחיף עץ

Hos 3:2 לתך שערים "a unit of dry measure"[34]--
Ug. *lṯh*

[34]See H. L. Ginsberg, כתבי אוגרית (Jerusalem, 1936), 102; *HALAT*, 510 and the literature cited there; E. Stern, "מידות ומשקלות", *EM* IV, 852; A. Salonen, *Die Hausgeräte der alten Mesopotamier I* (Helsinki, 1965), 277; *II* (Helsinki, 1966), 286-88. That *lṯh* is a dry measure cognate with Hebrew לתך may be seen from the occurrence of the former as a measure of such foodstuffs as *ššmn* "sesame" (*CTA* 142:4, 10), *ṣmqm* "raisins" (*CTA* 142:5, 17), and *dblt* "cakes of dried figs" (*CTA* 142:17), its occurrence alongside the measure *ḥmr* in *CTA* 142 and *PRU* II, 99, which parallels the sequence לתך-חמר in Hos 3:2, and the occurrence of *š'rm* "barley" as one of the foods measured in the two aforementioned texts, which corresponds to the measuring of שעורה "barley" in Hos 3:2. The interchange of *ḥ* and *k* is not common, but does occur notably in the Ugaritic abecedary with corresponding Akkadian syllabic signs, *PRU* II, 189:9, where Ugaritic *ḥ* corresponds to Akkadian *ku*. This correspondence is discussed by E. A. Speiser, "The Syllabic Transcription of Ugaritic [ḫ] and [ḥ]," *BASOR* 175 (1964), 42-47, and most recently by E. E. Knudsen, "Spirantization of Velars in Akkadian," *lišān mitḫurti* (Neukirchen-Vluyn, 1969), 147-55. Note that the comparison with Akkadian *litiktu* "true measure" (*CAD*, L, 216-17; *AHW*, 556) suggested by W. von Soden (most recently in *AHW*, 556), while phonologically sound, must be rejected (contrast also the aforementioned study of Salonen where the same comparison is made). *litiktu* is not a specific measure as is proven by its occurrence with pronominal suffix -*ša* (*litiktaša* "its full amount"--*CAD*, L, 217) in its single attestation in a non-lexical passage. *litiktu* is simply a regular substantive derived from *latāku* "to test, try out; check measurements, calculations" (*CAD*, L, 111-12; *AHW*, 540) and as such can not be equated with Hebrew לתך which is a specific dry measure. Note especially B. Landsberger's categorization of Akkadian *litiktu* and similar terms: "Zur gleichen Kategorie 'Massnorm', bzw. 'geeichtes Mass', aber ohne Bezug auf ein konkretes Hohlmass, gehören auch *litiktu*, *maštaqtu*..."; see B. Landsberger, "Assyriologische Notizen," *WO* 1 (1948-50), 376. Note finally Talmudic לתך, for which see *OLT* XXII, 1162.

Hos 13:1 רתת

Hos 13:5 תלאבות

Joel 1:17 עבשו

Joel 2:20 צחנתו

Amos 6:10 מרספו!

Amos 7:14 בולס שקמים

Jonah 4:6,7,9,10	קיקיון	
Hab 2:11	כפיס	
Hab 3:6	לתחתאנה!	"to smite, crush"[35]--Akk. *ḫatû*; Ug. *ḫt'*

[35]See *HALAT*, 349; W. F. Albright, "Two Letters from Ugarit (Ras Shamrah)," *BASOR* 82 (1941), 43-49; idem, "The Psalm of Habakkuk," *Studies in Old Testament Prophecy* (Edinburgh, 1950), 15 n. u; H. L. Ginsberg, "The Ugaritic Texts and Textual Criticism," *JBL* 62 (1943), 115; M. J. Dahood, "Ugaritic Lexicography," *Mélanges Eugène Tisserant* I (Rome, 1964), 89; *UHP*, 59; *AHW*, 336. For references to *ḫatû*, see *CAD*, Ḫ, 151-52 and *AHW*, 336. For references to *ḫt'*, see *CTA* 4:8:17-20; *CTA* 6:2:21-23; *CTA* 53:5-10. On the emphatic *l* in Ugaritic and biblical Hebrew, see, e.g., M. Dahood, "Ugaritic-Hebrew Syntax and Style," *UF* 1 (1969), 21 and the bibliography cited there. Note that Dahood's proposal (repeated in *NSGJ*, 139, with previous bibliography) to read חתאת in Job 41:25 derived from חתא "to crush," and then translate לבלי חתאת "without a flaw" is totally unacceptable semantically and must be rejected.

Hab 3:17	רפתים	
Zeph 2:9	<u>ממשק</u> חרול	
Zech 2:12	בבת עינו	
Zech 11:8	בחלה	
Ps 32:9	לבלום	
Ps 48:14	פסגו	
Ps 50:20	דפי	
Ps 55:9	סעה	"to sweep away"[36]--Ug. *sw/y'*

[36]See J. Gray, *The Krt Text in the Literature of Ras Shamra* (Leiden, 1964), 46-47; J. C. Greenfield, "Some Glosses on the Keret Epic," *EI* 9 (1969), 63; Dahood, "Syntax and Style," 20-21; idem, *Psalms II*, 33. For *sw/y'* see *CTA* 14:3:111-14; *CTA* 14:4-5:214-17. As suggested by Greenfield, Ugaritic *s't* in both these passages should be taken as a feminine plural passive participle of *sw/y'* and be translated "swept away." Greenfield's proposal was based on the variant סייעתו הרוח "the wind swept it" to the regular סערתו הרוח "the wind scattered it" in Mishnah Kila'yim 5:7, as noted by H. Yalon, מבוא לניקוד המשנה (Jerusalem, 1964), 83-84, 172, who derived סעה in Ps 55:9 from a middle-weak סוע or סיע "to sweep away." Dahood's derivation of both *s't* and סעה from Arabic *sa'aya* "He walked, went, or went along, quickly" (Lane IV, 1366-67) is far less satisfactory from both a semantic point of view and because he ignores the Mishnaic variant, the most important evidence of all; see Dahood, "Syntax and Style," 21, where it is also erroneously asserted that Yalon and Greenfield revocalize MT *sō'āh* to *sā'āh*. As shown by Yalon (p. 171) and endorsed by Greenfield, there are cases in both Mishnaic and biblical Hebrew where the qal participle of middle *w/y* verbs is written with *ō*, and therefore, no revocalization is necessary.

Ps 58:9 שבלול תמס

Ps 60:4 פצמתה

Ps 62:4 תהותתו

Ps 63:2 כמה

Ps 68:17 תרצדון

Ps 68:18 שנאן

Ps 68:32 חשמנים

Ps 72:6 זרזיף ארץ

Ps 74:6 כילפות "axes"[37]--Akk. *kalappātu*

[37]See above, Chapter III, #26.

Ps 78:47 חנמל

Ps 80:14 יכרסמנה

Ps 99:1 תנוט "to wobble, quake"[38]--Ug. *nṭṭ*

[38]See KB II, 171 (to KB I, 602); LP, #20 and the bibliography cited there; *UT* III, #1641; Dahood, *Psalms II*, 368; M. Weinfeld, "'Rider of the Clouds' and 'Gatherer of the Clouds,'" *JANESCU* 5 (1973), 421 n. 1. For *nṭṭ*, see *CTA* 3:3:29-31; *CTA* 4:2:16-19 [restored]; *CTA* 4:7:34-35; *CTA* 19:2:93-95; *PRU* II, 1:9. Note especially *CTA* 4:7:34-35; *qdm ym bmt a*[*ṛṣ*] *tṭṭn* "East and west, earth's high places quake" as restored by Gaster, Aistleitner, Ginsberg and others (see *ANET*, 135 and *CTA*, p. 29 n. 15). Clearly נוט and *nṭṭ* are by-forms of the same verb.

Ps 104:12 עפאים

Ps 119:103 נמלצו

Ps 119:131 יאבתי

Ps 139:8 אסק

Ps 140:4 עכשוב

Ps 140:11 מהמרות "pit, grave"[39]--Ug. *mhmrt*

[39]See N. J. Tromp, *Primitive Conceptions of Death and the Nether World in the Old Testament* (Rome, 1969), 54-56; M. Dahood, *Psalms III* (New York, 1970), 305; J. Hoftijzer, "Two Notes on the Baʿal Cyclus," *UF* 4 (1972), 157-58 n. 17; M. Held, "Pits and Pitfalls in Akkadian and Biblical Hebrew," *JANESCU* 5 (1973), 188-90; *HALAT*, 524; and all the previous literature cited in these most recent studies. For *mhmrt*, see *CTA* 5:1:7-9. From the same root, *hmr*, is derived one of the names of Mot's city, *Hmry* "Pit"; see *CTA* 4:8:10-14; *CTA* 5:2:13-16. In opposition to all the other aforementioned studies, Held has shown that the Ugaritic passages mentioned above in general, and the Ugaritic root *hmr* specifically, do not provide a "philological basis for describing the netherworld as a place of liquid filth." Held's major argument is that Ugaritic

ḫḫ, usually translated "filth" in *CTA* 4:8:10-14 and *CTA* 5:2:13-16, and taken as describing Mot's abode, must instead be understood as parallel to *mk* "low" and be translated "depressed." Held also notes that the usually cited etymological derivation of מהמרות from Arabic *hamara* "to pour (rain, water)" (Lane VIII, 2900) "has very little to recommend it" in light of its post-biblical usage in such passages as Ben Sirah 12:16: מהמרות עמוקות "deep pits", where there is "no relationship whatever to rain and water." Finally, note that the attempts of M. H. Pope, Dahood, and Tromp to find the root המר in other biblical verses must be rejected. For Job 17:7, as opposed to the suggestions advanced by Pope, *Job*, 128, and Tromp in his aforementioned study, see the interpretation of N. H. Tur-Sinai, *Job*, 272-73 (see now also פשוטו של מקרא IV/2, 42 and the Targum to this verse) which fits the general context much better, and does not depend on a highly doubtful rendering of *CTA* 4:8:4: *ʿm tlm ǵṣr arṣ* "Unto the (two) hills boarding the nether world" (contrast *ANET*, 135). For Ps 46:3, Dahood's translation of המיר ארץ as "the jaws of the netherworld" is based on the incorrect understanding of *CTA* 5:1:7-9 dealt with by Held in his aforementioned study. Contrast M. Dahood, *Psalms I* (New York, 1966), 278. Finally, contrast also the recent treatment of A. van Selms, "A Systematic Approach to CTA 5,1,1-8," *UF* 7 (1975), 482. Van Selms erroneously assumes that *mhmrt* must mean "gullet" in parallelism to *npš* "throat". For this erroneous assumption, see Held, "Pits and Pitfalls," 188.

Ps 144:13	מזוינו	
Prov 7:16	אטון מצרים	
Prov 18:8//26:22	מתלהמים	
Prov 21:8	וזר	
Prov 22:21	קשט	
Prov 26:18	מתלהלה	
Prov 26:23	ספסיגים!	"glaze"[40]--Ug. *spsg*

[40] See H. L. Ginsberg, "The North-Canaanite Myth of Anat and Aqhat II," *BASOR* 98 (1945), 21 n. 55; W. F. Albright, "A New Hebrew Word for 'Glaze' in Proverbs 26:23," *BASOR* 98 (1945), 24-25; A. Goetze, "Contributions to Hittite Lexicography," *JCS* 1 (1947), 311-15; S. Abramsky, "סיגים ובדילים בישעיהו פרק א", *EI* 5 (1958), 106 and especially n. 14; C. Rabin, "Hittite Words in Hebrew," *Orientalia* 32 (1963), 139; *UT* III, #1792; פשוטו של מקרא IV/1, 364-66; FFM, #85 and the bibliography cited there; Oppenheim, "The Cuneiform Texts," *Glass and Glassmaking*, 19. For Ugaritic *spsg*, see *CTA* 17:6:36-37; *PRU* II, 106:8 (*s̀ps̀g*); *PRU* II, 112:14 (*sb[?]sǵ*). Since Ginsberg's celebrated discovery in 1945, and Albright's addition of the alleged Hittite evidence in the same year, many scholars have discussed this comparison from all points of view, as may be seen from the select bibliography listed above. The truth

appears to be that the meaning "glaze" fits very nicely in both *CTA* 17:6:36-37 and Prov 26:23. In the case of the latter, contra Abramsky and Tur-Sinai, smooth glaze spread on worthless pottery is precisely the image called for in this verse, and no other suggested interpretation fits nearly so well. Albright's Hittite evidence, however, as corrected by Goetze, cannot stand. As noted by Rabin, with the corrected translation of the alleged Hittite cognate as "fine bowl" rather than "glaze," and with Goetze's suggestion to interpret Ugaritic *spsg* therefore as "bowlfull," "there would be no point in making the emendation in Proverbs." Therefore, despite the fact that Ugaritic *spsg* is almost surely a foreign word (written once *s̀ps̀g*), the alleged Hittite evidence must be rejected. Similarly, according to Oppenheim, the connection suggested in *CAD*, Z, 10, between the once attested *zabzab*[*gû*] and Ugaritic *spsg* is "equally unlikely." Note finally, that Rabin's suggestion to read כספסגים for סיגים כסף in Ezek 22:18 cannot be accepted. Read here סיגי-מ כסף "silver dross" (with enclitic *m*) in view of the close parallel in Isa 1:25 for which see the aforementioned study of Abramsky (read !בכור "in the furnace" for כבר "as with lye" in Isa 1:25 based on both Ezek 22:18 and Isa 48:10--contra Abramsky--see Ginsberg, *Isaiah*, 26).

Prov 27:15	סגריר	
Prov 29:21	מפנק	
Prov 30:15	עלוקה	
Prov 30:28	שממית	
Prov 30:31	<u>זרזיר</u> מתנים	
Job 2:8	להתגרד	
Job 3:5	<u>כמרירי</u> יום	
Job 4:18	תהלה	
Job 6:10	ואסלדה	
Job 7:5	רגוש	
Job 8:14	יקוט	
Job 9:26	יטוש	
Job 13:27//33:11	סד	
Job 15:12	ירזמון	
Job 16:15	גלדי	"skin, hide"[41]--Akk. *gil(a)du*

[41]See *HALAT*, 183; H. Holma, *Die Namen der Körperteile im Assyrisch-Babylonischen* (Helsinki, 1911), 3; *AHW*, 288. For references to *gil(a)du*, see *CAD*, G, 71, and *AHW*, 288. That *gil(a)du* is an Aramaic loanword in Akkadian has been noted in *HALAT*, 183, and *AHW*, 288. See also AW I, #26. For other Semitic cognates, see *HALAT*, 183, and *AHW*, 288. Note especially the references in *DISO*, 50, to Aramaic texts from various periods. See also the discussion in

AD, 85-86. Here it should be noted that the semantic range of terms for "animal hide" includes the notion of "human skin" as may be clearly seen from the usage of the Akkadian term *mašku* "hide, skin" (*AHW*, 627-28).

Job 16:19 — שהדי

Job 17:1 — נזעכו

Job 18:2 — קנצי

Job 21:24 — עטיניו

Job 26:11 — ירופפו

Job 26:13 — שפרה "net"[42]--Akk. *saparru*

[42]See above, Chapter III, #27.

Job 33:20 — וזהמתו

Job 37:3 — ישרה! "to flash (lightning)"[43]--Ug. *šrh*

[43]See H. L. Ginsberg, "נוספות לעלילת אלאין בעל", *Tarbiz* 4 (1933), 385; idem, "The Ugaritic Texts and Textual Criticism," *JBL* 62 (1943), 109-10 n. 1; M. Held, "The YQTL-QTL (QTL-YQTL) Sequence of Identical Verbs in Biblical Hebrew and in Ugaritic," *Studies and Essays in Honor of Abraham A. Neuman* (Leiden, 1962), 287 n. 5; *UHP*, 74; *UT* III, #2484; *NSGJ*, 129-30 and the additional bibliography in n. 304; LP, #18 and the additional bibliography cited there; Pope, *Job*, 280. For *šrh*, see *CTA* 4:5:70-71: *w<y>tn qlh bʿrpt šrh larṣ brqm* "And <he will> thunder in the heavens, flashing his lightning to the earth." For MT ישרהו, read simply with Ginsberg, ישרה "he flashes" with the extra ו having been added as a result of dittography with the following word. Note that the ה of ישרה must be considered consonantal due to its occurrence in the Ugaritic text. Finally, note that Dahood's attempt to retain the ו of ישרהו "with archaic *yaqtulu* ending" is completely pointless and must be rejected.

Job 38:28 — אגלי טל

Job 39:5 — ערוד

Job 40:18 — מטיל ברזל

Job 40:21,22 — צאלים

Job 41:10 — עטישתיו

Job 41:21 — תותח

Cant 1:10 — חרוזים

Cant 2:9 — כתלנו

Cant 2:11 — סתו

Cant 2:13 — פגיה

Cant 3:9 — אפריון

Cant 4:1//6:5 גלשו

Cant 4:4 תלפיות

Cant 4:14 כרכם

Cant 5:3 אטנפם "to soil, dirty"[44]--Akk. *ṭunnupu*

[44] See KB I, 354; O. Loretz, *Das althebräische Liebeslied* (Neukirchen-Vluyn, 1971), 35 n. 5. For *ṭunnupu*, see BWL 215:14: *mubaḫḫiš sūqāni* [*muṭ*]*ṭannipu bītāti* "(The pig) makes the streets stink, dirties the houses." Note also KAR 134: reverse 7 (= TuL #25: reverse 7) where *ṭanāpu* in the I/1 is opposite *zakû* "to be clean, pure" which clearly parallels the opposition of רחץ "to wash, cleanse" (see also Job 9:30 and the Akkadian passage cited in the discussion of שלג "soapwort" below in n. 80) and טנף in Cant 5:3. For other Semitic cognates, see KB I, 354, and note especially the references to Talmudic טנף "to dirty, soil" and its derivatives cited in *OLT* XV, 199-201.

Cant 5:11 תלתלים

Cant 6:11 אגוז

Cant 7:3 מזג

Cant 7:9 סנסניו "spadix"[45]--Akk. *sissinnu*

[45] See KB I, 662; *AF*, 54; Löw, *Flora* II, 336-37; B. Landsberger, *The Date Palm and its By-products according to the Cuneiform Sources* (Graz, 1967), 18; Loretz, *Liebeslied*, 44 n. 8 and the bibliography cited there; *AHW*, 1051. For references to *sissinnu*, see *AHW*, 1051. For other Semitic cognates, see especially Löw, *Flora* II, 336-37. Here it must be noted that the contention of R. Gordis that סנסניו means "branches" derived from Akkadian *sinsinnu* "the topmost branches of the palm", and that "a variant with Lamed instead of Nun occurs in Jer. 6:9 סלסלות" is completely groundless and based on a lack of understanding of the Akkadian evidence; see R. Gordis, *The Song of Songs* (New York, 1961), 94.

Cant 7:10 דובב

Cant 8:5 מתרפקת

Ruth 1:13 תעגנה

Lam 3:11 ויפשחני

Lam 4:8 צפד

Eccl 10:8 גומץ

Eccl 12:3 ובטלו "to cease, be idle"[46]--Akk. *baṭālu*

[46] See *HALAT*, 116; *AF*, 47; *AHW*, 116. For references to *baṭālu*, see *CAD*, B, 174-76 and *AHW*, 116. Note especially TCL 9, 116:8: *sinnišāti ša lā šipāti baṭlā* "The women

(workers) are idle because of a lack of wool." For other cognates, see *HALAT*, 116 and note especially biblical Aramaic בטל in Ezra 4:21, 23, 24; 5:5; 6:8.

Eccl 12:5	אביונה	
Esth 1:6	כרפס	
Esth 1:6	בהט	
Esth 7:4	נזק המלך	
Esth 8:10,14	אחשתרנים	
Esth 8:10	רמכים	
Esth 8:15	תכריך בוץ וארגמן	
Dan 9:24	נחתך	
Dan 10:21	רשום	
Dan 11:45	אפדנו	"audience hall"[47]--Akk. *appadānu*

[47]See *HALAT*, 75 and bibliography cited there; *AF*, 8; *FWOT*, 35. For *appadānu*, see *CAD*, A/2, 178, and *AHW*, 59, both of which cite only VAB 3, 123:2-3: *agâ šum appadān Dariyāmuš ab ab abiya ītepus* "This (building), called *appadāna*, Darius, my great grandfather, built." Note also Talmudic אפדנא for which see the references cited in *OLT* VI, 2777-78. That all these cognates must be derived from Old Persian *apadāna* "audience hall" has been noted in all the studies listed above. For the latter word used in Old Persian texts, and for its construction and suggested derivation from Sanskrit and Greek, see R. G. Kent, *Old Persian Grammar, Texts, Lexicon* (New Haven, 1953), 168 with references cited there. Note finally that such an audience hall belonging to Darius and Xerxes has now been excavated at Persepolis; for pictures of this structure, see *ANEP*, #766, 767.

Ezra 1:9	אגרטלי זהב; אגרטלי כסף
Ezra 4:7	כנותו
1 Chr 15:27	מכרבל
2 Chr 2:15	צרכך
2 Chr 2:15	רפסדות
2 Chr 3:10	צעצעים
2 Chr 36:16	מלעבים

B. HOMONYMIC *HAPAX LEGOMENA*

Gen 6:3	ידון	
Gen 6:14	וכפרת...בכפר	"bitumen"[48]--Akk. *kupru*

[48]See above, Chapter III, #1.

Gen 6:14 גפר

Gen 6:16 צהר

Gen 9:27 יפת

Gen 22:9 ויעקד

Gen 30:37 לוז

Gen 31:34 כר הגמל

Gen 32:25,26 ויאבק; האבקו

Gen 32:33 נשה

Gen 36:24 הימם

Gen 43:11 בטנים "pistachio nut"[49]--Akk. *buṭnu/buṭṭutu*

[49] See above, Chapter III, #4.

Gen 45:17 טענו "to load up"[50]--Akk. *ṣênu* (most often with respect to boats)

[50] See *HALAT*, 361. Aramaic טען "to carry, load up" seems to have developed a much broader meaning than its etymological equivalent *ṣênu* in Akkadian, which is used most often as a technical term for "to load cargo on a boat"; see *CAD*, Ṣ, 131-32; *AHW*, 1091. Both the form (with *ṭ*) and this more general meaning "to carry, load up" show that Heb. טען must be identified much more closely with Aramaic טען than with Akkadian *ṣênu*. For the latest discussion of Aramaic טען and its relationship with Hebrew טען, see J. C. Greenfield, "Scripture and Inscription," *Near Eastern Studies in Honor of William Foxwell Albright* (Baltimore, 1971), 261-62. Note also the oral communication of S. Lieberman and the remarks of H. L. Ginsberg in *LKK*, 34, concerning the semantic development "'to bear' hence 'to suffer'" exhibited in the root טען in Aramaic. For this semantic development in other roots from Hebrew, Ugaritic, and Akkadian, see M. Held, "The Root ZBL/SBL in Akkadian, Ugaritic and Biblical Hebrew," *JAOS* 88 (1968), 92-93. Note that while the separation of I טען (also a *hapax legomenon* occurring in Isa 14:19--see below in list B) and II טען (the term discussed immediately above) as set forth in *HALAT*, 361, is correct, most of the cognates listed for I טען are not at all semantically equivalent to I טען (whose meaning can only be approximately established through its single occurrence in Isa 14:19) and should therefore be deleted. The alleged Aramaic cognate defined as "(schwer) krank sein" should be listed as cognate to II טען according to the semantic development discussed immediately above. The alleged Ugaritic cognate *ṭʿn* occurs only in *CTA* 5:1:26 which is totally incomprehensible and should therefore be deleted (note that Gordon in *UT* III, #1040 compares *ṭʿn* to II טען which is likewise unacceptable). Finally, the alleged MH cognate defined as "Klage erheben, argumentieren" cannot be related semantically to I טען and should therefore be deleted as well.

Gen 48:14	שכל	
Gen 49:5	מכרתיהם	
Gen 49:22	פרת	
Exod 9:32	אפילת	"late (of crops)"[51]--Akk. *uppulu*

[51]For discussion, see B. Landsberger, "Schwierige akkadische Wörter. 2. 'Früh' und 'spät,'" *AfO* 3 (1926), 164-72, especially p. 170. See also idem, "Jahreszeiten im Sumerisch-Akkadischen," *JNES* 8 (1949), 248-97, where the above article is referred to constantly together with the occurrence of the phrase *eqlum ḫirrētum ḫarpātum eqlum ḫirrētum uppulātum* "the fields (with) early furrows and the fields (with) late furrows." For translation and sources, see *CAD*, Ḫ, 199. For discussion, see MSL I, 156-57. Note also the Talmudic cognate אפילה and related terms, for which see *OLT* VI, 2784. Contrast both KB I, 77, and *HALAT*, 76, where the attempt to derive this term from the root אפל "to be, make dark" is semantically impossible and must be rejected. Note finally the recent discussion of both this biblical *hapax legomenon* and its Akkadian and Aramaic cognates in M. Held, "Two Philological Notes on Enūma Eliš," *Kramer Anniversary Volume* (Neukirchen-Vluyn, 1976), 236 n. 62.

Exod 12:9	נא	
Exod 16:31	צפיחת	
Exod 16:31//Num 11:7	גד	
Exod 21:10	ענתה	
Exod 24:11	אצילי בני ישראל	
Exod 28:19//39:12	אחלמה	
Exod 28:19//39:12	שבו	"(kind of) precious stone"[52]--Akk. *šubû*

[52]See KB I, 939; *AF*, 58; *RLA* II, 268; *FWOT*, 155. That *šubû* is a precious stone is indicated both by its determinative NA_4 and its inclusion in such lexical lists as Uruanna III: 139, 141 (= MSL X, 69:11-12a) and Ḫḫ XVI:162-69 (= MSL X, 9:162-69 and commentary on pp. 20-21). These passages indicate that there were two colors associated with this precious stone: *arqu* "green-yellow" and *sāmu* "red-brown." Despite the assertion in *CAD*, I/J, 328, *šubû* has "nothing to do" with *yašpû (ašpû)* "jasper," and is unidentified at present. For discussion, see B. Landsberger, "Über Farben im Sumerisch-Akkadischen," *JCS* 21 (1967), 151 n. 66.

Exod 30:23	דרור	
Exod 30:34	שחלת	
Lev 3:9	עצה	
Lev 11:13//Deut 14:12	פרס	
Lev 11:16//Deut 14:15	תחמס	

Lev 11:17//Deut 14:17	שלך	
Lev 11:18//Deut 14:16	תנשמת	
Lev 11:18//Deut 14:17	רחמ(ה)	
Lev 11:19//Deut 14:18	אנפה	"(kind of) bird"[53]--Akk. *anpatu*

[53]See *AF*, 51; *HALAT*, 70. That *anpatu* is a kind of bird is clear from its inclusion in the lexical bird list Ḫḫ XVIII:336-37 (= MSL VIII/2, 151:336-37). For all known references, see *CAD*, A/2, 143, and *AHW*, 54; for other possible cognates, see *HALAT*, 70.

Lev 11:29	חלד	
Lev 11:29	צב	
Lev 11:30	תנשמת	
Lev 11:30	כח	
Lev 11:30	אנקה	
Lev 16:21	עתי	
Lev 19:10	פרט כרמך	
Lev 19:20	בקרת	"indemnity"[54]--Akk. *baqru/paqru*

[54]See *HALAT*, 145; E. A. Speiser, "Leviticus and the Critics," *Oriental and Biblical Studies* (Philadelphia, 1967), 128-31. Speiser's suggestion has been adopted by JPS Torah, 217 (see JPS Torah Notes, 217), and it is from there that the translation "indemnity" has been taken. For the usage of *baqru/paqru* in Akkadian texts, see *AHW*, 105; for other possible cognates, see *HALAT*, 145 (contrast *AIA*, 80 n. 252).

Lev 21:20	מרוח אשך	
Lev 22:23	וקלוט	
Lev 25:47	עקר משפחת גר	
Num 5:21,22,27	צבה; לצבות; וצבתה	
Num 6:3	משרת ענבים	
Num 11:5	חציר	
Num 11:5	אבטחים	
Num 14:44	ויעפלו	
Num 19:15	צמיד	
Num 23:9	צרים	"mountain"[55]--Ug. *ǵr*

[55]See above, Chapter III, #7.

Num 23:10	תרבע(ת)!	"dust-cloud"[56]--Akk. *tarbu'u/turbû/turbu'tu*

[56]See above, Chapter III, #8.

Num 24:20,24	אבד	
Num 25:8	קבה	
Deut 1:41	ותהינו	
Deut 14:5	זמר	
Deut 16:10	מסת נדבת ידך	
Deut 22:8	מעקה	
Deut 23:14	אזנך	
Deut 23:26	מלילת	
Deut 28:27	חרס	
Deut 32:2	שעירם	
Deut 32:17	שערום	
Deut 32:26	אפאיהם	
Deut 33:14	גרש ירחים	
Josh 5:11,12	עבור הארץ	"harvest, produce"[57]--Akk. *ebūru*

[57]See above, Chapter III, #10.

Judg 7:13	צלול לחם שערים	
Judg 7:15	שברו	
Judg 8:7,16	ברקנים	
Judg 19:2	ותזנה	"to be angry"[58]--Akk. *zenû*

[58]See *HALAT*, 264 and the bibliography cited there. For *zenû*, see *CAD*, Z, 85-86, and note the many passages in which this verb is used in contexts of marital difficulties and lovers' quarrels. Note especially *RA* 18, 25:2:17: *lū sabus litū*[*ra*] *lū zeni šudbibīšu itti*[*ya*] "If he (my lover) is offended, let him return to me; if he is angry, (O Ishtar), make him speak to me (again). Note finally that the Greek rendering of ותזנה in LXX^{A} clearly supports this interpretation as does the fact that the verb זנה "to practice prostitution" is never connected elsewhere in the Bible with the preposition על "on, upon" (which is very commonly used with verbs denoting "to be angry" such as קצף). For the rendering of LXX^{A} and its significance, see R. G. Boling, *Judges* (New York, 1975), 273-74. After correctly rejecting the traditional understanding of ותזנה on the basis of the evidence stated above as well as the general context, Boling, unaware apparently of Akkadian *zenû*, is forced to radically emend the text and to regard the MT as "interpretive." The above comparison of ותזנה with Akkadian *zenû* renders all such emendations completely unnecessary.

1 Sam 2:36	אגורת כסף	
1 Sam 3:13	כהה	
1 Sam 13:21	פצירה	

1 Sam 13:21	פים	
2 Sam 1:9	שבץ	
2 Sam 6:14,16	מכרכר	
2 Sam 6:19//1 Chr 16:3	אשפר	
2 Sam 17:29	שפות בקר	
2 Sam 21:16	קינו	
2 Sam 22:12//Ps 18:12!	חשרת מים	"sieve"[59]--Ug. *ḫṯr*

[59]See *HALAT*, 348; S. I. Feigin, "The Heavenly Sieve," *JNES* 9 (1950), 40-43; *SAYP*, 146 n. 33. For Ugaritic *ḫṯr*, see *CTA* 6:2:30-35, and for a possible connection with *ḫṯr* in *PRU* V, 50:2, which is a list of clothes, see the discussion in *SP*, 210, where a full bibliography is also given. Undoubtedly, חשכת in Ps 18:12 should be emended to the more difficult reading חשרת. For other Semitic cognates, see *HALAT*, 348. Contrast Y. Kutscher, "למילון המקראי", *Leshonenu* 21 (1957), 252 [my thanks to Professor M. Weinfeld for this reference].

1 Kgs 5:23	דברות	
1 Kgs 6:9	גבים	
1 Kgs 7:30	סרני נחשת	
1 Kgs 7:33	חשריהם	
1 Kgs 7:50	פתות	
1 Kgs 10:25//2 Chr 9:24	נשק	
1 Kgs 20:27	חשפי עזים	
1 Kgs 20:38,41	אפר	"head covering"[60]--Akk. *apāru* ("to provide with a head covering")

[60]See *AF*, 36; *HALAT*, 78; *AHW*, 57. For references to *apāru*, see *CAD*, A/2, 166-68 and *AHW*, 57.

2 Kgs 4:35	ויזורר	
2 Kgs 6:25	קב	
2 Kgs 23:7	בתים	
Isa 2:16	שכיות החמדה	"(type of) ship"[61]--Ug. *ṯkt*

[61]See above, Chapter III, #13.

Isa 3:16	טפוף	
Isa 3:18	שביסים	
Isa 3:19	רעלות	
Isa 5:7	משפח	
Isa 7:19	בתות	

Isa 8:16,20 — תעדה — "message"[62]--Ug. *tʿdt* ("delegation")

[62]See H. L. Ginsberg, "An Unrecognized Allusion to Kings Pekah and Hoshea of Israel (Isa. 8:23)," *EI* 5 (1958), 62*; Ginsberg, *Isaiah*, 36. Ginsberg rightly compares *tʿdt* "delegation" which occurs parallel to *mlakm* "messengers" in *CTA* 2:1:21-22, 25-26, 28, 30, 44, and is also restored in *CTA* 2:1:11, 40-41. He also compares עדדן "soothsayers" in the Zkr inscription (*KAI* 202:11-12), assuming that it is derived from the same root עדד "with special reference to messages from god to man." On the basis of these comparisons, Ginsberg vocalizes תְּעֻדָּה from the assumed Hebrew root עדד* "to send a message." See now also J. F. Ross, "Prophecy in Hamath, Israel, and Mari," *HTR* 63 (1970), 4-8, and the bibliography cited there.

Isa 13:21 — אחים

Isa 14:19 — מטעני חרב

Isa 17:6 — גרגרים

Isa 19:3 — אטים — "spirit of the dead"[63]--Akk. *eṭemmu*

[63]See above, Chapter III, #14.

Isa 19:4 — וסכרתי

Isa 19:7 — ערות

Isa 19:9 — שריקות

Isa 22:18 — כדור

Isa 22:24 — צפעות

Isa 24:6 — חרו

Isa 27:9 — גר

Isa 28:10,13 — קו לקו

Isa 28:10,13 — צו לצו

Isa 30:6 — דבשת גמלים — "hump"[64]--Ug. *gbṯt*

[64]See H. L. Ginsberg, "Baʿlu and His Brethren," *JPOS* 16 (1936), 143-44 n. 14; *HALAT*, 204. For *gbṯt*, see *CTA* 12:1:30-32, where it is parallel to *qrnm* "horns". The interchange of *g* and *d* is dealt with by Ginsberg in his aforementioned article, and he cites among other examples Aramaic גּוּנבא alongside the more original דונבא "tail" (reflecting *ḏ*--compare Hebrew זנב). Note, for example, TB Shabbat 77b: "Why is a camel's tail (גנובתיה) short? - Because it eats thorns. Why is an ox's tail (גנובתיה) long? - Because it grazes in meadows and must beat off the gnats." Other references may be found in *OLT* IX, 304.

Isa 33:8 — !עדים — "vassal treaty"[65]--Akk. *adû*

[65]See above, Chapter III, #15.

Isa 34:14 לילית "(kind of) demon"[66]--Akk. *lilītu*

[66]See *HALAT*, 502 and the literature cited there; *AHW*, 553; *MLC*, 578-80; Weinfeld, *Deuteronomy*, 113 n. 1. *lilītu* is the feminine form of Akkadian *lilû* which is a loanword from Sumerian *LÍL* "wind" (for this derivation and the semantic development involved, see *CAD*, Z, 60). For references to *lilû* and *lilītu*, see *CAD*, L, 190, and *AHW*, 553. Note also the occurrence of another associated demon called *ardat lilî* "*lilû*-woman," for which see *CAD*, A/2, 241-42, and *AHW*, 553. For many parallels in both Semitic and non-Semitic cultures including the amulet from Arslan Tash (*KAI*, 27), see *MLC*, 578-80, and G. Scholem, "Lilith," *EncJud* XI, 245-49. Note finally that it has been suggested (*HALAT*, 502 and especially Weinfeld, *Deuteronomy*, 113 n. 1) to read לילית in Job 18:15 for the unintelligible מבלי לו of the MT. While this emendation certainly fits the context admirably, it still seems a bit too drastic to accept without additional evidence.

Isa 38:12 קפדתי

Isa 38:21 וימרחו

Isa 40:15 מר

Isa 40:20 מסכן "(type of) tree"[67]--Akk. *musukkanu*

[67]See *AF*, 53; *HALAT*, 573; *FWOT*, 106-7. For the identification of this tree as the Dalbergia Sissoo, see A. Salonen, *Die Türen des alten Mesopotamien* (Helsinki, 1961), 40, 99; idem, *Die Möbel des alten Mesopotamien* (Helsinki, 1963), 221-22 and the bibliography cited there. For references to *musukkanu*, see the aforementioned studies and *AHW*, 678. On the relationship of this tree to its gloss in Isa 40:20 (עץ לא ירקב "a wood that does not rot"), see E. Lipiński, "SKN et SGN dans le sémitique occidental du nord," *UF* 5 (1973), 206. Note also Ginsberg, *Isaiah*, 79 n. e. Finally, for the commercial importing and use of this wood in the Neo-Assyrian empire, see M. Elat, קשרי כלכלה בין ארצות המקרא (Jerusalem, 1977), 60-61 (with reference to מסכן in Isa 40:20 as well).

Isa 41:3 ארח

Isa 42:14 אפעה

Isa 44:13 שרד

Isa 44:14 ארן "cedar"[68]--Akk. *erēnu*

[68]See above, Chapter III, #17.

Isa 44:19 בול עץ

Isa 46:1,2 קרס; קרסו

Isa 46:8 והתאששו

Isa 48:19 מעותיר

Isa 51:17,22 קבעת "chalice"[69]--Ug. *qb't*

[69]See above, Chapter III, #18.

Isa 54:12 אקדח

Isa 63:1 חמוץ בגדים

Isa 66:11 זיז כבודה "teat"[70]--Akk. *zīzu*

[70]See above, Chapter III, #19-20.

Isa 66:20 כרכרות

Jer 2:22 נכתם

Jer 2:23 משרכת

Jer 9:7 שחוט

Jer 13:22 נחמסו

Jer 30:13//46:11 תעלה

Jer 36:22,23 אח

Jer 43:9 מלט

Jer 49:7 נסרחה

Jer 51:34 הממני

Jer 51:38 נערו "to roar"[71]--Akk. *na'āru*

[71]See KB I, 622; *AHW*, 694, 709. For occurrences of *na'āru* and *nā'iru* (I/1 participle), see *AHW*, 694, 709. Note especially those references with *nêšu/labbu/girru* "lion" which parallel the context of Jer 51:38, e.g., Cagni Erra V:11: *ina pī labbi nā'iri ul ikkimū šalamtu* "They cannot take away a carcass from the mouth of a roaring lion." For other suggested cognates, see KB I, 622.

Ezek 1:7//Dan 10:6 קלל

Ezek 4:15 צפיעי הבקר

Ezek 5:1 גלבים "barber"[72]--Akk. *gallābu*

[72]See *HALAT*, 183; *AF*, 28; Howie, *Ezekiel*, 52 (#7); *AHW*, 274-75. For references to *gallābu*, see *CAD*, G, 14-17, and *AHW*, 274-75. Note also the related forms *gullubu* "to shave" (*CAD*, G, 129-31; *AHW*, 297), *gallabūtu* "barbering" (*CAD*, G, 17-18; *AHW*, 275), and *naglabu* "razor" (*AHW*, 711-12; A. Salonen, *Die Hausgeräte der alten Mesopotamier I* [Helsinki, 1965], 102-4). Note finally the cognates גלב and גלבא in Phoenician, Punic, and Nabatean (see *DISO*, 50 and *AIA*, 51).

Ezek 7:25 קפדה

Ezek 13:20 פרחות

Ezek 16:30 לבתך "rage"[73]--Akk. *libbātu*

[73]See above, Chapter III, #22.

Ezek 16:36 נחשתך

Ezek 19:9 סוגר "neck-stock"[74]--Akk. *šigāru*

[74]See above, Chapter III, #23.

Ezek 23:15 טבולים

Ezek 26:9 קבלו

Ezek 27:19 <u>דני</u>! יין "vat"[74A]--Akk. *dannu*

[74A]See A. Millard, "Ezekiel XXVII.19: The Wine Trade of Damascus," *JSS* 7 (1962), 201-3; *HALAT*, 218; H. J. van Dijk, *Ezekiel's Prophecy on Tyre* (Rome, 1968), 80-81; FFM, #41; *CPOT*, 189-90, 325; F. L. Moriarty, "The Lament over Tyre (Ez. 27)," *Gregorianum* 46 (1965), 87. Contrast M. Elat, קשרי כלכלה בין ארצות המקרא (Jerusalem, 1977), 54 n. 59. By emending the totally incomprehensible ודן ויון מאוזל to ודני יין מאיזל! "and vats of wine from Izalla", Millard in his aforementioned article has succeeded in restoring what must have been the original sense of these words. The major evidence cited for this emendation is the equation of *karānu ša Izalli* "wine of Izalla" with *karānu Hulbūnû* "wine of Hulbūnu" in the Practical Vocabulary from Nineveh (IIR, 44, #3:9'; see B. Landsberger and O. Gurney, "Practical Vocabulary of Assur," *AfO* 18 [1957-58], 340:9') and the association of these same two types of wine in the Neo-Babylonian inscriptions of Nebuchadrezzar II (VAB 4, 90:22-23; 154:50-51). This equation and association are then compared with the association of יין חלבון "wine of Helbon" (see now Elat, קשרי כלכלה, 154) with יין מאיזל! "wine from Izalla" in Ezek 27:18-19. Millard also notes that the reading יין מאיזל! "wine from Izalla" is supported by the Septuagint as well. For other occurrences of *karānu ša Izalli*, see Millard's aforementioned article and *CAD*, K, 205. For the reading ודני! "and vats of", Millard compares Akk. *dannu* "vat" (*CAD*, D, 98-99; *AHW*, 161; A. Salonen, *Die Hausgeräte der alten Mesopotamier II* [Helsinki, 1966], 160-62) and especially the occurrence of *dannu ša karāni* "vat of wine" (e.g., *4! dannūtum ša karāni* "4 vats of wine"--TCL 9, 105:9). Here it should be noted that Millard's contention that Akk. *dannu* is cognate with Ug. *dn* "receptacle for corn" must be rejected (others who have accepted this comparison include *LKK*, 47; ענת, 75; FFM, #41; *CPOT*, 190; Moriarty, "Lament over Tyre," 87; Salonen, *Hausgeräte II*, 160; *AHW*, 161; *CML*, 154 n. 12; *HALAT*, 218; *AIA*, 46; M. Dietrich and O. Loretz, "Zur ugaritischen Lexikographie I," *Bibliotheca Orientalis* 23 [1966], 129). First of all, of the two Ugaritic passages for *dn* which Millard cites (p. 202 n. 8), neither one contains the word *dn* according to the readings of A. Herdner (*CTA* 3:A:12 [*r'idn*]; *CTA* 16:3:14 [(*b*) ʿ*dnhm*]).

Secondly, even if the reading [*b*]*dnhm* were to be allowed in *CTA* 16:3:14, the objections to this proposed identification as set forth in *CAD*, D, 99 are still quite valid:

> The word *dannu*...is late and seems to sppear in Arabic and Aram. as a loan word....It should not be connected with Ugaritic *dn* (a container for bread--Gordon Handbook No. 493). Derived from the adj. *dannu* describing containers..., it refers in NB exclusively to large storage jars for beer, wine or dates.

The attempt by A. Salonen to oppose this conclusion concerning the usage of Akk. *dannu* by citing the phrase *akli danni* in ADD 1011:6 and translating it "Krugbrote" following *AHW*, 161 must also be considered unsuccessful. *akli danni* occurs several times (see, e.g., the passages cited in *CAD*, A/1, 244) and should be translated "big loaf of bread" (*CAD*, D, 96) or the like with *dannu* being used in a regular adjectival way (see also Landsberger and Gurney, "Practical Vocabulary," 338; G. van Driel, *The Cult of Aššur* [Assen, 1969], 214). That this must be the case is proven both by the fact that in all the other passages cited, *dannu* "vat" never occurs *after* the word describing its contents and by the plural form of the phrase *akli danni* which occurs as *12 aklī dannūte* "12 big loaves of bread" (Ebeling Parfumrez. 21:7). Finally, note that the attempt by van Dijk to retain the initial ו of MT ויון by reading ודנו with "archaic construct masculine plural in û" seems completely illogical especially in view of the fact that he himself accepts the change of the second ו in MT ויון to י, the same exact change required to read ודני; see van Dijk, *Ezekiel's Prophecy on Tyre*, 81. [I would here like to express my thanks to Dr. M. Sokoloff who first called my attention to this very interesting biblical *hapax legomenon*.]

Ezek 27:20	חפש
Ezek 27:24	<u>גנזי</u> ברמים
Ezek 27:24	ארזים
Ezek 28:14	ממשח
Ezek 43:15,16	הראל; אריאל
Ezek 44:20	כסום יכסמו
Ezek 46:22	קטרות
Ezek 47:3	אפסים
Hos 2:12	נבלתה
Hos 5:12	עש
Hos 8:6	שבבים
Hos 10:1	בוקק
Joel 1:7	קצפה
Joel 1:8	אלי

Joel 1:17 פרדות

Joel 2:6//Nah 2:11 פארור

Joel 2:7 יעבטון

Amos 3:12 בדל אזן

Amos 5:11 שבסכם! "to gather; collect a (straw) tax"[75]--Akk. *šabāšu*

[75]See above, Chapter III, #25.

Amos 6:5 פרטים

Amos 6:11 רסיסים

Amos 7:7,8 אנך "tin"[76]--Akk. *annaku*

[76]See *HALAT*, 69; *AF*, 59; *FWOT*, 31; *AHW*, 49; B. Landsberger, "Tin and Lead: The Adventures of Two Vocables," *JNES* 24 (1965), 285-96. For references to *annaku*, see *CAD*, A/2, 127-30, and *AHW*, 49. For the translation of *annaku* as "tin" rather than "lead" (= Akkadian *abaru*--*CAD*, A/1, 36-38; *AHW*, 4), see Landsberger's aforementioned study. Here it should be noted that, while the vision in Amos 7:7-9 is still far from clear, the remarks of Landsberger on these verses, which have been ignored in recent commentaries, do help in a general way to understand why אנך "tin" was used here. Landsberger (p. 287) suggests that tin "is a symbol of (a) softness, (b) uselessness, unless alloyed to another metal, (c) perishability." On the commercial importing and use of tin in the Neo-Assyrian empire, see now Elat, קשרי כלכלה, 43-45.

Obadiah 7 מזור

Jonah 1:5 ספינה "ship"[77]--Akk. *sapīnatu*

[77]See KB I, 664; A. Salonen, *Die Wasserfahrzeuge in Babylonien* (Helsinki, 1939), 19; S. Aḥituv, "ספנות", *EM* V, 1072-73. *sapīnatu* is clearly an Aramaic loanword in Akkadian, for which see AW II, #130. For additional references, see *AHW*, 1027. For references to Aramaic ספינה, see *DISO*, 196. For other Semitic cognates, see KB I, 664.

Jonah 4:8 חרישית

Mic 1:13 רתם

Mic 3:3 פצחו

Nah 2:8 מנהגות

Nah 3:17 מנזריך

Hab 3:6 וימדד

Zeph 3:6 נצדו

Ps 29:7 חצב

Ps 35:3 סגר

Ps 45:2	רחש	
Ps 45:9	קציעות	
Ps 73:4	אולם	
Ps 90:5	זרמתם	
Ps 118:10,11,12	אמילם	
Ps 139:16	גלמי	
Prov 3:10	שבע	
Prov 6:11//24:34	מגן	"to beseech, entreat"[78]--Ug. *mgn*

[78]See W. F. Albright, "Some Canaanite-Phoenician Sources of Hebrew Wisdom," VTSup 3 (1960), 9-10; M. Held, "Rhetorical Questions in Ugaritic and Biblical Hebrew," *EI* 9 (1969), 75 n. 36; W. McKane, *Proverbs* (Philadelphia, 1970), 324-25; O. Margalith, "ארבעה פסוקים במשלי", *Beth Miqra* 67 (1976), 517-18. For *mgn*, see *CTA* 4:1:20-23; *CTA* 4:3:25-37; *CTA* 8:1-2; *CTA* 16:1:44-45. This last passage is restored and translated by Held in his aforementioned study as follows: *šqrb* [*bḥntk*] *bmgnk* "Present [your plea] with your entreaty." The restoration is based on the idiom *qrb bḥnt* "to approach with a plea" which occurs in *CTA* 17:1:17. In all other cases, *mgn* is an A-word parallel to the B-word *ǵẓy* "to do homage, propitiate." Here it should be noted that, while Ugaritic *mgn* is rightly compared to איש מגן "beggar" in Prov 6:11//24:34, the finding of this root in such passages as Prov 2:7 and 4:9 must be completely rejected. Contrast *UT* III, #1419, and W. A. van der Weiden, *Le Livre des Proverbes* (Rome, 1970), 26-27, 45. Both of these attempts are based on the misunderstanding of the meaning of Ugaritic *mgn* as "to beseech (with gifts)" and "faire cadeau" respectively. Note also Dahood's attempts to find this root in no less than nine additional passages, all based on his erroneous assumption that *mgn* means "to bestow" (*WUS*, #1513: "beschenken"); see M. J. Dahood, "Ugaritic Lexicography," *Mélanges Eugène Tisserant* I (Rome, 1964), 94; idem, *Psalms I*, 16-17. See now *CMHE*, 4 n. 4, where Dahood's view is accepted by F. M. Cross, Jr., who, however, admits the contrary evidence of Deut 33:29. This whole issue has now been discussed anew by O. Loretz who comes to the conclusion that, since *mgn* can only mean "Schild" or "Geschenk, schenken", and only the former can possibly fit Prov 6:11//24:34, איש מגן must be translated "Schildträger"! See O. Loretz, "Psalmstudien III," *UF* 6 (1974), 177-83; idem, "'jš mgn in Proverbia 6,11 und 24,34," *UF* 6 (1974), 476-77; M. Dietrich, O. Loretz and J. Sanmartín, "Zur ugaritischen Lexikographie XI," *UF* 6 (1974), 31-32. This new analysis is based largely on the view of W. von Soden that Akkadian *mag/kannu* and *mag/kannūtu* "Geschenk" which occur in documents from Nuzi, Alalaḫ and Ugarit have their origin in "sskr. *magha-* + *-nnu*; > ug. *mgn*; > aram. *maggān*, ar. *maǧǧānan*." See *AHW*, 574-75 and the bibliography cited there; *AIA*, 67. Here, it cannot be emphasized too strongly that *the only meaning* for Ugaritic *mgn* that fits both the context and the parallelism of the

Ugaritic passages cited above is "to beseech, entreat". Whether or not the aforementioned Akkadian terms are related to Ugaritic *mgn* (and they may well not be!), it is clear that Ugaritic *mgn* "to beseech, entreat" fits biblical איש מגן perfectly and there is thus no reason why the latter comparison should be rejected. Such may not be said, however, for the comparison recently suggested by O. Loretz for Gen 15:1. Loretz compares *mgn* "Geschenk" and translates the verse as follows: "Fürchte dich nicht, Abram! Ich (selbst) bin dein Geschenk, dein überreicher Lohn!"; see O. Loretz, "mgn - 'Geschenk' in Gen 15,1," *UF* 6 (1974), 492. This translation which replaces the well-established notion of God's protecting His subject with the completely unattested concept of God's declaring that He is a gift to His subject should surely be rejected on both conceptual and philological grounds.

Prov 6:13 מולל

Prov 7:16 חטבות

Prov 12:27 יחרך

Prov 21:9//25:24 בית חבר "noise, clamor"[78A]-- Akk. *ḫubūru*

[78A]See J. J. Finkelstein, "Hebrew חבר and Semitic Ḫ̮BR," *JBL* 75 (1956), 328-31; O. Margalith, "ארבעה פסוקים במשלי", *Beth Miqra* 67 (1976), 522-23; C. Cohen, "לצרוף 'בית חבר' (משלי כ"א,ט; כ"ה,כד)", *Beth Miqra* 67 (1976), 598-99 and all the literature cited in these works. For Akkadian *ḫubūru* "noise, clamor" and its verbal form *ḫabāru* "to make noise", see the aforementioned article by Finkelstein, *CAD*, Ḫ, 7, 220-21 and *AHW*, 302-3, 352. The present author in his aforementioned study has compared VAS 16, 153: 1-9 (= AbB 6, 98), which shows that Akkadian *ḫabāru* "to make noise" can be used in conjunction with, and with respect to, *bītu* "house": [*ana bē*]*liya* [*qi*]*bīma umma Marduk-išmēannīma Yamzu-atnû mār Yaplaḫum ina mūšim ayyumma laḫanna issukšumma killi bīt bēliya iḫburma*... "To my lord speak: Thus (says) Marduk-išmēannīma - As regards Yamzu-atnû, someone threw a bottle at him during the night and he made a clamor in the house of my lord...." This evidence combined with Prov 21:19 (which parallels the two verses in question and shows that the meaning of בית חבר must be connected with כעס "anger"--see the aforementioned study of Margalith) demonstrates that בית חבר should be translated "noisy house (literally 'house of noise')." That such an adjectival construction (rather than a fixed phrase referring to a specific place which has been the underlying assumption in virtually all previous studies of בית חבר) may occur within a construct chain together with בית "house of..." is evidenced by the fairly common *bīt ekleti* "dark house (literally 'house of darkness')" which is used to refer to many different dark houses (for references, see *CAD*, I/J, 61). Note that in at least one case *bīt ekleti* alternates with *bīti eṭê* "dark house" where *eṭê* "dark" is a verbal adjective of the synonomous verb *eṭû* "to be dark" (compare CT 15, 45:4

bīti eṭê with Gilg. VII, IV:33 *bīt ekleti*). Note further that Landsberger has compared *bīt ekleti* to *bīt asakki* "forbidden house (literally 'house of taboo')"; see B. Landsberger, "asakku II = 'tabu,'" *ZA* 41 (1933), 219. The resultant general context of Prov 21:9//25:24 may now be compared to CT 40,5:13-14 which includes the term *ikkillu* "clamor" (a synonom of both *ḫubūru* and *rigmu* "noise"): *šumma bītu ikkil*[*la*] *īšu āšib libbišu nakrū šumma bītu ikkil*[*la*] *lā īšu libbi āšibišu ṭâb* "If a house is noisy, its residents will be hostile; If a house is not noisy, its residents will be contented." Finally, it should be noted that the attempt by Finkelstein in his aforementioned study to compare Akkadian *ḫabārum* "to make noise" with Hebrew חבר "to charm (with words)" in such passages as Deut 18:11; Isa 47:9, 12; Ps 58:6; Job 16:4 cannot be accepted because Akkadian *ḫabārum* is never used in this way.

Prov 25:13 צנת שלג

Prov 26:14 צירה "door pivot"[79]--Akk. *ṣerru*

[79]See KB I, 803; BDB, 852; *AF*, 30. For *ṣerru*, see *CAD*, Ṣ, 137; *AHW*, 1093; A. Salonen, *Die Türen des alten Mesopotamien* (Helsinki, 1961), 66-67. Note, for example, OIP II 127:I 13:3-6: *kašurrû aqaru...ina šapal serrī dalāti bābanī ēkalliya ukīn* "Costly stones from Gasur...I set up under the pivots of the door leaves of my palace gates." Note also *ṣerrāniš* "past the cap of the door pivot" (*CAD*, Ṣ, 134). For Aramaic and Arabic cognates, see KB I, 803; *AF*, 30; Salonen, *Die Türen*, 67; *AIA*, 96 and the literature cited in these studies. Note especially *AP*, #30:10-11: וציריהם זי דששיא אלך נחש "And the pivots of these door leaves were copper."

Prov 31:2 ברי; בר בטני; בר נדרי

Prov 31:19 כישור

Job 9:7 חרס

Job 9:26 אבה

Job 9:30 שלג "soapwort"[80]--Akk. *ašlāku* ("fuller, washerman")

[80]See KB I, 972; Tur-Sinai, *Job*, 171; Pope, *Job*, 75; *AF*, 28. For references to *ašlāku*, see *CAD*, A/2, 445-47; *AHW*, 81; E. Salonen, *Über das Erwerbsleben im alten Mesopotamien* (Helsinki, 1970), 286-97. See, for example, UET 6, 414:1: *alkam ašlak luwa''irkāma ṣubāti zukki* "Come on, O fuller! I will give you an order: Cleanse my garment!" For the relevant late Hebrew and Aramaic cognates, see J. Preuss, *Biblisch-Talmudische Medizin* (reprint; New York, 1971), 431; Löw, *Flora* I, 648-49. Note, however, that Löw's statement that Akkadian *ašlāku* cannot be compared to שלג because the former must be derived from √שלק has no basis whatsoever.

Job 10:10 גבינה "cheese"[81]--Akk. *gubnatu*

[81]See *HALAT*, 166; *CAD*, G, 118; *AHW*, 295; H. Hoffner, "A Native Akkadian Cognate to West Semitic *GBN 'cheese,'" *JAOS* 86 (1966), 27-31. For references to *gubnatu*, see the aforementioned articles in the two Akkadian dictionaries. That Akkadian *gubnatu* is an Aramaic loanword in Akkadian has been noted in all the studies listed above and see also AW I, #29. Hoffner, in his aforementioned work, has attempted to identify *GA-BÁ-AN* in an isolated Hittite text (KUB 9, 28: 2:2-4 obverse) as an Akkadogram for an assumed Akkadian **gab(bā)nu* "Gab(bā)nu - cheese" which he then terms a "native (East Semitic) designation of cheese attested for the earlier period of the language cognate to the terms for cheese in the West Semitic languages based upon the proto-Semitic root **gbn*." This proposal, however, cannot be accepted due to methodological considerations, until **gab(bā)nu* is actually attested *in Akkadian* as a native Akkadian term. For other attested Semitic cognates, see *HALAT*, 166, and *AHW*, 295. Note finally that the proposed connection between גבינה "cheese", גבן "hunchback", and גבנן "knoll" based apparently on the shape of the cheese and adopted by both *HALAT*, 167, and Hoffner (p. 31) is completely groundless and must be rejected.

Job 13:28 רקב

Job 15:24 כידור

Job 15:27 פימה

Job 18:5 שביב אשר

Job 18:9 צמים

Job 30:6 ערוץ

Job 32:6 זחלתי "to fear"[82]--Ug. *dḥl* (!)

[82]See *HALAT*, 257; *PRU* II, p. 29; *WUS*, #737; *UHP*, 55 and the bibliography cited there. For Ugaritic *dḥl*, see *PRU* II, 13:20-21: *wat umy al tdḥl* (!) "And as for you, my mother, fear not!" Note that the text reads *tdḥṣ* with 𐎕 as the last sign, but there is little doubt that this sign should be emended to 𐎍 = *l*, in view of the formula at the end of the letter (lines 22-24) which is identical to the end of the letter in *PRU* V, 59:26-27, and which expresses reassurance from the writer of the letter to its recipient that he should not worry (for a provisional translation of this formula, see *UT* III, #1439). Thus, *al tdḥl* (!) in this context should be compared to the biblical formula אל תירא "do not fear" especially in such verses as Jer 30:10; 46:27; Ezek 2:6 (note also Isa 41:8-10). For general parallels to this formula in Akkadian and Aramaic, as well as a short bibliography, see Weinfeld, *Deuteronomy*, 45 n. 5, 50-51. Note especially אל תזחל in the *Zkr* Inscription (*KAI* 202A:13) for which see Ross, "Prophecy," 8-9, where additional bibliography is also cited. While *dḥl* "to fear" has hitherto been limited chiefly to Aramaic

(see *HALAT*, 257, and *DISO*, 73), it must now be looked upon as having an earlier existence in Ugaritic as well. For a similar case, see M. Held, "Philological Notes on the Mari Covenant Rituals," *BASOR* 200 (1970), 34 n. 11.

Job 32:19 אבות

Job 33:9 חף "to cleanse"[83]--Akk. *ḫapāpu*

[83]See *HALAT*, 326 (where incorrect reference is made to *AHW*, however); *CAD*, Ḫ, 84; *AHW*, 321. For references to *ḫapāpu*, see the latter two works. That *ḫapāpu* is an Aramaic loanword in Akkadian has been noted in all the aforementioned works, and see also AW I, #45. For other Semitic cognates, see *HALAT*, 326. Note especially the Talmudic references to חפף "to wash (especially the head)" in *OLT* XIV, 674-75. That the semantic range of terms for "to wash" includes the notion "to be innocent, free of guilt" may be clearly seen from the usage of such terms as Akkadian *zukkû* "to cleanse, declare free of guilt" and its Hebrew counterpart, זכך. For both the former and the latter meaning "to cleanse," see Job 9:30, and n. 80 above. For *zukkû* meaning "to declare free of guilt," see *CAD*, Z, 29. For זכך in that meaning, see Job 33:9.

Job 36:2 כתר

Job 39:4 בר "open country"[84]--Akk. *bāru*

[84]*bāru* occurs only once in Akkadian as a synonom to *ṣēru* "open country, plain" in an astrological commentary, and must be considered a loanword from Sumerian *BAR*, which is a synonom of *EDIN*, the regular Sumerian logogram for *ṣēru*; see *CAD*, B, 120, and for references to the bilingual equation *BAR* = *ṣēru*, see *CAD*, Ṣ, 138. For references to Aramaic בר "open country, field", note especially the phrase חיות ברא "beast of the field" (Dan 2:38; 4:9, 18, 20, 22, 29) which is equivalent to Hebrew חית השדה (e.g., Gen 2:19, 20) and בול הרים (see above, Chapter III, #28). Note also the other cognates listed in *HALAT*, 146. Note finally, however, that the contention in the last named dictionary that there exists an Akkadian *barru* which is a loanword from Aramaic is incorrect. This contention is based on *AHW*, 107 and see also AW I, #11. All passages listed under von Soden's *barru* III (*AHW*, 107) have now been placed under *birītu* (*CAD*, B, 252-53) and have been interpreted convincingly as "balk (between fields and gardens)."

Job 39:19 רעמה

Job 40:17 פחדו

Job 40:17 יחפץ

Job 40:20 <u>בול</u> הרים "wild animals"[85]--Akk. *būlu*

[85]See above, Chapter III, #28.

Job 40:31	צלצל דגים	
Job 41:11	כידודי אש	
Cant 1:17	רהיטנו	
Cant 2:9	חרכים	
Cant 2:13	חנטה	
Ruth 2:16	של תשלו	
Lam 4:1	יועם	
Eccl 9:1	עבדיהם	
Esth 1:6	דר	
Esth 1:6	סחרת	
Dan 11:43	מכמני הזהב והכסף	
Neh 3:15	ויטללנו	
Neh 5:7	וימלך	"to reflect, consider"[86]-- Akk. *mitluku*

[86] See BDB, 576; J. M. Myers, *Ezra, Nehemiah* (New York, 1965), 128. For references to *malāku*, see *AHW*, 593-94. Note especially Gilg. XI:167-68: *Enlil ā illika ana surqinni aššu lā imtalkūma iškunu abūbu* "Enlil must not come to the offering because he did not reflect and (thoughtlessly) brought about the flood." Note also the many parallels to this passage in Atraḫasis and related texts; see Lambert and Millard, *Atra-Ḫasīs*, 188 (passages cited under *malāku*). For other Semitic cognates, see *HALAT*, 559. Note especially biblical Aramaic מלכי "my advice, counsel" in Dan 4:24.

Neh 7:3	יגיפו
1 Chr 10:12	גופת שאול; גופת בניו
1 Chr 21:27	נדנה
2 Chr 9:18	כבש

BIBLIOGRAPHY

Excluding primary Akkadian sources

Abramsky, S. "סיגים ובדילים בישעיהו פרק א'." *EI* 5 (1958), 105-7.

________. "חמר." *EM* III, 187-90.

Aharoni, Y. "Three Hebrew Ostraca from Arad." *BASOR* 197 (1970), 16-42.

________. כתובות ערד (Jerusalem, 1975).

Aḥituv, S. "ספנות." *EM* V, 1071-74.

________. "Divination." *EncJud* VI, 111-16.

Aistleitner, J. *Wörterbuch der ugaritischen Sprache* (Berlin, 1963).

Albright, W. F. *The Vocalization of the Egyptian Syllabic Orthography* (New Haven, 1934).

________. "Two Letters from Ugarit (Ras Shamrah)." *BASOR* 82 (1941), 43-49.

________. "New Light on the Early History of Phoenician Colonization." *BASOR* 83 (1941), 14-22.

________. "The Oracles of Balaam." *JBL* 63 (1944), 207-33.

________. "A New Hebrew Word for 'Glaze' in Proverbs 26:23." *BASOR* 98 (1945), 24-25.

________. "Baal-Zephon." *Festschrift Alfred Bertholet* (Tübingen, 1950), 1-14.

________. "The Psalm of Habakkuk." *Studies in Old Testament Prophecy* (Edinburgh, 1950), 1-18.

________. *JBL* 69 (1950), 385-93.

________. "A Catalogue of Early Hebrew Lyric Poems (Psalm LXVIII)." *HUCA* 23/1 (1950-51), 1-39.

________. *From the Stone Age to Christianity* (New York, 1957).

________. "Some Remarks on the Song of Moses in Deuteronomy XXXII." *VT* 9 (1959), 339-46.

________. "Some Canaanite-Phoenician Sources of Hebrew Wisdom." VTSup 3 (1960), 1-15.

________. *Yahweh and the Gods of Canaan* (New York, 1969).

Albright, W. F. *Archaeology and the Religion of Israel* (New York, 1969).

________. "Some Comments on the Ammān Citadel Inscription." *BASOR* 198 (1970), 38-40.

Allony, N. "שני קטעים נוספים מהנוסח המקורי של שבעים מלים בודדות." *Sinai* 37 (1955), רמה-רס.

________. "כתאב אלסבעין לפט׳ה לרב סעדיה גאון." *Ignace Goldziher Memorial Volume* II (Jerusalem, 1958), 1-48.

________. "מיכה בשבעים מלים בודדות לרס"ג." ספר דים (Jerusalem, 1958), 362-66.

________. "המלים הבודדות בשאלות עתיקות." *HUCA* 30 (1959), א-יד.

________. "ישעיה בשבעים מלים בודדות לרס"ג." ספר טור-סיני (Jerusalem, 1960), 279-88.

________. "ירמיה בשבעים מלים בודדות לרס"ג." *Beth Miqra* 7/2 (1962), 43-49.

________. "השקפות קראיות במחברת מנחם והמלים הבודדות בערך גלב." אוצר יהודי ספרד V (1962), 21-54.

________. "הקדמת רס"ג לספרו שבעים המלים הבודדות." ספר זיידל (Jerusalem, 1962), 233-52.

________. "קטע חדש מספר הקרחה לר׳ יהודה חיוג׳." Appended to P. Kokovzov, מספרי הבלשנות העברית בימי הבינים (reprint; Jerusalem, 1970), א-טו.

________. "שבעיט מלים בודדות ברסאלה ליהודה אבן קריש." ספר ייבין (Jerusalem, 1970), 409-25.

Alt, A. "Ägyptisch-Ugaritisches." *AfO* 15 (1945-51), 69-75.

________. "Die phönikischen Inschriften von Karatepe." *WO* 1 (1948), 272-87.

Amiaud, A. "De la prononciation du פ en assyrien." *ZA* 2 (1887), 205-7.

The Ancient Near East in Pictures Relating to the Old Testament, ed. J. B. Pritchard (2nd ed.; Princeton, 1969).

Ancient Near Eastern Texts Relating to the Old Testament, ed. J. B. Pritchard (3rd ed.; Princeton, 1969).

Artzi, P. "ראשית עליתה של ממלכת אשור לפי מכתבי אל עמרנה." *EI* 9 (1969), 22-28.

Astour, M. C. "Ma'ḫadu, the Harbor of Ugarit." *Journal of the Economic and Social History of the Orient* 13 (1970), 113-27.

Bacher, W., ed. ספר השורשים (reprint; Jerusalem, 1966).

Baer, S. *Liber Ezechielis* (Leipzig, 1884).

Baneth, D. H. "Bemerkungen zu den Achikarpapyri." *OLZ* 17 (1914), 248-52.

________. "Zu dem aramäischen Brief aus der Zeit Assurbanipals." *OLZ* 22 (1919), 55-58.

Bargès, J. J. L., and Goldberg, D. B. *Risala* (Paris, 1857).

Barnett, R. D. "Monkey Business." *JANESCU* 5 (1973), 1-5.

Baron, S. *A Social and Religious History of the Jews* V (New York, 1957).

Barr, J. *Comparative Philology and the Text of the Old Testament* (Oxford, 1968).

Barth, J. *Die Nominalbildung in den semitischen Sprachen* (Leipzig, 1894).

Basmachi, F. "An Akkadian Stela." *Sumer* 10 (1954), 116-19.

Baumgartner, W. "Untersuchungen zu den akkadischen Bauausdrücken." *ZA* 36 (1924-25), 29-40, 123-38, 219-53.

________. "Das semitische Wort für 'Leiter, Treppe.'" *TZ* 7 (1951), 465-67.

________ et al. *Hebräisches und aramäisches Lexikon zum Alten Testament* (Leiden, 1967-.).

Bendavid, A. *Parallels in the Bible* I-IV (Jerusalem, 1965-69).

Benjacob, Y. דברים עתיקים (Leipzig, 1844).

Benor, J. L. "בענין 'דכים' (תהל' צ"ג)." *Beth Miqra* 63 (1975), 530-35.

ben Yehuda, E. מלון הלשון העברית I-VIII (New York/London, 1960).

Bezold, C. *Babylonisch-Assyrisches Glossar* (Heidelberg, 1926).

Biblia Hebraica Stuttgartensia.

Blau, J. "Hapax Legomena." *EncJud* VII, 1318-19.

Blommerde, A. C. M. *Northwest Semitic Grammar and Job* (Rome, 1969).

Boling, R. G. *Judges* (New York, 1975).

Borger, R. *Die Inschriften Asarhaddons Königs von Assyrien* (reprint; Osnabrück, 1967).

________. "Weitere ugaritologische Kleinigkeiten." *UF* 1 (1969), 1-4.

Breasted, J. H. *Ancient Records of Egypt* IV (New York, 1906).

Briggs, C. A., et al. *The Book of Psalms* I-II (Edinburgh, 1907).

Bright, J. *Jeremiah* (New York, 1965).

Brinkman, J. A. "Merodach Baladan II." *Studies Presented to A. Leo Oppenheim* (Chicago, 1964), 6-53.

________. *A Political History of Post-Kassite Babylonia* (Rome, 1968).

Brown, F.; Driver, S. R.; and Briggs, C. A. *A Hebrew and English Lexicon of the Old Testament* (Oxford, 1929).

Buber, S. בית אוצר הספרות I (1887), 33-52.

Büchler, A. "Zu Sachaus aramäischen Papyrus aus Elephantine." *OLZ* 15 (1912), 126-27.

de Buck, A. "The Judicial Papyrus of Turin." *JEA* 23 (1937), 152-64.

Budde, K. "Zu Jesaja 1-5." *ZAW* 49 (1931), 182-211.

Burchardt, M. *Die altkanaanäischen Fremdworte und Eigennamen im Aegyptischen* II (Leipzig, 1910).

van Buren, E. D. "The ṣalmê in Mesopotamian Art and Religion." *Orientalia* 10 (1941), 65-92.

Burney, C. F. *Notes on the Hebrew Text of the Books of Kings* (reprint; New York, 1970).

Cagni, L. *L'epopea di Erra* (Rome, 1969).

________. *Das Erra-Epos Keilschrifttext* (Rome, 1970).

Caminos, R. A. *Late Egyptian Miscellanies* (London, 1954).

Casanowicz, I. M. "Hapax Legomena - Biblical Data." *The Jewish Encyclopedia* VI (New York, 1904), 226-28.

Cassuto, M. D. "תהלים ס"ח." *Tarbiz* 12 (1940-41), 1-27.

________. "מותו של בעל." *Tarbiz* 12 (1941), 169-80.

________. "ספרות מקראית וספרות כנענית." *Tarbiz* 14 (1942), 1-10.

________. "שירת העלילה בישראל." *Knesset* 8 (1943), 121-42.

________. האלה ענת (Jerusalem, 1951).

________. פרוש על ספר בראשית (Jerusalem, 1965).

________. *Biblical and Oriental Studies* II (Jerusalem, 1975).

Chayes, Z. ספר תהלים (reprint; Jerusalem, 1970).

Childs, B. S. *Isaiah and the Assyrian Crisis* (Illinois, 1967).

Cogan, M. *Imperialism and Religion: Assyria, Judah and Israel in the Eighth and Seventh Centuries B.C.E.* (Montana, 1974).

Cohen, C. "Was the P Document Secret?" *JANESCU* 1/2 (1969), 39-44.

________. "'Foam' in Hosea 10:7." *JANESCU* 2/1 (1969), 25-29.

________. "Poison." *EncJud* XIII, 702-4.

________. "Treasure, Treasury." *EncJud* XV, 1360-62.

________. "Widow." *EncJud* XVI, 487-91.

________. "Hebrew TBH: Proposed Etymologies." *JANESCU* 4/1 (1972), 36-51.

________. "The Widowed City." *JANESCU* 5 (1973), 75-81.

________. "Studies in Early Israelite Poetry I: An Unrecognized Case of Three-Line Staircase Parallelism in the Song of the Sea." *JANESCU* 7 (1975), 13-17.

________. "לצרוף 'בית חבר' (משלי כ"א, ט; כ"ה, כד)." *Beth Miqra* 67 (1976), 598-99.

Conybeare, F. C., et al. *The Story of Aḥiḳar* (Cambridge, 1913).

Cooke, G. A. *The Book of Ezekiel* (Edinburgh, 1936).

Cowley, A. E. *Aramaic Papyri of the Fifth Century B.C.* (Oxford, 1923).

________. *Gesenius' Hebrew Grammar* (reprint; London, 1966).

Craig, J. A. "Prayer of the Assyrian King Asurbanipal." *Hebraica* 10 (1893), 75-87.

Cripps, R. S. *A Critical and Exegetical Commentary on the Book of Amos* (Cambridge, 1960).

Cross, F. M. "Epigraphic Notes on the Ammān Citadel Inscription." *BASOR* 193 (1969), 13-19.

________. *Canaanite Myth and Hebrew Epic* (Cambridge, 1973).

________ and Freedman, D. N. *Early Hebrew Orthography* (New Haven, 1952).

________. *Studies in Ancient Yahwistic Poetry* (Montana, 1975).

Dahood, M. "Some Ambiguous Texts in Isaias." *CBQ* 20 (1958), 41-49.

Dahood, M. *Biblica* 43 (1962), 544-46.

________. "Ugaritic Lexicography." *Mélanges Eugène Tisserant* I (Rome, 1964), 81-104.

________. "Ugarit." *Enciclopedia de la Biblia* VI (Barcelona, 1965), 1121-29.

________. *Ugaritic-Hebrew Philology* (Rome, 1965).

________. *Psalms I* (New York, 1966).

________. *Psalms II* (New York, 1968).

________. "Ugaritic-Hebrew Syntax and Style." *UF* 1 (1969), 15-36.

________. *Psalms III* (New York, 1970).

________. "Hebrew-Ugaritic Lexicography IX." *Biblica* 52 (1971), 337-56.

________. "Ugaritic-Hebrew Parallel Pairs." *Ras Shamra Parallels* I (Rome, 1972), 71-382.

________. "Ugaritic-Hebrew Parallel Pairs." *Ras Shamra Parallels* II (Rome, 1975), 3-39.

Daiches, S. "Lexikalisches." *ZA* 17 (1903), 91-93.

Davies, N. *The Tomb of Rekh-m'i-Rē'* at *Thebes* (New York, 1943).

Delitzsch, Fr. *Assyrische Studien* I (Leipzig, 1874).

________. *Prolegomena eines neuen hebräisch-aramäischen Wörterbuchs zum Alten Testament* (Leipzig, 1886).

________. *Assyrische Lesestücke* (Leipzig, 1900).

Deller, K. "Zur Terminologie neuassyrischer Urkunden." *WZKM* 57 (1961), 29-42.

________. *Orientalia* 34 (1965), 259-74.

Dhorme, E. *L'emploi metaphorique des noms de parties du corps en hébreu et en akkadien* (reprint; Paris, 1963).

Diakonoff, I. M. *Semito-Hamitic Languages* (Moscow, 1965).

Dietrich, M., and Loretz, O. "Zur ugaritischen Lexikographie I." *Bibliotheca Orientalis* 23 (1966), 127-33.

________ and Sammartín, J. "Ugaritisch ILIB und hebräisch '(W)B 'Totengeist.'" *UF* 6 (1974), 450-51.

________. "Zur ugaritischen Lexikographie XI." *UF* 6 (1974), 19-38.

van Dijk, H. J. *Ezekiel's Prophecy on Tyre* (Rome, 1968).

Dijkstra, M., and de Moor, J. C. "Problematical Passages in the Legend of Aqhâtu." *UF* 7 (1975), 171-215.

Diringer, D. *Le Iscrizioni Antico-Ebraiche Palestinesi* (Firenze, 1934).

Donner, H., and Röllig, W. *Kanaanäische und aramäische Inschriften* I-III (Wiesbaden, 1966-69).

Dotan, A. "Masorah." *EncJud* XVI, 1401-82.

van Driel, G. *The Cult of Aššur* (Assen, 1969).

Driver, G. R. "Some Hebrew Words." *JTS* 29 (1928), 390-96.

________. "Studies in the Vocabulary of the Old Testament III." *JTS* 32 (1930-31), 361-66.

________. "Difficult Words in the Hebrew Prophets." *Studies in Old Testament Prophecy* (Edinburgh, 1950), 52-72.

________. *Canaanite Myths and Legends* (Edinburgh, 1956).

________. *Aramaic Documents of the Fifth Century B.C.* (Oxford, 1957).

________. "Abbreviations in the Massoretic Text." *Textus* 1 (1960), 112-31.

Driver, S. R. *Deuteronomy* (Edinburgh, 1895).

________. *The Book of Genesis* (London, 1911).

________. *Notes on the Hebrew Text and the Topography of the Books of Samuel* (London, 1913).

Duhm, B. *Das Buch Jesaia* (reprint; Göttingen, 1968).

Dukes, L. "Erklärung seltener biblischer Wörter von Saadias Gaon." *ZKM* 5 (1844), 115-36.

Dupont-Sommer, A. *Les inscriptions araméenes de Sfiré* (Paris, 1958).

________. "Ancient Aramaic Monumental Inscriptions." *An Aramaic Handbook* I/2 (Wiesbaden, 1967), 1-7.

Ebeling, E. "Erdöl, Erdpech." *RLA* II, 462-63.

Ehrlich, A. B. *Randglossen zur hebräischen Bibel* I-VII (Leipzig, 1908-14).

________. מקרא כפשוטו I-III (reprint; New York, 1969).

Eichrodt, W. *Ezekiel* (Philadelphia, 1970).

Eissfeldt, O. *Das Lied Moses Deuteronomium 32:1-43 und das Lehrgedicht Asaphs Psalm 78* (Berlin, 1958).

———. "Wahrsagung im Alten Testament." *La divination en Mésopotamie ancienne* (Paris, 1966), 141-46.

Eitan, I. *A Contribution to Biblical Lexicography* (New York, 1924).

Elat, M. קשרי כלכלה בין ארצות המקרא (Jerusalem, 1977).

Ellenbogen, M. *Foreign Words in the Old Testament* (London, 1962).

Ellis, M. de J. "Taxation in Ancient Mesopotamia: The History of the Term *miksu*." *JCS* 26 (1974), 211-50.

Ember, A. *Egypto-Semitic Studies* (Leipzig, 1930).

Enciclopedia Judaica Castellana V (Mexico, 1949).

Epstein, Y. N. מבוא לנוסח המשנה II (Tel-Aviv, 1964).

Erman, A. "Das Verhältnis des Aegyptischen zu den semitischen Sprachen." *ZDMG* 46 (1892), 93-129.

——— and Grapow, H. *Wörterbuch der aegyptischen Sprache* I-VII (reprint; Berlin, 1971).

Ewald, H., and Dukes, L. *Beiträge zur Geschichte der ältesten Auslegung und Spracherklärung des Alten Testamentes* (Stuttgart, 1844).

Falkenstein, A., and von Soden, W. *Sumerische und akkadische Hymnen und Gebete* (Zürich, 1953).

Faulkner, R. O. "Egypt: From the Inception of the Nineteenth Dynasty to the Death of Ramesses III." *Cambridge Ancient History*, Fascicle #52 (Cambridge, 1966).

Feigin, S. I. "The Heavenly Sieve." *JNES* 9 (1950), 40-43.

Fenton, T. L. "Ugaritica-Biblica." *UF* 1 (1969), 65-70.

Fink, D. לשון למודים III (Berlin, 1926).

Finkelstein, J. J. "The Middle Assyrian Šulmānu Texts." *JAOS* 72 (1952), 77-80.

———. "Hebrew חבר and Semitic ḪBR." *JBL* 75 (1956), 328-31.

Fischer, H. G. "The Butcher Pḥ-r-nṯr." *Orientalia* 29 (1960), 168-90.

Fitzmyer, J. A. "The Aramaic Suzerainty Treaty from Sefîrē in the Museum of Beirut." *CBQ* 20 (1958), 444-76.

Fitzmyer, J. A. "A Note on Ezek. 16:30." *CBQ* 23 (1961), 460-62.

________. *The Aramaic Inscriptions of Sefîre* (Rome, 1967).

Fleischer, E. "לצבירן השאלות העתיקות ולבעית זהות מחברן." *HUCA* 38 (1967), א-כג.

Frankena, R. "The Vassal Treaties of Esarhaddon and the Dating of Deuteronomy." *OTS* 14 (1965), 122-54.

Frankfort, H., et al. *Before Philosophy* (Baltimore, 1949).

Garcia-Treto, F. O. "Genesis 31:44 and 'Gilead.'" *ZAW* 79 (1967), 13-17.

Gardiner, A. H. *Egyptian Hieratic Texts* I (Leipzig, 1911).

Garelli, P. *Les Assyriens en Cappadoce* (Paris, 1963).

Gaster, T. H. "A Canaanite Ritual Drama." *JAOS* 66 (1946), 46-76.

________. *Thespis* (New York, 1961).

________. *Myth, Legend, and Custom in the Old Testament* (New York, 1969).

Gattiker, H. *Das Verhältnis des Homerlexikons des Appolonius Sophistes zu den Homerscholien* (Zürich, 1945).

Geers, F. W. "The Treatment of Emphatics in Akkadian." *JNES* 4 (1945), 65-67.

Geiger, A. *Wissenschaftliche Zeitschrift* V (1844), 317-24.

Gelb, I. J., et al. *The Assyrian Dictionary of the University of Chicago* (Glückstadt, 1956-.).

________. *Bibliotheca Orientalis* 19 (1962), 159-62.

Gevirtz, S. *Patterns in the Early Poetry of Israel* (Chicago, 1963).

Gibson, J. C. L. *Textbook of Syrian Semitic Inscriptions* II (Oxford, 1975).

Ginsberg, H. L. "Lexicographical Notes." *ZAW* 51 (1933), 308-9.

________. "נוספות לעלילת אלאין בעל." *Tarbiz* 4 (1933), 380-90.

________. "Aramaic Dialect Problems, II." *AJSL* 52 (1935-36), 95-103.

________. "חדשות אפיגרפיות מאוגרית." *BJPES* 3 (1935-36), 49-56.

________. כתבי אוגרית (Jerusalem, 1936).

Ginsberg, H. L. "The Rebellion and Death of Baʿlu." *Orientalia* 5 (1936), 161-98.

________. "Baʿlu and His Brethren." *JPOS* 16 (1936), 138-49.

________. "The Ugaritic Texts and Textual Criticism." *JBL* 62 (1943), 109-15.

________. "Ugaritic Studies and the Bible." *BA* 8 (1945), 41-58.

________. "The North-Canaanite Myth of Anath and Aqhat II." *BASOR* 98 (1945), 15-23.

________. *The Legend of King Keret* (New Haven, 1946).

________. "Judah and the Transjordan States from 734 to 582 B.C.E." *Alexander Marx Jubilee Volume* (New York, 1950), 347-68.

________. "סיום שירת האזינר." *Tarbiz* 24 (1954-55), 1-3.

________. "An Unrecognized Allusion to Kings Pekah and Hoshea of Israel (Isa. 8:23)." *EI* 5 (1958), 61-65.

________. קהלת (Tel-Aviv, 1961).

________. "למילון לשון המקרא." ספר ח. ילון (Jerusalem, 1963), 167-73.

________. "Lexicographical Notes." VTSup 16 (1967), 71-82.

________. "Reflexes of Sargon in Isaiah after 715 B.C.E." *JAOS* 88 (1968), 47-53.

________. *The Five Megilloth and Jonah* (Philadelphia, 1969).

________. "Abram's Damascene Steward." *BASOR* 200 (1970), 31-32.

________. "First Isaiah." *EncJud* IX, 49-60.

________. *The Book of Isaiah* (Philadelphia, 1973).

________. "Ugaritico-Phoenicia." *JANESCU* 5 (1973), 131-47.

Goetze, A. "Contributions to Hittite Lexicography." *JCS* 1 (1947), 307-20.

Goodwin, D. W. *Text-Restoration Methods* (Naples, 1969).

Gordis, R. *The Song of Songs* (New York, 1961).

Gordon, C. H. "Homer and Bible." *HUCA* 26 (1955), 43-108.

________. *Ugaritic Textbook* I-III (Rome, 1965).

Gordon, C. H. *Ugarit and Minoan Crete* (New York, 1966).

Gordon, E. I. "Of Princes and Foxes: The Neck-Stock in the Newly-Discovered Agade Period Stela." *Sumer* 12 (1956), 80-84.

________. *Sumerian Proverbs* (Philadelphia, 1959).

Grasovsky, Y., and Yellin, D. המלון העברי (Tel-Aviv, 1919).

Gray, G. B. *The Book of Isaiah I-XXVII* (Edinburgh, 1912).

Gray, J. *The Krt Text in the Literature of Ras Shamra* (Leiden, 1964).

________. *I and II Kings* (2nd ed.; Philadelphia, 1970).

Greenfield, J. C. "Lexicographical Notes I." *HUCA* 29 (1958), 203-28.

________. "Stylistic Aspects of the Sefire Treaty Inscriptions." *Acta Orientalia* 29 (1965-66), 1-18.

________. "Some Glosses on the Keret Epic." *EI* 9 (1969), 60-65.

________. "Scripture and Inscription." *Near Eastern Studies in Honor of William Foxwell Albright* (Baltimore, 1971), 253-68.

Greenstein, E. "Two Variations of Grammatical Parallelism in Canaanite Poetry and their Psycholinguistic Background." *JANESCU* 6 (1974), 87-105.

Gröndahl, F. *Die Personennamen der Texte aus Ugarit* (Rome, 1967).

Guillaume, A. "A Note on Numbers 23:10." *VT* 12 (1962), 335-37.

Gurney, O. R. "The Tale of the Poor Man of Nippur." *AnSt* 6 (1956), 145-62.

________. "The Myth of Nergal and Ereshkigal." *AnSt* 10 (1960), 105-31.

Hammershaimb, E. *The Book of Amos* (Oxford, 1970).

Harper, W. R. *Amos and Hosea* (Edinburgh, 1905).

Haupt, P. "Wateh-Ben-Hazael." *Hebraica* 1 (1884-85), 217-31.

________. "Über den Halbvocal u̯ im Assyrischen." *ZA* 2 (1887), 259-86.

Heidel, A. *The System of the Quadriliteral Verb in Akkadian* (Chicago, 1940).

Heidel, A. "The Meaning of *mummu* in Akkadian Literature." *JNES* 7 (1948), 102-5.

________. *The Gilgamesh Epic and Old Testament Parallels* (Chicago, 1963).

Helck, W. *Die Beziehungen Ägyptens zu Vorderasien im 3. und 2. Jahrtausend v. Chr.* (Wiesbaden, 1971).

Held, M. "עוד זוגות מלים מקבילות במקרא ובכתבי אוגרית." *Leshonenu* 18 (1953), 144-60.

________. "סתומה מקראית ומקבילתה באוגריתית." *EI* 3 (1954), 101-3.

________. "Studies in Ugaritic Lexicography and Poetic Style." (Unpublished Ph.D. dissertation; Johns Hopkins University, 1957).

________. "mḫṣ/*mḫš in Ugaritic and Other Semitic Languages." *JAOS* 79 (1959), 169-76.

________. "A Faithful Lover in an Old Babylonian Dialogue." *JCS* 15 (1961), 1-26.

________. "The YQTL-QTL (QTL-YQTL) Sequence of Identical Verbs in Biblical Hebrew and in Ugaritic." *Studies and Essays in Honor of Abraham A. Neuman* (Leiden, 1962), 281-90.

________. "The Action-Result (Factitive-Passive) Sequence of Identical Verbs in Biblical Hebrew and Ugaritic." *JBL* 84 (1965), 272-82.

________. "Studies in Comparative Semitic Lexicography." *Studies in Honor of Benno Landsberger on His Seventy-Fifth Birthday* (Chicago, 1965), 395-406.

________. The Root zbl/sbl in Akkadian, Ugaritic and Biblical Hebrew." *JAOS* 88 (1968), 90-96.

________. "Rhetorical Questions in Ugaritic and Biblical Hebrew." *EI* 9 (1969), 71-79.

________. "Philological Notes on the Mari Covenant Rituals." *BASOR* 200 (1970), 32-40.

________. "Pits and Pitfalls in Akkadian and Biblical Hebrew." *JANESCU* 5 (1973), 173-90.

________. "Two Philological Notes on Enūma Eliš." *Kramer Anniversary Volume* (Neukirchen-Vluyn, 1976), 231-39.

Herdner, A. *Corpus des tablettes en cunéiformes alphabétiques découvertes à Ras Shamra-Ugarit de 1929 à 1939* (Paris, 1963).

Hillers, D. R. "A Hebrew Cognate of unuššu/unṯ in Isa. 33:8." *HTR* 64 (1971), 257-59.

Hirschfeld, H. *Literary History of Hebrew Grammarians and Lexicographers* (London, 1926).

Hoffner, H. A., Jr. "A Native Akkadian Cognate to West Semitic *GBN 'cheese.'" *JAOS* 86 (1966), 27-31.

________. "Second Millennium Antecedents to the Hebrew *'ÔB*." *JBL* 86 (1967), 385-401.

Hoftijzer, J. "Two Notes on the Baʿal Cyclus." *UF* 4 (1972), 155-58.

Holma, H. *Die Namen der Körperteile im Assyrisch-Babylonischen* (Helsinki, 1911).

Honeyman, A. M. "The Pottery Vessels of the Old Testament." *PEQ* (1939), 76-90.

Honor, L. L. *Sennacherib's Invasion of Palestine* (New York, 1926).

Horn, S. H. "The Ammān Citadel Inscription." *BASOR* 193 (1969), 2-13.

Howie, C. G. *The Date and Composition of Ezekiel* (Philadelphia, 1950).

Hurvitz, A. בין לשון ללשון (Jerusalem, 1972).

Jacobsen, T. "On the Textile Industry at Ur under Ibbī Sîn." *Toward the Image of Tammuz and Other Essays on Mesopotamian History and Culture* (Cambridge, 1970), 216-29.

Jastrow, M. *A Dictionary of the Targumim, the Talmud Babli and Yerushalmi, and the Midrashic Literature* I-II (New York, 1950).

Jean, C.-F., and Hoftjizer, J. *Dictionnaire des inscriptions sémitiques de l'Ouest* (Leiden, 1965).

Jellink, A. In Benjacob, Y. דברים עתיקים (Leipzig, 1844).

Jensen, P. "De Incantamentorum Sumerico-Assyriorum seriei quae Dicitur šurbu Tabula VI, II." *ZK* 2 (1885), 15-61.

________. "Hymnen auf das Wiedererscheinen der drei grossen Lichtgötter II." *ZA* 2 (1887), 191-204.

Jirku, A. *Die Dämonen und ihre Abwehr im Alten Testament* (Leipzig, 1912).

________. "Eṭimmu und אטים." *OLZ* 17 (1914), 185.

Johns, C. H. W. *Assyrian Deeds and Documents* IV (Cambridge, 1923).

Kallai, Z., and Tadmor, H. "בית נינורתה = בית חורון." *EI* 9 (1969), 138-47.

Kasovsky, H. J. אוצר לשון התלמוד I-XXVIII (Jerusalem, 1954-.).

Katz, M. אגרת ר' יהודה בן קוריש (Tel-Aviv, 1950).

Kaufman, S. A. *The Akkadian Influences on Aramaic* (Chicago, 1974).

Kaufman, Y. תולדות האמונה הישראלית I-VIII (Tel-Aviv, 1937-57).

________. ספר יהושע (Jerusalem, 1966).

Kelso, J. L. *The Ceramic Vocabulary of the Old Testament* (New Haven, 1948).

Kent, R. G. *Old Persian Grammar, Texts, Lexicon* (New Haven, 1953).

Kirschner, B. "Hapax Legomena." *Jüdisches Lexikon* II (Berlin, 1928), 1430.

Kissane, E. J. *The Book of Isaiah* I-II (Dublin, 1941-43).

Kitchen, K. A. *Ancient Orient and Old Testament* (Chicago, 1968).

Klar, B. מחקרים ועיונים (Tel-Aviv, 1954).

Klauber, E. *Assyrisches Beamtentum* (Leipzig, 1910).

Knudsen, E. E. "Spirantization of Velars in Akkadian." *Lišān Mitḫurti* (Neukirchen-Vluyn, 1969), 147-55.

Kocher, F. "Ein Inventartext aus Kār-Tukulti-Ninurta." *AfO* 18 (1957-58), 300-13.

Koehler, L. "Hebräische Etymologien." *JBL* 59 (1940), 35-40.

________ and Baumgartner, W. *Lexicon in Veteris Testamenti Libros* (Leiden, 1958).

________ and ________. *Supplementum ad Lexicon in Veteris Testamenti Libros* (Leiden, 1958).

Kokovtsov, P. *Nowiye Materyaly* II (Leningrad, 1916).

________. מספרי הבלשנות העברית בימי הבינים (reprint; Jerusalem, 1970).

Koopmans, J. J. *Aramäische Chrestomathie* (Leiden, 1962).

Kopf, L. "המילון הערבי כאמצעי עזר לבלשנות העברית." *Leshonenu* 19 (1954), 72-82.

________. "Das arabische Wörterbuch als Hilfsmittel für die hebräische Lexikographie." *VT* 6 (1956), 286-302.

________. "Arabische Etymologien und Parallelen zum Bibelwörterbuch." *VT* 8 (1958), 161-215.

________. "Arabische Etymologien und Parallelen zum Bibelwörterbuch." *VT* 9 (1959), 247-87.

Kraus, F. R. *Ein Edikt des Königs Ammi-ṣaduqa von Babylon* (Leiden, 1958).

Kraus, H.-J. *Psalmen 64-150* (Neukirchen-Vluyn, 1972).

Kraus, S. "Saadya's Tafsir of the Seventy Hapax Legomena Explained and Continued." *Saadya Studies* (Manchester, 1943), 47-77.

________. ספר ישעיהו (reprint; Jerusalem, 1969).

Kuchler, F. *Beiträge zur Kenntniṡ der assyrisch-babylonischen Medizin* (Leipzig, 1904).

Kutscher, E. Y. "למילון המקראי." *Leshonenu* 21 (1957), 251-58.

________. הלשון והרקע הלשוני של מגילת ישעיהו השלמה ממגילות ים המלח (Jerusalem, 1959).

________. מלים ותולדותיהן (Jerusalem, 1965).

________. "Mittelhebräisch und Jüdisch-Aramäisch im neuen Köhler-Baumgartner." VTSup 16 (1967), 158-75.

________. "Ugaritica V בעקבות." *Leshonenu* 34 (1969-70), 5-19.

Kutscher, R. "כתובת חדשה מרבת עמון." *Qadmoniot* 17 (1972), 27-28.

________. "māḫāzu המקבילות השומריות של." *Leshonenu* 34 (1969-70), 267-69.

Lambdin, T. O. "Egyptian Loan Words in the Old Testament." *JAOS* 73 (1953), 145-55.

Lambert, W. G. *Babylonian Wisdom Literature* (Oxford, 1960).

________. "An Incantation of the Maqlû Type." *AfO* 18 (1957-58), 288-99.

________ and Millard, A. R. *Atra-Ḫasīs* (Oxford, 1969).

Landman, I. ed. *The Universal Jewish Encyclopedia* V (New York, 1941).

Landsberger, B. "Schwierige akkadische Wörter. 2. 'Früh' und 'spät'." *AfO* 3 (1926), 164-72.

________. "asakku II = 'tabu'." *ZA* 41 (1933), 218-19.

________. "Zu Meissner, Beiträge zum assyrischen Wörterbuch II." *ZA* 41 (1933), 224-33.

________. *Die Fauna des alten Mesopotamien* (Leipzig, 1934).

________. "Zu ZA 41, 230." *ZA* 42 (1934), 166.

________ and Güterbock, H. G. "Das Ideogramm für simmiltu ('Leiter, Treppe')." *AfO* 12 (1937-39), 55-57.

________. "Assyriologische Notizen." *WO* 1 (1948-50), 362-76.

________. "Jahreszeiten im Sumerisch-Akkadischen." *JNES* 8 (1949), 248-97.

________ and Gurney, O. R. "Practical Vocabulary of Assur." *AfO* 18 (1957-58), 328-41.

________. "Corrections to the Article 'An Old Babylonian Charm against Merḫu.'" *JNES* 17 (1958), 56-58.

________ and Kinnier Wilson, J. V. "The Fifth Tablet of Enūma Eliš." *JNES* 20 (1961), 154-79.

________. "Einige unerkannt gebliebene oder verkannte Nomina des Akkadischen." *WO* 3 (1964), 48-79.

________. "Tin and Lead: The Adventures of Two Vocables." *JNES* 24 (1965), 285-96.

________. *The Date Palm and its By-products According to the Cuneiform Sources* (Graz, 1967).

________. "Über Farben im Sumerisch-Akkadischen." *JCS* 21 (1967), 139-73.

Lane, E. W. *An Arabic-English Lexicon* I-VIII (reprint; Beirut, 1968).

Langdon, S. "An Incantation for Expelling Demons from a House." *ZA* 36 (1924-25), 209-14.

Lehrs, K. *De Aristarchi Studiis Homericia* (Königsberg, 1833).

Levine, B. "כיפורים." *EI* 9 (1969), 88-95.

________. *In the Presence of the Lord* (Leiden, 1974).

Levita, E. *Massoreth Ha-Massoreth*; ed. C. D. Ginsburg (reprint; New York, 1968).

Lewy, J. "Studies in Old Assyrian Grammar and Lexicography." *Orientalia* 19 (1950), 1-36.

Leyde, L. *De Apollonii Sophistae Lexico Homerico* (Leipzig, 1844).

Licht, Y. "יונה." *EM* III, 608-13.

Lichtenstein, M. "Psalm 68:7 Revisited." *JANESCU* 4/2 (1972), 97-112.

Liddell, H. G., and Scott, R. *A Greek-English Lexicon* (Oxford, 1940).

Lipínski, E. "SKN et SGN dans le semitique occidental du nord." *UF* 5 (1973), 191-207.

Loewenstamm, S. E. "הערות לתולדות המליצה המקראית." ספר סגל (Jerusalem, 1964), 180-87.

________. "עדות." *EM* VI, 89.

________. "The Expanded Colon, Reconsidered." *UF* 7 (1975), 261-64.

Loretz, O. *Das althebräische Liebeslied* (Neukirchen-Vluyn, 1971).

________. "Psalmstudien III." *UF* 6 (1974), 175-210.

________. "Psalmstudien IV." *UF* 6 (1974), 211-40.

________. "'jš mgn in Proverbia 6,11 und 24,34." *UF* 6 (1974), 476-77.

________. "mgn - 'Geschenk' in Gen. 15,1." *UF* 6 (1974), 492.

Löw, I. *Die Flora der Juden* I-IV (reprint; Hildesheim, 1967).

Ludwich, A. *Aristarchs Homerische Textkritik* (Leipzig, 1884-85).

Luzatto, S. D. פרוש על ספר ישעיהו (reprint; Tel-Aviv, 1970).

Maisler, B. "Zur Urgeschichte des phönizisch-hebräischen Alphabets." *JPOS* 18 (1938), 278-91.

Malter, H. *Saadia Gaon, His Life and Works* (Philadelphia, 1921).

Margalith, O. "ארבעה פסוקים במשלי." *Beth Miqra* 67 (1976), 517-23.

Marti, K. *Das Buch Jesaja* (Tübingen, 1900).

Martinazzoli, F. *Hapax Legomenon* I/2 (Rome, 1957).

May, H. G. "Some Cosmic Connotations of Mayim Rabbim, 'Many Waters.'" *JBL* 74 (1955), 9-21.

McCarthy, D. J. *Treaty and Covenant* (Rome, 1963).

McKane, W. *Proverbs* (Philadelphia, 1970).

McKenzie, J. L. *Second Isaiah* (New York, 1968).

Meier, G. "Ritual für das Reisen über Land." *AfO* 12 (1937-39), 141-44.

Melammed, E. Z. מפרשי המקרא - דרכיהם ושיטותיהם (Jerusalem, 1975).

Milik, J. T. "Une lettre de Simeon Bar Kokheba." *RB* 60 (1953), 276-94.

Millard, A. "Ezekiel XXVII.19: The Wine Trade of Damascus." *JSS* 7 (1962), 201-3.

Miller, E. F. *The Influence of Gesenius on Hebrew Lexicography* (reprint; New York, 1966).

Montgomery, J. A. "Archival Data in the Book of Kings." *JBL* 53 (1934), 46-60.

________. *The Books of Kings* (Edinburgh, 1951).

de Moor, J. C. "Frustula Ugaritica." *JNES* 24 (1965), 355-64.

________. "The Semitic Pantheon of Ugarit." *UF* 2 (1970), 187-228.

________. "Studies in the New Alphabetic Texts from Ras Shamra II." *UF* 2 (1970), 303-27.

________. *The Seasonal Pattern in the Ugaritic Myth of Ba'lu* (Neukirchen-Vluyn, 1971).

Moriarty, F. L. "The Lament over Tyre (Ez. 27)." *Gregorianum* 46 (1965), 83-88.

Moscati, S., et al. *An Introduction to the Comparative Grammar of the Semitic Languages* (Wiesbaden, 1964).

Müller, K. F. "Das assyrische Ritual I." MVAG 41/3 (Leipzig, 1937).

Muller, W. M. *Asien und Europa* (Leipzig, 1893).

Muss-Arnoldt, W. "Notes on the Publications Contained in Volume II of E. Schraeder's Keilschriftliche Bibliothek. II. The Inscriptions of Esarhaddon." *Hebraica* 7 (1890-91), 81-103.

Muss-Arnoldt, W. *Assyrisch-english-deutsches Handwörterbuch* I-II (Berlin, 1905).

Myers, J. M. *II Chronicles* (New York, 1965).

________. *Ezra, Nehemiah* (New York, 1965).

Neubauer, K. W. "Erwägungen zu Amos 5:4-15." *ZAW* 78 (1966), 292-316.

New English Bible (Oxford, 1970).

Noeldeke, T. *ZDMG* 40 (1886), 718-43.

North, C. R. *The Second Isaiah* (Oxford, 1964).

Oppenheim, A. L. "Mesopotamian Mythology II." *Orientalia* 17 (1948), 17-58.

________. *Ancient Mesopotamia* (Chicago, 1964).

________. "The Cuneiform Texts." *Glass and Glassmaking in Ancient Mesopotamia* (New York, 1970), 2-102.

Oppert, J. *Mémoire sur les rapports de l'Égypte et de l'Assyrie dans l'antiquité* (Paris, 1869).

Orlinsky, H. M. *Notes on the New Translation of the Torah* (Philadelphia, 1969).

Pallis, S. A. *The Babylonian Akîtu Festival* (København, 1926).

Parnas, M. "'עדֹת', 'עדוֹת', 'עדוות' במקרא על רקע תעודות חיצוניות." *Shnaton* 1 (1975), 235-46.

Paul, S. M. "Deutero-Isaiah and Cuneiform Royal Inscriptions." *JAOS* 88 (1968), 180-86.

________. "Psalm 72:5 - A Traditional Blessing for the Long Life of the King." *JNES* 31 (1972), 351-55.

Perles, F. "Eṭimmu im Alten Testament und im Talmud." *OLZ* 17 (1914), 108-10.

________. "Noch einmal eṭimmu im AT und im Talmud." *OLZ* 17 (1914), 233.

Piankoff, A. *Le 'coeur' dans les textes égyptiens* (Paris, 1930).

Pilipowski, Z. מחברת מנחם (reprint; Jerusalem, n.d.).

________. ספר תשובות דונש (reprint; Jerusalem, n.d.).

Pinckert, J. *Hymnen und Gebete an Nebo* (Leipzig, 1920).

Polotsky, H. J. "Egyptian." *World History of the Jewish People I* (Tel-Aviv, 1964), 121-34.

Pope, M. H. *Job* (New York, 1973).

Porten, B., and Greenfield, J. C. "The Aramaic Papyri from Hermopolis." *ZAW* 80 (1968), 216-31.

Postgate, J. N. *Neo-Assyrian Royal Grants and Decrees* (Rome, 1969).

________. *Taxation and Conscription in the Assyrian Empire* (Rome, 1974).

Praetorius, F. "Zur äthiopischen Grammatik und Etymologie." BASS 1 (1890), 21-47, 369-78.

Preuss, J. *Biblisch-talmudische Medizin* (reprint; New York, 1971).

Procksch, O. *Jesaia I* (Leipzig, 1930).

Rabin, C. "Hittite Words in Hebrew." *Orientalia* 32 (1963), 113-39.

________. "מלים בודדות." *EM* IV, 1066-70.

________. "פנג." *EM* VI, 509.

von Rad, G. *Genesis* (Philadelphia, 1961).

Raḥman, L. Y. "גביע." *EM* II, 401-2.

Rainey, A. F. מבנה החברה באוגרית (Jerusalem, 1967).

________. "הערות לווקאבולארים החברתיים שבאוגרית." *Leshonenu* 34 (1969-70), 180-84.

________. "Observations on Ugaritic Grammar." *UF* 3 (1971), 151-72.

________. "Institutions: Family, Civil, and Military." *Ras Shamra Parallels* II (Rome, 1975), 71-107.

Reiner, E. "Another Volume of Sultantepe Tablets." *JNES* 26 (1967), 177-200.

________. *Šurpu* (reprint; Osnabrück, 1970).

Revised Standard Version (reprint; New York, 1962).

Ring, Y. מבוא לספרות התנ"ך (Tel-Aviv, 1967).

Robertson, D. A. *Linguistic Evidence in Dating Early Hebrew Poetry* (Montana, 1972).

Roemer, A. *Die Homerexegese Aristarchs in ihren Grundzügen* Ed. E. Belzner (Paderborn, 1924).

Römer, W. H. P. *Sumerische Königshymnen der Isin-Zeit* (Leiden, 1965).

Rosenthal, J. "שאלות עתיקות בתנ"ך." *HUCA* 21 (1948), כט-צא.

Ross, J. F. "Prophecy in Hamath, Israel, and Mari." *HTR* 63 (1970), 1-28.

Saggs, H. W. F. *The Greatness that was Babylon* (New York, 1962).

________. *Everyday Life in Babylonia and Assyria* (New York, 1965).

Salonen, A. *Die Wasserfahrzeuge in Babylonien* (Helsinki, 1939).

________. *Die Türen des alten Mesopotamien* (Helsinki, 1961).

________. *Die Möbel des alten Mesopotamien* (Helsinki, 1963).

________. *Die Hausgeräte der alten Mesopotamier I* (Helsinki, 1965).

________. *Die Hausgeräte der alten Mesopotamier II* (Helsinki, 1966).

________. *Agricultura Mesopotamica* (Helsinki, 1968).

________. *Die Fussbekleidung der alten Mesopotamier* (Helsinki, 1969).

Salonen, E. *Die Waffen der alten Mesopotamier* (Helsinki, 1965).

________. *Über das Erwerbsleben im alten Mesopotamien* (Helsinki, 1970).

Sandys, J. E. *A History of Classical Scholarship* I (reprint; New York, 1958).

Sarna, N. M. *Understanding Genesis* (New York, 1966).

Sasson, J. M. "Canaanite Maritime Involvement in the Second Millennium B.C." *JAOS* 86 (1966), 126-38.

________. "Flora, Fauna and Minerals." *Ras Shamra Parallels* I (Rome, 1972), 383-452.

Säve-Söderbergh, T. *The Navy of the Eighteenth Egyptian Dynasty* (Uppsala, 1946).

Scheiber, A. "Unknown Leaves from שאלות עתיקות." *HUCA* 27 (1956), 291-303.

Scheiber, A. "Fernere Fragmente aus שאלות עתיקות." *HUCA* 36 (1965), 227-59.

Schloessinger, M. "Hapax Legomena in Rabbinical Literature." *The Jewish Encyclopedia* VI (New York, 1904), 228-29.

Scholem, G. "Lilith." *EncJud* XI, 245-49.

Schoors, A. "Literary Phrases." *Ras Shamra Parallels* I (Rome, 1972), 3-70.

Schrader, E. *The Cuneiform Inscriptions and the Old Testament* I-II (London, 1885).

Schwally, F. "Lexikalische Studien." *ZDMG* 53 (1889), 197-201.

Scott, R. B. Y. "Weights and Measures of the Bible." *BA* 22 (1959), 22-40.

Segal, M. H. ספרי שמואל (Jerusalem, 1964).

________. מבוא המקרא IV (Jerusalem, 1965).

van Selms, A. "A Systematic Approach to CTA 5,1,1-8." *UF* 7 (1975), 477-82.

Seux, M.-J. *Épithètes royales akkadiennes et sumériennes* (Paris, 1967).

Shalit, A. "חבשים וארזים במרכלתך." *Leshonenu* 7 (1935-36), 131-35.

Skinner, J. *Isaiah, Chapters I-XXXIX* (Cambridge, 1915).

Smith, H. P. *The Books of Samuel* (Edinburgh, 1899).

von Soden, W. *Grundriss der akkadischen Grammatik* (Rome, 1952).

________. "Eine altbabylonische Beschwörung gegen die Dämonin Lamaštum." *Orientalia* 23 (1954), 337-44.

________. *OLZ* 49 (1954), 36-39.

________. "Gibt es ein Zeugnis dafür, dass die Babylonier an die Wiederauferstehung Marduks geglaubt haben?" *ZA* 51 (1955), 130-66.

________. *Akkadisches Handwörterbuch* (Wiesbaden, 1959-.).

________. *OLZ* 61 (1966), 356-60.

________. "Aramäische Wörter in neuassyrischen und neu- und spätbabylonischen Texten. Ein Vorbericht. I." *Orientalia* 35 (1966), 1-20.

von Soden, W. "Aramäische Wörter in neuassyrischen und neu- und spätbabylonischen Texten. Ein Vorbericht. II." *Orientalia* 37 (1968), 261-71.

________. *Ergänzungen zu GAG* (Rome, 1969).

Soggin, J. A. *Joshua* (Philadelphia, 1972).

Speiser, E. A. "The Syllabic Transcription of Ugaritic [ḫ] and [ḥ]." *BASOR* 175 (1964), 42-47.

________. *Genesis* (New York, 1964).

________. "Leviticus and the Critics." *Oriental and Biblical Studies* (Philadelphia, 1967), 123-42.

Sperber, A. *The Bible in Aramaic* I-IV (Leiden, 1959-73).

Sperling, D. "Rab-Saris and Rab-Mag." *EncJud* XIII, 1481.

Stadelman, L. I. J. *The Hebrew Conception of the World* (Rome, 1970).

Steinberg, E. "Weights and Measures." *EncJud* XVI, 376-88.

Steinschneider, M. *Die arabische Literatur der Judea* (reprint; Hildesheim, 1964).

Stern, E. "מידות ומשקלות." *EM* IV, 846-78.

________. "נעל." *EM* V, 888-91.

Stieglitz, R. R. "Ugaritic Mḫd--The Harbor of Yabne-Yam?" *JAOS* 94 (1974), 137-38.

Strong, S. A. "A Prayer of Aššurbanipal." *Transactions of the Ninth International Congress of Orientalists* II (1893), 199-208.

Stummer, F. "אמלה (EZ XVI 30A)." *VT* 4 (1954), 34-40.

Tadmor, H. "הרקע ההסטורי להצהרת כורש." ספר בן-גוריון (Jerusalem, 1964), 450-73.

Tallqvist, K. *Akkadische Götterepitheta* (Helsinki, 1938).

Teloni, B. "Appunti intorno all'iscrizione di Nabonid V.R. 65." *ZA* 3 (1888), 159-73, 293-310.

Tene, D. "Linguistic Literature, Hebrew." *EncJud* XVI, 1352-90.

Thompson, J. A. "Expansions of the עד Root." *JSS* 10 (1965), 222-40.

Thureau-Dangin, F. *Rituels accadiens* (Paris, 1921).

The Torah (Philadelphia, 1962).

Tromp, N. J. *Primitive Conceptions of Death and the Nether World in the Old Testament* (Rome, 1969).

Tur-Sinai (Torczyner), N. H. *Altbabylonische Tempelrechnungen* (Wien, 1913).

________. *Das Buch Hiob* (Wien and Berlin, 1920).

________. "Hapax Legomena." *Encyclopaedia Judaica* VII (Berlin, 1931), 997-1000.

________. "דרישה אל המתים בתקופת המקרא." מנחה לדוד (Jerusalem, 1935), סט-עז.

________. "Presidential Address." *JPOS* 16 (1936), 1-8.

________. ספר איוב II (Jerusalem, 1941).

________. הלשון והספר I-III (Jerusalem, 1954).

________. "A Contribution to the Understanding of Isaiah I-XII." *Studies in the Bible* (Jerusalem, 1961), 154-88.

________. פשוטו של מקרא I-IV/2 (Jerusalem, 1962-67).

________. *The Book of Job* (Jerusalem, 1967).

Vieyra, M. "Ištar de Ninive." *RA* 51 (1957), 83-102.

________. "Les noms du 'mundus' en hittite et en assyrien et la pythonisse d'Endor." *RHA* 69 (1961), 47-55.

Virolleaud, Ch. "La naissance des dieux gracieux et beaux." *Syria* 14 (1933), 128-51.

________. *La légende phénicienne de Danel* (Paris, 1936).

________. "Textes administratifs de Ras-Shamra." *RA* 37 (1940-41), 11-44.

________. "Le mariage du Roi Kéret." *Syria* 23 (1942-43), 137-72.

________. *Le Palais royal d'Ugarit* II (Paris, 1957).

________. *Le Palais royal d'Ugarit* V (Paris, 1965).

________. *Ugaritica* V (Paris, 1968).

Vogt, E. "Ioiakîn Collari Ligneo Vinctus (Ez 19,9)." *Biblica* 37 (1956), 388-89.

Volkwein, B. "Masoretisches ʿēdūt, ʿēdwōt, ʿēdōt - 'Zeugnis' oder 'Bundesbestimmungen'?" *BZ* 13 (1969), 18-40.

Waldman, N. "A Note on Canticles 4:9." *JBL* 89 (1970), 215-17.

Waldorf, N. O. "The *Hapax Legomena* in the English Vocabulary: A Study Based upon the Bosworth-Toller Dictionary." (Unpublished Ph.D. dissertation; Stanford University, 1953).

Waterman, L. *Royal Correspondence of the Assyrian Empire* I-IV (Ann Arbor, 1936).

van der Weiden, W. A. *Le Livre des Proverbes* (Rome, 1970).

Weidner, E. F. "Der Stattsvertrag Assurniraris VI mit Mati'ilu von Bit-Agusi." *AfO* 8 (1932-33), 17-26.

________. "Die Feldzüge und Bauten Tiglatpilesers I." *AfO* 18 (1957-58), 342-60.

Weinfeld, M. "'הברית והחסד'." *Leshonenu* 35 (1972), 85-105.

________. *Deuteronomy and the Deuteronomic School* (Oxford, 1972).

________. "Covenant Terminology in the Ancient Near East and its Influence on the West." *JAOS* 93 (1973), 190-99.

________. "'Rider of the Clouds' and 'Gatherer of the Clouds.'" *JANESCU* 5 (1973), 421-26.

________. ספר בראשית (Tel-Aviv, 1975).

Weisberg, D. B. *Guild Structure and Political Allegiance in Early Achaemenid Mesopotamia* (New Haven, 1967).

Wertheimer, S. A. באור תשעים מלות בודדות בתנ"ך (Jerusalem, 1931).

Whitaker, R. E. *A Concordance of the Ugaritic Literature* (Cambridge, 1972).

Wiseman, D. J. "A New Stela of Aššurnaṣirpal II." *Iraq* 14 (1952), 24-44.

________. *The Vassal Treaties of Esarhaddon* (London, 1958).

Wohlstein, H. "Zu den altisraelitischen Vorstellungen von Toten und Ahnengeistern." *BZ* 5 (1961), 30-38.

Wolff, H. W. *Dodekapropheton 2* (Neukirchen-Vluyn, 1969).

Wright, G. E. "The Lawsuit of God: A Form-Critical Study of Deuteronomy 32." *Israel's Prophetic Heritage* (London, 1962), 26-67.

Würthwein, E. *Der Text des Alten Testament* (4th ed.; Stuttgart, 1973).

Yahuda, A. S. "Hapax Legomena im Alten Testament." *JQR* 15 (1903), 698-714.

Yalon, H. מבוא לניקוד המשנה (Jerusalem, 1964).

Yeivin, S. "אטים." *EM* I, 237.

Yeivin, Z. "Bitumen." *EncJud* IV, 1062.

Yellin, D. חקרי מקרא, ישעיהו (Jerusalem, 1939).

Zelson, L. G. "A Study of *Hapax Legomena* in the Hebrew Pentateuch." (Unpublished Ph.D. dissertation; University of Wisconsin, 1924).

________. "Les Hapax Legomena du Pentateuque Hebraique." *RB* 36 (1927), 243-48.

Ziegler, J. *Isaias* (Würzburg, 1948).

van Zijl, P. J. *Baal* (Neukirchen-Vluyn, 1972).

Zimmerli, W. *Ezechiel 1* (Neukirchen-Vluyn, 1969).

________. *Ezechiel 2* (Neukirchen-Vluyn, 1969).

Zimmern, H. *The Babylonian and the Hebrew Genesis* (London, 1901).

________. *Akkadische Fremdwörter als Beweis für babylonischen Kultureinfluss* (Leipzig, 1917).

________. "Kleine Mitteilungen und Anzeigen." *ZA* 36 (1925), 80-85.

Zohary, M. "ארן." *EM* I, 596-97.

________. "לט." *EM* IV, 496.

________. "צרי." *EM* VI, 770-71.

INDEX OF BIBLICAL *HAPAX LEGOMENA*, EX-*HAPAX LEGOMENA*,* AND "GHOST" WORDS** DISCUSSED IN THIS STUDY

---

*For ex-*hapax legomena* in the Bible, see page 24 above. These words are designated in this index with one asterisk (*).

**For "ghost" words which would otherwise be biblical *hapax legomena*, see pages 5 and 107 above. These words are designated in this index with two asterisks (**).

INDEX OF KEY WORDS AND EXPRESSIONS BESIDES BIBLICAL *HAPAX LEGOMENA* DISCUSSED IN THIS STUDY

A. Hebrew

B. Akkadian

C. Ugaritic

ADDENDA

To page 6 line 15:

Here should also be noted the study of E. Ullendorff, *Is Biblical Hebrew a Language? Studies in Semitic Languages and Civilizations* (Wiesbaden, 1977), 14-16. While Ullendorff refers to many of the works cited here, he is most concerned with the percentage of words in the Bible which qualify (according to him) as *hapax legomena* and the number of *hapax legomena* in each biblical book. He deals neither with the problem of obtaining a functional definition for biblical *hapax legomena* nor with questions of methodology for their interpretation.

To pages 135-36 n. 74A:

Dr. M. Lichtenstein has kindly called my attention to *PRU* V, 64:14-15: *w.lqḥ/y?n*[-].*bdnh*. If this reading is correct (note the question mark), it would be a first instance of Ugaritic *dn* referring to a vat of wine and should logically be connected to Akkadian *dannu* and the Hebrew *hapax legomenon* under discussion. Dr. Lichtenstein agrees with me, however, that the other occurrence(s) of Ugaritic *dn* should still be kept separate and not be associated with the word in question in any case.